PRINNY
AND HIS PALS

PRINNY
AND HIS PALS

GEORGE IV AND HIS
REMARKABLE GIFT OF FRIENDSHIP

Tom Ambrose

PETER OWEN PUBLISHERS
LONDON AND CHESTER SPRINGS, PA, USA

PETER OWEN PUBLISHERS
73 Kenway Road, London SW5 0RE

Peter Owen books are distributed in the USA by
Dufour Editions Inc., Chester Springs, PA 19425-0007

First published in Great Britain 2009 by
Peter Owen Publishers

ISBN 978-0-7206-1326-1

Printed and bound in Great Britain by
CPI Antony Rowe

Every effort has been made to contact owners of copyright material. The author and
publishers regret if there are missing acknowledgements; if copyright holders contact the
publishers with these they will be included in future editions.

CONTENTS

ILLUSTRATIONS
between pages 128 and 129

PREFACE

'. . . a violator of his word, a libertine over head and ears in debt and disgrace, a despiser of domestic ties, the companion of gamblers and demi-reps, a man who has just closed half a century without one single claim on the gratitude of this country or the respect of posterity . . .'
– James Henry Leigh Hunt, *The Examiner*, 1812

L EIGH Hunt's poor opinion of George IV would have been shared by many of his contemporaries, particularly George's first biographer, Robert Huish, writing in 1831 within a year of the king's death. Sadly, much of the popular odium that surrounded George in his later years was the result of one disastrous event: his failed marriage and bitter divorce from Caroline of Brunswick. By clever manipulation of the radical press and by courting the sympathy of the London mob Caroline was able to present her husband to the nation as a heartless monster and herself as his innocent victim. As has been the case with a more recent Prince of Wales, George's positive qualities were ignored in favour of a simplistic interpretation of complicated and highly personal events.

George's fall from public grace was particularly sad given the people's early obsession with him and his undoubted abilities. Even as a child George Augustus was an unusually gifted and charming person, whose true worth in simple human terms can be evaluated through the scores of sincere friendships that he made and kept with some of the most colourful characters of his age. Furthermore, no other British monarch before or since has developed such a wide spread of friendships, ranging from the political philosopher Edmund Burke to Louis Weltje, a German pastry cook who made his fortune in England. Highly creative in temperament, George was naturally drawn to artists, writers and musicians. All the greatest British painters of the age, from Thomas Gainsborough to David Wilkie, became his friends, and his artistic comprehension and affable manner led to an excellent working relationship with architects such as John Nash and Jeffry Wyatville. Musically, he was a highly talented amateur, and it is difficult to image any other monarch capable of singing a duet with a great composer as George once did with Giacchino Rossini. What is remarkable about these artistic friendships is that they were not principally dependent on patrimony because men such as the writers Richard Brinsley Sheridan and Sir Walter Scott genuinely liked him as a person and admired his undoubted qualities as a man.

Equally unusual – and possibly unique for a British monarch – was George's lack of concern for social class and his insistence on judging a man by what he did rather than by his background. For this reason he constantly formed friendships with his servants and people of humble origins. How many other British monarchs have spontaneously joined the servants for dinner in the palace kitchen – and brought their friends with them? Again, George's relationships with children are remarkable for a man who suffered an emotionally deprived childhood himself. The gentle and amusing letters he wrote to young girls such as Minney Seymour and Maria Conyngham reveal a remarkable insight into a child's mind all the more unusual considering his own father's cold and critical attitude towards him. The very qualities that George IV possessed in abundance – generosity of spirit, flamboyance of character, disdain for conventional morality and, above all, the capacity to openly enjoy the pleasures of a finite life – became increasingly irrelevant in the changing moral climate of the country. Even before his niece Queen Victoria came to the throne Britain was becoming a more sober and pious nation with religious conformity taking the place of natural generosity of spirit. Significantly, no subsequent monarch, with perhaps the exception of Edward VII, ever again attempted to live in the relaxed and sybaritic manner of George IV.

If one were to consider which British monarch one would most enjoy having dinner with, the choice would surely be either Charles II, whose amused cynicism restored the unity of his country, or George IV, the most enjoyable of companions and the best of friends.

1

THE SEARCH FOR FRIENDS

APPROPRIATELY for a man who would spend the rest of his life in the public eye, Prince George Augustus made his first public appearance in the grand drawing-room at St James's Palace at the age of just two weeks. There, in late August 1762, he was put on display between the hours of one o'clock and three o'clock each day. Even at that early age he began to make friends for each afternoon curious members of the respectable classes flocked to St James's to gawp at the infant. So intrusive did the crowd become that his mother, Queen Charlotte, ordered that he be secluded in a highly ornate cradle surrounded by lattice screens decorated with Chinese designs so preventing the people from touching him. It was the perfect setting for someone who would one day create the exotic oriental interiors of Carlton House and the Brighton Pavilion. But his public appearance provoked the first of many attacks by his critics. The vitriolic biographer Robert Huish claimed that displaying the baby to the public in this vulgar manner was undoubtedly a dreadful German custom and would be deeply resented by all right-thinking British people.

That summer baby George was the greatest attraction in town, with visitors queuing to see him and to sample the delicious free refreshments thoughtfully provided in the German fashion by his mother. When news of this royal largesse spread, even more people arrived, and in the first week alone more than £500 worth of rich fruit cake was consumed and eight gallons of sweet wine drunk. After viewing the baby each visitor was encouraged to raise a glass of welcome to the little newcomer – an appropriate gesture to a prince whose own prodigious appetite for the pleasures of life would later astonish and infuriate the nation. Exactly one month after his birth George was taken out for his first airing. As his nurse wheeled him in a pram through Hyde Park an excited mob began following and jostling one another to catch a glimpse of the first royal baby for many years. Lord Bath, who accompanied the procession, was amused to hear one ruffian call out the prophetic words: 'God bless him; he is a lusty, jolly young dog truly!' Already the baby prince had been allocated a full retinue of servants, including the obligatory wet nurse, a necessary woman to change his nappies, a seamstress to supervise his clothes and two official rockers of the royal cradle. All were under the authority of the royal governess, the formidable Lady Charlotte Finch, who was described as 'a woman of remarkable sense and philosophy'. Whatever their disagreements in the years to come, Queen Charlotte was besotted with her first child and sought to preserve his image for posterity with the first of many childhood portraits. The artist chosen was Francis Cotes, who pictured him lying serenely cradled in his mother's arms. To commemorate his christening a few days later, in what some considered a singularly odd German custom, a tiny wax model of him was made and placed on a little velvet cushion under a glass bell jar. This the queen kept in her drawing-room for many years, always in position beside her like a miniature exhibit from a waxworks museum.

Surrounded by servants, courtiers and family members, George was seldom alone in those first years of life, and the busy atmosphere at St James's Palace encouraged the sociability that would enable him to form friendships easily for the rest of his life. When asked, fifty years later, by a guest at the Brighton Pavilion, what had been his first memory as a child, George replied that he distinctly recalled being picked up by his great-uncle, the infamous Duke of Cumberland, the Butcher of Culloden, who was wearing a snuff-coloured coat, and being astonished at the vast bulk of this elderly man who seemed like a giant. When it was time to begin his education, George III insisted that his son receive a course of instruction that would instil in him the same dedication to royal duties as he had himself. So, at the age of two and a half, when other children were confined to the nursery, Prince George was precociously introduced to public life. His first public engagement was to present a cheque for £100 on behalf of his father to members of a charitable institution. He did it faultlessly, behaving according to one witness 'with great propriety and suitableness of action'. This was no surprise to those around him for already he could be seen to be a bright child who responded well to his governess's innovative educational system, which included rearranging cut-up maps, an early form of the jigsaw puzzle. What impressed his instructors most was his precocious command of language, which often gave him an air of youthful pomposity. Obliged to remain in bed with the window curtains drawn after being inoculated for smallpox, he was asked by the Keeper of the Robes, Mrs Schwellenberg, if he found the experience irksome. 'Not in the least,' he replied laconically. 'I lie here and make reflections.'

Perhaps this precocity accounted for his father's odd choice of fifth-birthday present for his son, consisting of twenty miniature one-pound brass cannon, each mounted on a carriage and complete with live ammunition. This was an ironic gift considering his father's later implacable opposition to George's determination to pursue a military career. Yet, in spite of this apparent martial encouragement, George III was in all other matters anxious for his son not to show any signs of dangerous maturity. Rather, he attempted to keep him in a strange kind of enforced infancy, insisting even when the boy was ten that he continue being dressed as a young child. The cambric frocks with Valenciennes lace cuffs that he appeared in were thought by many at court to be wholly inappropriate for such a robust, intelligent and fast-growing boy. This embarrassing costume was but the first of many indignities that George III was to inflict on his eldest son, who responded with sullen resentment at what he considered a deliberate affront to his personal dignity. His later obsession with his appearance and his fixation with fashionable clothes may well have been the consequence of this early sartorial humiliation imposed on him by his father. Always sensitive to ridicule, a trait that became a serious impediment to public appearances in later life, he once caught a servant smiling mockingly at him as they passed each other in a corridor at Windsor. Catching hold of his frilly collar in childish frustration George called out to the man: 'See how I am treated!'

At first there were few other children to make friends with, but as the years passed increasing numbers of brothers and sisters were produced with remorseless efficiency by Queen Charlotte. Lacking natural good looks and possessing a harsh Germanic manner, she had little appeal for an English aristocracy that found her irredeemably dull. The wit Horace Walpole did comment, however, that after she had been in England for some time the bloom of her ugliness was beginning to wear off. The appearance of each new sibling delighted the royal couple, much as it did the little Prince of Wales, who welcomed each new addition to the family as a distraction that he hoped would divert his father's increasingly critical attention away from himself. By 1771 the rapidly expanding family was too large for either of the London palaces then available. The only alternative, the king decided, was to move them all to the more rural environment of the White House at Kew. Although barely twenty-eight, Queen Charlotte had already given birth to eight children, and even Kew Palace, as it was renamed, soon proved too small to house the still-growing family and its attendants. As the adjacent Dutch House was empty, the king decided to ease the overcrowding by sending George and his younger brother Frederick, Duke of York, to board there under their recently appointed governor, the Earl of Holderness, and his assistants Leonard Smelt and Dr William Markham.

Holderness – a man dismissed by Horace Walpole as 'a formal piece of dullness' – was a most uninspiring person, but Markham was to prove both an able tutor and a good friend to the boys. It was George's first experience of a man who had used his own natural ability rather than his connections to rise in society, and for the rest of his life George would always prize natural talent over inherited position. Markham was a typical product of the social changes that resulted from England's new prosperity in the eighteenth century. Although from a humble background he had won scholarships to Westminster School and Christ Church, Oxford. At the time of his appointment as royal tutor he had risen to be Bishop of Chester and was set for a successful career in the Church. Had George III known that Markham's outwardly pompous manner disguised an open mind and a liberal heart he might well have regretted choosing him to teach his sons. Ordered to impose a rigid system of both learning and discipline on the young princes, Markham tempered the need to instil information with a friendly and approachable manner. The boys were taught French, German and Italian as well as the more conventional Classics and English grammar. Yet it was still a hard regime for the boys as, at the king's insistence, lessons began in the early morning and continued far into the evening. With just two of them in the class, without the company of other children, they learnt quickly. They had few pleasures to enjoy other than the piece of garden they were given to cultivate. Here they were shown how to plant wheat, watch it ripen, mill the grain into flour and finally to bake bread. For George, the fascination with this process would encourage an interest in cooking that culminated in the innovative kitchens he installed at the Brighton Pavilion.

Thrown together in a form of educational adversity, George and Frederick formed an intimate bond of friendship that was to unite them, in spite of later disagreements and conflicts, for the rest of their lives. Both boys could well have excused their later dissolute ways as an inevitable reaction to a repressive upbringing that, even in eighteenth-century England, was far more rigorous in character than that endured by their aristocratic contemporaries at English public schools. Convinced that sparing the rod would certainly spoil the child, the king insisted that the slightest transgression in either boy be rigorously punished – and punished they were. One of their sisters recalled how, on a visit to the Dutch House, she had seen both boys 'held by their tutors and flogged like dogs with a long whip' for some minor wrongdoing. Neither was spared, and Prince Frederick recalled that both of them were frequently beaten about the head with a silver pencil case by one tutor, Cyril Jackson, 'until blood flowed'. As George was clearly the brighter of the two as well as heir to the throne, more attention was devoted to him, and more expected, than from his slightly dim but easygoing brother. From the start the problem with the young Prince of Wales was his quietly rebellious manner, which manifested itself as insouciance. It was this and an ill-disguised disregard for his elders' opinions that came to infuriate George III.

In response to his father's incessant bullying George began to disguise his true abilities, revealing them only to those he felt he could trust. Proof of this was a highly accomplished letter that he wrote to his great-aunt Amelia when barely ten years old. She was impressed by its maturity of expression and replied by complimenting him on his use of language that was 'far beyond what I could have expected for a prince of your age'. His father remained unaware of his son's true capabilities and continued to bombard him with demands that he should work harder. Just as annoying to the prince were the constant exhortations from both his parents and from the Earl of Holderness to behave more morally and to beware of vice, self-indulgence and dishonesty. 'Truth is the first quality of a man; the higher the rank the more to be adhered to,' Holderness sanctimoniously informed his young charge as well as exhorting him to avoid gluttony and to be wary of the flattery of false friends. Many of the supposed virtues George was advised to adopt – such as a simple lifestyle, hard work and punctuality – were not only ignored but their polar opposites rapidly adopted to become part of his own idiosyncratic lifestyle. To someone of George's innate intelligence and liberalism this attempt to suppress his natural good spirits had little effect other than to confirm his resolution to escape the moral shackles of life at the Dutch House as soon as possible.

There were other humiliations and frustrations to be endured there, the most damaging of which was George III's insistence that no adult other than their own tutors be allowed to talk to the princes for the king was convinced that their minds would be contaminated by contact with less-principled people. Again, this restriction was to prove counterproductive, making the young Prince of Wales determined to develop as wide a circle of friends as possible, drawn from as wide an intellectual and social background as possible. Unlike any other British monarch George IV would be as relaxed in the company of a boxer or coachman as he would be in the presence of the philosopher Edmund Burke or the Duke of Wellington. Men and women, he believed, should be judged by their true worth and not by the trappings of office or position. By this criterion, only Dr Markham earned his genuine respect, and when Lord Holderness resigned his governorship in May 1776 George was bold enough to ask his father to allow Markham to remain as tutor. The request was, predictably, refused on the grounds that if George got his way on this matter then he would count it as a victory over his father. Even when he had left the Dutch House Markham remained in contact with the prince, and in 1800 was still being addressed by him as 'my dear, much loved friend'. When, in 1806, Markham was appointed Archbishop of York at George's request, his old pupil was seen to fall to his knees to receive his blessing when he visited the city. Indeed, Markham was cherished by the prince as his first genuine adult friend and was held in such respect that whenever he visited London he was invited to dine at Carlton House, the prince's London home. For any pupil, least of all the heir to the throne, to remain in such close contact with a tutor was most unusual in that or any age and shows the gratitude that George held for a man who had opened his eyes to the world while showing him the respect and affection that his father consistently denied him.

(A sad postscript to George III's hostility to his eldest son occurred when the old king was dying in 1820. One evening he summoned George to St James's Palace, and they sat down to dinner alone – the first time such an event had ever happened. The king drank three glasses to wine to toast the prince's health then burst into tears and expressed his pleasure that for the first time in his life he had dined tête-à-tête with 'his beloved son'. If such affection could have been expressed years earlier perhaps the good aspects of character would have been more apparent.)

With Markham's departure life at Kew became even gloomier. There was little contact with the outside world other than the occasional visit to a concert or an opera performed for the royal family at the White House. The closest the princes came to encountering English society was on Thursdays, when they were taken up to London to attend one of their mother's formal drawing-room receptions at either St James's Palace or Buckingham House. On summer Sundays the gardens at Kew were open to the public, and parties of visitors either drove or were rowed up the river from London. On such days the princes were able to escape their father's attention and mingle with the guests largely unchaperoned. But George III's remorseless quest to exclude frivolity and drum piety and application into his eldest son continued. Suspecting that leniency had infiltrated the Dutch House, the king suddenly dismissed all the servants and tutors and replaced them with sterner men. The new governor was Richard Hurd, Bishop of Lichfield, a man of far tougher mettle than the aesthetically inclined and urbane Markham. Moral rectitude was now more than ever the order of the day, and Hurd set about instilling improving texts into the young princes with such determination that even on Sunday mornings they were forced to attend classes in the Greek Testament. Obedient to the king's wishes and a determined martinet, Hurd was held in great contempt by George, who compared him most unfavourably to his friend Markham, 'a much greater, wiser, and more learned man', who had bothered to explain difficult passages rather than resorting, like Hurd, to punishment for supposed inattention. Yet Hurd did make one highly positive contribution to the development of the prince's cultural tastes by encouraging an interest in music. A renowned cellist, John Crosdill, was hired to give George lessons on the instrument, and he was soon discussing music with the composer Johann Christian Bach, Master of Music to Queen Charlotte. The discovery that he had a fine melodic voice did much to boost the boy's battered self-esteem and provoked an interest in opera that would remain with him for the rest of his life. His guests at the Brighton Pavilion in later years might well have regretted this enthusiasm for they were often subjected to interminable after-dinner recitals of popular arias by their inebriated host.

This dawning interest in the arts extended to painting, and George was allowed to receive lessons from the renowned landscape artist Alexander Cozens, the natural son of Peter the Great of Russia, conceived when the tsar had studied shipbuilding at Deptford, near London. Cozens's artistic ability and bold technique greatly appealed to the boy and stimulated his interest in design. This early exposure to the visual arts, combined with his natural good taste, would lead him to become a perceptive collector of art in later years. Moreover, a maverick character such as Cozens greatly appealed to the young prince's rebelliousness as did his equally eccentric Italian-born fencing master, Henry Angelo, who became the first of his many sporting friends.

In spite of the repressive attitude of his father, all of George's tutors agreed that at the age of sixteen he had become an intelligent, accomplished and attractive young man. Even the elderly courtiers were charmed by his elegant and engaging manners, although he occasionally displayed an irritating fascination with childish practical jokes. When a notoriously greedy musician came to dinner, the prince shocked him by serving a live rabbit that escaped from the table the moment the dish cover was lifted. But it was his innate courtesy and consideration for others that most impressed everyone who came into contact with him. In a letter to one of his sister's attendants he described himself accurately as 'now approaching the bloom of youth, he is rather above the common size, his limbs well-proportioned and upon the whole well made though rather too great a penchant to grow fat'. His assessment of his own character in that same letter is also revealing:

> He is above doing anything mean . . . grateful and friendly to excess where he finds *a real friend*. He has a strict notion of honour, rather too familiar to his inferiors but will not suffer to be browbeaten or

> treated with haughtiness by his superiors. Now for his vices or rather
> let us call them weaknesses – too subject to give loose or vent to his
> passions, too subject to be in a passion, but he never bears malice or
> rancour in his heart . . . he is rather too fond of wine and women.

Few of his later biographers would disagree with that assessment, but few have since given the prince credit for the remarkable gift of friendship that he was to display throughout his life. No other British monarch ever developed such a wide circle of friends. This persistent quest for comradeship may well have been an attempt to compensate for the loneliness of childhood and the implacable hostility of a father in whose eyes he could do nothing right. Although George III has been described as the first truly 'English' of the Hanoverian kings, his own repressive upbringing governed an approach to the education of children that remained distinctly Germanic in character. This was hardly surprising, given that the royal family, as Kings of Hanover, retained a strong connection with German society. In the eighteenth century, Germany was the home of the educational treatise in which pedagogues recommended that children be looked upon more as wild animals in need of taming rather than as naturally spirited young people. In these influential works fathers are repeatedly warned that dissent and disobedience must be beaten out of them. The doyen of this school, J.G. Kruger, writing in the same decade that the prince was born, warned parents that 'the blows you administer should not be merely playful ones, but should convince him you are the master . . . if he has seen that he is vanquished the first time and has been obliged to humble himself before you, this will rob him of his courage to rebel anew'. If George III was personally unaware of this draconian approach to education then he would certainly have approved of its principles.

Any account of George III's childhood makes it perfectly clear that in dealing with his eldest son he was merely acting in the same controlling manner as his own father had with him. The damage had been done a generation earlier for George III was not the son but the grandson of George II. His own father, Prince Frederick, having died before he could inherit the throne, was a scheming and unpleasant bully who was totally alienated from his own parents. His mother, Queen Caroline, loathed him so intensely that she once said of him: 'If I was to see him in hell I should feel no more for him than I should for any other rogue that ever went there.' After Frederick's death, the queen mother, the domineering Princess Augusta of Saxe-Gotha, took charge of the future George III's upbringing, imbuing him with her own self-righteousness and keeping him away from other boys whom she felt might corrupt him. She was equally stern towards George's four other brothers. Once, seeing the young Duke of Gloucester in an unhappy mood, she sharply asked why he was so silent. 'I am thinking,' he replied sadly, 'that if ever I have a son I will not make him so unhappy as you make me.' With both parents dying pre-maturely George III became responsible for his sisters, two of whom were chronic invalids and the others soon married off to unsuitable husbands. George was shattered by the misery he had unwittingly brought upon his sisters and mortified that he was unable to control the increasingly dissolute behaviour of his brothers. But rather than learning the lesson of the past and encouraging his son with help and the occasional word of praise, George III resorted to bullying him, with predictable results. As Lord Melbourne later told Queen Victoria, because of his father's harshness the young Prince of Wales was 'monstrously afraid of him'.

The prince's undoubted virtues of a sweet nature, fine manners and an unusual sociability meant nothing to his father, who saw them merely as dangerous weaknesses of character that ought to be rigorously suppressed. Moreover, a tendency to duplicity and the bad habits that the king claimed to observe in his son posed a current and increasing threat to the very survival of the monarchy. As the prince would also one day be King of Hanover – the bolt-hole for the family in the event of ejection from England – it was important that as he approached manhood he should mend his ways and behave in a more responsible manner. There was also the need to improve his proficiency in the German language and become more Germanic and less French in his attitude. Such advice was explained to him in great detail in a letter written by his father soon after George's sixteenth birthday. It ended by urging him to mend his ways, to work harder and to behave more responsibly. The letter is written in a tone of anxious piety that almost pleads for George to turn away from sin while there is still time and to follow the path of righteousness as demanded by the 'Great Creator'. Once again the letter was self-defeating, only serving to make the prince more determined than ever to ignore his father's advice and, for good measure, to provide him with as much trouble and embarrassment as possible. What had alarmed the king and provoked him to write the letter were reports in the London newspapers of his eldest son's bad behaviour in public and obvious 'love of dissipation', when he should have been setting a good example to the nation. George had clearly fallen into bad company and must be persuaded to seek out more suitable companions, 'those who seem of worthy characters and wish to make themselves of utility and ornament to their country'. Nor did it help matters that two of his son's most infamous friends were the king's own two brothers.

These men, the Dukes of Gloucester and of Cumberland, had behaved so badly that they were forbidden to come to Windsor. Their infamy, naturally, made them highly attractive to the young Prince of Wales. Gloucester, the elder of the two, had secretly married the Dowager Countess Waldegrave in 1766 at her house in Pall Mall. Not only had the lady's late husband been George III's own despised governor, and loathed by him as a 'depraved and worthless man', but she was also the illegitimate daughter of Sir Edward Walpole, a leading Whig who had frequently spoken out against the House of Hanover. On both counts the bride was abhorrent to the king, who immediately banished his brother from the court, forcing him into exile in Italy from where he returned for an occasional foray into the lowlife of London. In contrast to his elder brother, Gloucester was a colourful character and a great favourite of the popular press of the day, which eagerly chronicled his every misdeed with whores and actresses.

The younger brother Cumberland had, if anything, behaved

even worse by committing adultery so ineptly with the Countess of Grosvenor that her husband was about to sue him in open court for £10,000 compensation. To avoid this damaging public humiliation George III persuaded his other brothers to join him in raising that sum to buy off the earl. If that disgrace was not enough, Cumberland then began an affair with a commoner named Olive Wilmot, who was soon calling herself Princess Olive of Cumberland. Finally, Cumberland, on the rebound from Mrs Wilmot, rushed into a marriage with the beautiful but dissolute young widow Mrs Ann Horton, who was much given to 'vulgar, noisy and indelicate behaviour and to jokes of unparalleled coarseness'. Horace Walpole described her as being 'extremely pretty and well made, and remarkable for the great length of her eyelashes, which veiled a pair of most artful and coquettish eyes'.

As a result of his brothers' serious misbehaviour George III had become obsessed that history might repeat itself and that his own sons would develop similar tastes to their uncles and marry unsuitable women. It was partly for this reason that he took such a close interest in the Prince of Wales's moral education, watching intensely for the first signs of similar depravity. So anxious was he that he persuaded his ministers to bring in the Royal Marriage Act of 1772 as a precaution. This bill expressly forbade any member of the royal family to marry without the sovereign's consent, the one concession being that if the person was over the age of twenty-five, an appeal could be made to the Privy Council. As punishment for their transgressions both Gloucester and Cumberland were ordered to remain in voluntary, if sullen, exile. When they were finally allowed to return eight years later in 1780 Cumberland, at least, appeared not have learnt his lesson and set up a faro gaming-table at his house in Pall Mall and consorted with the Whig opposition. Seeing an opportunity to annoy and embarrass his father further, George began seeking out their company.

The choice of one's uncles as boon companions seems odd, if not positively bizarre. The suspicion is that he did it more as a gesture to annoy his father than because his uncles were particularly stimulating company. This may explain why he was so keen to take up the cause of his uncle Gloucester when he returned to England. Knowing that his involvement would infuriate his father, the prince joined Gloucester in appealing to end the ban on the Duchess of Gloucester appearing at court. George even provoked his father more by stating that he intended to visit the duke and duchess at their new house in London. This so outraged the king that even Gloucester appealed to the prince to change his mind and stay away. The Cumberlands, too, cheerfully joined in the farce by inviting their young nephew to their boisterous parties and dinners. These rowdy evenings were immediately reported to the king, who blamed his brother for a further deterioration in his son's behaviour.

By this time the Prince of Wales was actually appearing drunk in public, and this, according to the king, was exactly what the Duchess of Cumberland specialized in together with shocking polite company by swearing like a trooper. Even Horace Walpole noticed the change in the prince's behaviour and claimed that his new family friends were encouraging him to belittle and mock the king. According to Walpole, the Duke of Cumberland 'spoke nothing but the dialect of footmen and grooms', and his coarseness continued to deny him a presence at court – even if he wanted one. Clever enough to avoid London, the scene of his past disgrace, Cumberland had taken up residence in the new, fashionable resort of Brighthelmstone, or Brighton. From there he bombarded his nephew with invitations to visit him and his wife and to escape the restrictions imposed by his father. Cumberland's reputation as a reprobate proved well justified for he engineered a meeting between his nephew and a local girl that resulted in George's first sexual liaison.

For a young man newly released from parental captivity the relaxed atmosphere of Brighton must have been very appealing. As his first biographer Robert Huish gushingly stated, he was 'a prisoner released from confinement and plunged at once into the joys of Society with all the avidity of the fainting traveller who hastens to the gushing spring to allay the torments of his thirst'. These visits to the seaside were to be the inspiration for George's ambition to build a pleasure dome of his own on the Sussex coast – which would one day be realized as the Brighton Pavilion. His uncle Cumberland and the town of Brighton thus became the formative experiences for the young Prince of Wales, launching him as one of the most famous libertines of the age. As the historian Sir Edward Parry lamented: 'Cumberland enabled the Prince to discover and practise most of the vices of the rich and corrupt few.' Or, as Huish put it melodramatically, the prince, with the encouragement of his uncle, managed to 'imitate the daring and boundless flight of the eagle, which had been long chained to the earth by some tyrannical power'.

In August 1780 an evermore confidant Prince of Wales celebrated his eighteenth birthday with the knowledge that having reached legal majority he would now accede directly to the throne in the event of his father's death. But if he had hoped to enjoy the freedom to form new friendships without the interference of his father he was much mistaken, as George III's obsession with controlling every aspect of his son's life continued unabated. To his dismay the Prince was informed that he could not have an establishment of his own and would be required to reside under the parental eye at either Buckingham House in London or in an apartment at Windsor Castle. He must also remain under the direct control and moral guidance of Bishop Hurd for another four months. One can imagine with what despondency George received this news, but worse was to come. In another long and detailed letter the king informed him that when in London he must dine with the family each night unless given prior permission to entertain his friends. Royal permission was also required if he wanted to go to the theatre or the opera, and then he must take his official attendant with him. Occasionally he could hold dances at the palace, but on no account was he to attend balls or assemblies at private houses. As to masked balls, notorious occasions for flirtations, they were strictly prohibited. Church attendance on Sunday was compulsory. As a further humiliation he was also ordered to take an attendant with him as chaperone whenever he drove out in a carriage or went riding in Hyde Park. Presumably, such attendants would be ordered to report to the king any bad behaviour or illicit flirtations. If the king himself rode out the prince would then be expected to accompany him briskly for there was to be 'no lounging about in Hyde Park' as 'in the exalted station you are placed in, every step is of consequence and your future character will greatly depend in the world on the propriety of your character at the present period'. Yet again had George III provided his eldest son with good reasons to rebel and a new determination to assert his moral and territorial independence.

Soon after this letter was received George was separated from his younger brother for the first time. Frederick was appointed a full colonel by his father – his elder brother would have to wait years to receive a similar commission – and sent off to complete his military education in Hanover. For seventeen years the brothers had been inseparable companions, sharing the loneliness of the Dutch House together. The loss of Frederick, who had provided the intimate contact lacking in the rest of his young life, had a profound effect on George, an emotional person whenever faced with the loss of a close friend. At first he seemed unable to deal with the separation and was reported to have spent a whole day walking about in a state of shock. The debt he owed his younger brother for his unquestioning support in childhood would be fully repaid in later years. Frederick, in Hanover, appeared almost as bereft as his elder brother, writing constantly to advise him, for his own sake, to make every attempt possible to improve the relationship with their father:

> For Gods [*sic*] sake do everything which you can to keep well with him, at least upon decent terms, consider he is vexed enough in publick affairs. I . . . You know, my dearer brother. I hate preaching full as much as you do, and constraint as if possible more, but still for both your sakes I entreat you to keep as well together as possible. Excuse what I write you because it comes from the heart.

Yet Frederick's own behaviour was scarcely more virtuous than that of George, appearing all the more hypocritical given that since the age of just seven months he had been titular Bishop of Osnaburg, Westphalia – the thought of the dissolute Frederick as a bishop amused many in the London clubs. This 'secular dignity' was a useful addition to the frugal allowance provided by his father for it was worth £20,000 a year. Already he seemed set on causing as much scandal as possible. An anecdote told by Captain Rees Gronow in his memoirs relates a conversation between the duke, soon after his return from Hanover, and a friend, Arthur Upton, concerning a newly arrived visitor from Paris:

'Who the deuce is this Montrand?' asks Frederick.

'They say, sir,' replied Upton, 'that he is the most agreeable scoundrel and the greatest reprobate in France.'

'Is he, by Jove!' Frederick replied. 'Then let us ask him to dinner immediately.'

2

BAD COMPANY

SINCERE as Frederick's advice to his brother had been, it had little effect for George was more determined than ever to disobey and thwart his father's persistent attempts to dominate and control him. Both parents, he claimed, continued to treat him badly, with the king being always 'excessively cross, ill-tempered and uncommonly grumpy' and the queen constantly accusing him of 'various high crimes and misdemeanours'. In response to what he considered her ill-natured and unjust treatment he now began answering her back and giving as good as he got. Although his mother was irritating, it was his father who was the real villain of the piece, with the queen merely obeying her husband's orders.

Ironically, Frederick's own behaviour at this time was far more compromising than that of his elder brother. Even before he had left for Hanover he had formed an intimate relationship with one of the most unsuitable women in London, the infamous Letitia Smith. Her notoriety came from having been the mistress of the late highwayman 'Sixteen-String' John Rann. One of the most celebrated criminals of the age, Rann combined ruthlessness with an unusual sense of style as exhibited in the multicoloured ribbons with which he fastened the knees of his breeches. Finally apprehended near Brentford in 1774, he supposedly entertained seven women to a farewell dinner at Newgate Prison on the eve of his execution, at which he danced a jig and exchanged cheerful banter with the hangman and the crowd. After the demise of her colourful lover, Letitia had become involved with the young Frederick, who was captivated by her uninhibited attitude to life. Even when his removal to Hanover ended the affair he still recalled her fondly in letters to his brother. George was so intrigued that he sought Letitia out, introducing himself at a masked ball – an event he had been expressly forbidden to attend. He then wrote to Frederick, saying that the lady was missing him so badly that she was planning to follow him over to Hanover. 'I believe no woman ever loved a man more passionately', George told his brother, 'than she does you.'

Clearly both brothers were still driven by a youthful romanticism that contrasted strongly with the hard-headed reality represented by the beautiful Letitia. Wasting no time after Frederick had departed, she set her sights on a wealthy landowner, the rake and sportsman Sir John Lade. Heir to a vast fortune derived from brewing, Lade's father had died young, and no less a person than Dr Samuel Johnson, a family friend, was regularly consulted on his upbringing. Johnson formed a very low opinion of the boy, advising his mother to 'procure him knowledge; for really ignorance to a rich man is like fat to a sick sheep, it only serves to call the rooks about him'. After their marriage the Lades became close friends with George, who was fascinated by their almost complete disregard for convention and their bold and sybaritic approach to life – the very qualities he wished for himself. Yet the obsession with this most unusual woman does not appear to have led him to attempt an affair, although he constantly showered her with presents. Not the least of Letitia's accomplishments was the ability to use the foulest language to make her point. Brought up in the tight-lipped atmosphere at Kew, George listened in wonderment to a tirade of oaths that amused rather than repelled him. Other qualities they possessed impressed him, too, particularly their mastery of horsemanship – Sir John was one of the most accomplished carriage drivers of his day, while Letitia could handle even the most difficult horse – something then much admired by the prince. His obsession with Letitia led him to commission George Stubbs to paint what became one of his finest portraits, *Laetitia, Lady Lade* (1793), which depicts Letitia riding side-saddle on a spirited horse.

The Lades may well have been the models for Rawdon Crawley and his wife Becky Sharp in Thackeray's *Vanity Fair* for both husbands were compulsive gamblers and their wives fascinating but unprincipled schemers. A compulsive gambler from an early age, John Lade lost vast sums of money on all forms of gambling. Many of his bets involved feats of skill such as betting that he could drive the off-wheels of his phaeton exactly over a small object like a six-pence or manipulate a large four-in-hand carriage around the cramped yard at Tattersall's at Hyde Park Corner – no wonder he became one of the founder members of the Four-in-Hand Club, named after the number of horses' reins held in one hand. Lade was also acknowledged as the finest judge of a thoroughbred horse in England. His disdain for risk and his sporting style of dress – he always wore riding clothes and had a penchant for laconically brandishing a riding whip – proved highly attractive to the young Prince of Wales. This imitation in dress and manners of common coachmen was a strange obsession of the age. Wealthy young men adopted coachmen and ostlers as friends and copied their costumes and manner of speech, particularly their constant swearing. Such behaviour would not be seen again until the 1960s when upper-class young men from Chelsea aped the speech and manners of working-class Cockneys and Liverpudlians.

Yet Dr Johnson's warnings about the fate that awaited the young John Lade in later life proved only too prescient, and bad company and heavy gambling soon ate up the Lade fortune, driving him into the arms of the London moneylenders. Inevitably Sir John ended up in the debtors' prison, from where his good friend the Prince of Wales rescued him and persuaded him to accept a pension of £300 a year as his driving tutor. To save face the money was made out in the name of a Reverend Dr Tolly. The discreet rescue of a friend in need was typical of George's generous nature as was his contempt for the condemnation that Lade received from others. Friendship mattered more than public opinion, and even such a morally reprehensible character as John Lade deserved the help and support that respectable society denied him.

Many of the stories of snubs that the Regent received on

behalf of his rakish friends centre on Lade, and many of them appear to have been delivered by the acerbic Lord Thurlow. On one occasion Thurlow was invited to dinner at the Brighton Pavilion, but, knowing that Lade and another notorious rake, Lord Barrymore, would be present, he sent the sanctimonious reply: 'I cannot do so until your Royal Highness keeps better company.' Even as late as 1805 Thurlow was still fulminating against George's dissolute friends. Once again invited to dinner at the Pavilion by its good-natured host, he deigned to appear but was then ushered into an anteroom where George apologized for the unexpected presence of Sir John Lade, whom he could not avoid asking to stay for dinner. To this Lord Thurlow responded in an ill-tempered growl: 'I have no objection, Sir, to Sir John Lade in his proper place, which I take to be your Royal Highness's coach-box, and not your table.' When Letitia died in 1825, Sir John retired to the one asset he had left, his stud farm in Sussex, where he continued to receive the pension from his old friend, now King George IV. Queen Victoria, when a young girl new to the throne, records disapprovingly in her diaries that she had just discovered that she was still paying a pension to 'a Sir John Lade, one of George IV's intimates'.

Lord Thurlow's disdain for another of George's closest companions at the time, Richard Barry, Lord Barrymore, would have been shared by the great majority of polite society. Barrymore, known as Hellgate, was the head of a particularly eccentric Irish family. All were given disparaging nicknames: his elder brother, a gambling clergyman thought destined for prison, was known as Newgate; his club-footed younger brother was dubbed Cripplegate; and their sister, the foul-mouthed Lady Melfort, was universally referred to as Billingsgate. Succeeding to the Earldom of Barrymore when just four years old, Lord Barrymore arrived at Eton with £1,000 in his pocket and two large estates in England and Ireland behind him. A London cabbie who used to drive him to the brothels several times a week recalled – in Henry Mayhew's *London Labour and the London Poor* – witnessing Barrymore's wild lifestyle:

he used always to take his own wine with him. After waiting till near daylight, or till daylight, I've carried my lord, girls and all – fine dressed-up madams – to Billingsgate, and there I've left them to breakfast at some queer place, or to slang with the fishwives.

On another occasion the cabbie drove him to a Mother Cummins's in Lisle Street, but she refused to let him in because he had broken so many things the last time he had been there and had disgraced her to the neighbourhood. 'Knock at the door, tiger; and knock till they open it,' Barrymore ordered, and so they continued until 'every drop of water in the house was emptied over us, out of the windows'.

Apart from such rakish behaviour and his undoubted prowess as a horseman, Lord Barrymore did little other than earn a reputation as a practical joker. His many pranks included pretending to kidnap young women on the London streets and leaving coffins outside houses to frighten the servants. This irresponsibility greatly appealed to the Prince of Wales, who once encouraged him to ride his horse up to the top floor of Mrs Fitzherbert's house in Brighton. As Maria Fitzherbert was a woman of strict propriety this was a provocative and dangerous act. When the terrified horse refused to descend, two burly blacksmiths had to be called out to push it down the stairs by force. However, Barrymore's most famous bet was a wager that he could eat a very large live tomcat at one sitting. When the time came to perform the feat even this gamest of men admitted defeat. But what most endeared him to the prince was his profligate generosity that closely resembled his own capacity for largesse. Barrymore thought nothing of spending almost £2,000 on a banquet in honour of the prince, and their shared passion for drama provoked him into spending over £60,000 on building a theatre on his estate at Wargrave that saw little drama, although it proved an ideal venue for parties, including a particularly licentious masked ball held there in 1790. Falling on hard times, and oblivious to aristocratic convention, Barrymore finally married the daughter of a sedan-chair porter, who proved to be as much of a wastrel as himself.

Another of the prince's companions, George Hanger, Baron

Colerain, was equally eccentric in his choice of bride, marrying a gipsy woman only for her to run off with a penniless Irish tinker. Hanger, too, inherited large estates that were soon gambled away. Unlike many of the prince's companions, however, Hanger had a proper career as a soldier and had served in the army of Frederick the Great of Prussia. Returning home, he joined the British Army and fought with distinction in the American War of Independence. When that war ended he tried his luck in Hanover where he became friendly with Prince Frederick, frequently acting as his personal courier by taking his private letters to the Prince of Wales in London. At the king's birthday ball in 1782 Hanger appeared in his own eccentric version of court dress, featuring a short blue coat with an enormous feathered hat and an odd-looking sword. Totally unknown in society at that time, he took the hand of one of the great beauties of the age, Miss Gunning, put on his hat and led her out to dance. Even George III was forced to smile at this preposterous spectacle while the Prince of Wales was convulsed into uncontrollable laughter. George was so taken with Hanger's performance that evening and with his exuberant manner and obvious good nature that he later appointed him an equerry. With little more than his salary from the prince to live on, Hanger supplemented his income by riding as a jockey and by sponging off friends. The new equerry also shared his master's appetite for lively women, once pursuing a runaway mistress down to Brighton only to discover that she was staying with the prince at the Pavilion. Amiable as ever, George took pity on his friend, thinking him more in need of the lady than he was himself. Summoning his carriage, he ordered them both to be taken back to London that night.

One of Hanger's most ludicrous exploits was to organize a cross-country race between a flock of turkeys and a flock of geese, an event attended by both the Prince of Wales and the Duke of York. The race was held over a ten-mile course, with George, the leader of the turkey faction, driving them along with a pole. As dusk approached, the turkeys decided to fly up to roost in the trees. The prince and his supporters were unable to dislodge them so leaving the geese to win the race. The painter Joseph Farington recalls in his diary another famous anecdote that demonstrates Hanger's capacity for quick thinking, even when drunk. At one of the entertainments given by the prince, His Royal Highness filled a glass with wine and wantonly threw it in Hanger's face. Hanger, without being disconcerted, immediately filled his glass and threw the wine in the face of the person who sat next to him and bid him pass it round, an admirable instance of presence of mind and judgement upon an occasion of coarse rudeness. Yet another of Hanger's misadventures became the subject of a famous cartoon of the time. It occurred when Hanger visited Plymouth in the company of the Prince of Wales. As they ambled along the street arm-in-arm, Hanger rather disrespectfully pushed a local fishwife aside. The woman responded by punching Hanger so hard that she knocked him head over heels into a dog kennel, much to the amusement of the prince and his friends. But George Hanger's fast-accumulating debts were no laughing matter, and he was soon, like Sir John Lade, carried off to debtors' prison by his creditors. In the year that he languished there he wrote his memoirs, blaming his failings on keeping bad company, although he does not name the prince personally:

> with men and women of every description, and of every rank, from the highest to the lowest, from St James's to St Giles's; in palaces and night cellars; from the drawing-room to the dust cart . . . human nature is in general frail, and mine I confess has been wonderfully so.

When released, he scraped together a small amount of money to establish himself somewhat incongruously as a London coal merchant. Against all expectations and ignoring the scandalized reactions of his wealthy and well-bred acquaintances such as the diarist Nathaniel Wraxall – who described him as 'an outcast from decent society' – the business flourished. In a final gesture of contempt for public opinion, Hanger married his cook.

Among the prince's other dissolute companions in these early years were two dukes both old enough to have known better. One was the Catholic grandee, the Duke of Norfolk, a man of virtually no education but possessed of a native cunning that had made him a successful gambler when sober. Although hereditary Earl Marshall of England, he had earned the reputation of being the dirtiest aristocrat in the kingdom. Constantly in a foul condition, Norfolk could only occasionally be washed by his servants when lying dead drunk on the floor.

The other reprobate was William Douglas, fourth Duke of Queensberry, popularly known as Old Q after the single initial boldly painted on his carriage door. Immensely wealthy, Queensberry was the leading racehorse owner of the age and an inveterate gambler. He had met the prince when Lord of the Bedchamber to George III, although he clearly did not share his sovereign's poor opinion of his son and heir or the need for sobriety for he was later dismissed by the king for drunkenness. Certainly, Queensbury, who had obtained almost mystical status as a raddled old libertine, made an ideal role model for a young prince determined to live extravagantly and to flout social convention. Apart from drinking, Old Q's speciality vice was whoring, and he became famous as the most public lecher in the kingdom, a reputation all the more incongruous because of his short stature and shrivelled features. His lair was a fine mansion in Piccadilly into which he was said to take young girls obtained for him by an elderly procuress who combed the local lodging-houses, servant-hiring fairs and even girls' boarding schools. The press and the cartoonists transformed Queensbury into a figure of almost fairytale lust and attributed to him all the characteristics of failing sexuality such as paying young women to undress but not touching them. In an attempt to regain his youth and potency he was said to have bathed in milk and slept with veal cutlets on his face. Such stories appeared in the cheap scandal sheets of the time, in one of which a fictitious young woman claimed that she had slept with the 'the old goat of Piccadilly', having got into his bed a maid and left it in the same condition. From such public exposure it is easy to see the Duke of Queensberry as the inspiration for the phrase 'a dirty old man'. Why the young and stylish heir to the throne would have welcomed the company of such an elderly and infamous reprobate remains a mystery, but the friendship was maintained for many years.

From this particular circle of friends George derived the enthusiasm for horse racing that led him to win the Derby in 1788 with a horse named *Sir Thomas*. His favourite racecourse was Lewes, near Brighton, which he attended well into old age, forming casual friendships with owners and jockeys alike. His early success on the turf was impressive for his horses won almost two hundred races in just three years. His decision to give up the sport and sell off his stable of thoroughbreds followed an embarrassing scandal at Newmarket in 1791. His horse Escape, ridden by his jockey Sam Chiffney, failed to win a race for which he was the favourite. The following day, with the odds against him considerably lengthened by his previous failure, Escape did exactly that, running away with the race and causing a considerable loss to the punters. The rumour spread that Chiffney had pulled the horse in the first race at the instruction of either the prince or his racing manager, Warwick Lake. The scandal and furore was so distressing that George immediately decided to abandon racing altogether, even though Escape was cleared in a Jockey Club inquiry. The reason for George's swift action was a visit from Sir Charles Bunbury, a Jockey Club Steward, who informed him discretely that if George were ever to allow Chiffney to ride one of his horses again 'no gentleman would start against him'. In a typically magnanimous gesture the prince informed Chiffney that he believed him completely innocent of the allegations and intended to pay him an allowance of £200 a year for the rest of his life. Perhaps his faith in Chiffney's character was misplaced for the jockey soon sold his annuity cheaply for a £1,260 lump sum and ended his days in a debtors' prison.

From the moment of his release from Kew at the age of eighteen the Prince of Wales had appeared determined to emulate his new and dissolute companions in bad behaviour, particularly when staying in Brighton with his uncle Cumberland. Soon George had persuaded his younger brother Frederick, Duke of York, to join him there, and together they enjoyed, according to the diarist

Thomas Creevey, 'all the extravagances and debaucheries of this most virtuous metropolis'. While George encouraged his brother to drink to excess Frederick in return persuaded his brother to indulge in his own particular vice of gambling at cards. It was not long before the king was receiving almost daily reports of his sons' bad behaviour together. When in London George, the more adventurous of the two, was seen 'riding like a madman' in Hyde Park or involved in drunken brawls at the pleasure gardens of Vauxhall or Ranelagh.

If this was not enough, there were the liaisons with very unsuitable women, with George behaving, as Huish archly puts it, 'like the bee, roaming from flower to flower, sipping the honey, but never visiting the flower again'. Seen as a stratagem to deeply annoy his father, the prince's new lifestyle was a great success, and he had the pleasure of receiving a letter from his father containing further reprimands. What annoyed the king most was that his son's irresponsible adventures were now being chronicled daily in the newspapers. The king told him, more in sorrow than in anger:

> Draw your own conclusion, whether you must not give me many an uneasy moment. I wish to live with you as a friend but then by your behaviour you must deserve it . . . When you have read this carefully over you will find an affectionate father trying to save his son from perdition.

But the boy who could once be bullied into submission was now a man, and the only effective sanction the king could impose on his unruly son was to withhold an increase in his allowance. To fund his extravagant lifestyle the prince depended almost entirely on the royal Privy Purse. Already the king had grudgingly provided the £5,000 needed to buy off the first of his son's clinging and potentially blackmailing mistresses, Mrs Robinson. In return he asked, quite reasonably, that George make a serious attempt to mend his ways and in particular not continue to dine with such reprobates as Lord Chesterfield, Colonel Anthony St Leger or Charles William Windham. Completely ignoring the request,

George went straight round to Lord Chesterfield's house at Black-heath where he became so drunk he collapsed with alcoholic poisoning. In another roistering evening at Blackheath a dog badly savaged a servant and Lord Chesterfield himself fell down the stairs, after which the prince, now too drunk to walk, had to be carried to his carriage and then driven home by his equally inebri-ated uncle, the Duke of Cumberland. These adventures were, to his father's chagrin, eagerly reported in the press. Inevitably there was a price to pay for this wild lifestyle, and a few days later George became so seriously ill that a royal surgeon, Sir Richard Jebb, informed the king that his son was in serious danger of dying. Even the patient now realized that he had gone too far. For a fort-night he remained confined to his bedroom, his face covered with ugly red blotches that were 'dreadful to behold'. To his dismay he was forced to drink only barley water during the course of a slow recovery. The drunken orgies that had brought the prince to this state might well have triggered off the constant bad health that he was now to endure for the rest of his life. Yet, once recovered, he continued to drink heavily and acquired a harmful addiction to opium in its popular form of laudanum.

As well as deteriorating health there was a second, equally damaging price to pay for consorting with the likes of Lade, Barry-more and Queensberry. The Prince of Wales, so popular when a child, had begun to lose the respect of the public. Stories of his misdeeds filled the papers and cartoons, and over the years his illustrated image was transformed from that of a fresh-faced and highly civilized young prince into that of the fat, debauched Regent of the Brighton Pavilion and finally into the buffoonish King George IV, shut away from the people at Windsor Lodge. Youthful promise had mutated into mature irrelevance as George slowly drifted away from the public at a time when great inter-national events concerned the nation.

The start of the damage can be attributed to a single cartoon by one of the leading satirists of the day, Charles Pigott. It was entitled *The Jockey Club: or a Sketch of the manners of the Age* and mocked the prince's close circle of sporting friends and their many vices. This was one of the most widely circulated cartoons of the time and did considerable damage to George's reputation by exposing him to moral censure combined with personal ridicule. Yet George carried on his merry way, ignoring an important levee at St James's Palace in favour of a day's hunting in Northampton-shire with Anthony St Leger. Again the king wrote, reprimanding him for his absence and warning that he must never do it again. The prince coolly replied that although he recognized that his behaviour was different from 'the limited plans' drawn up for him by his father it was far from deserving the king's censure. George was convinced that nothing could be done to alter the situation. As he told the diplomat Sir James Harris in April 1785: 'What can I do my dear Harris? The King hates me, he always did from seven years old . . . We are too wide asunder ever to meet.'

3

FOLLOWING THE FOX

GAMBLING, whoring and drinking were bad enough, but what if the Prince of Wales fell into the clutches of unscrupulous politicians? This was the question that obsessed George III as he struggled to contain the irresponsible behaviour of his eldest son. If this happened then George would no longer be simply an embarrassment to his family but a threat to the very survival of the British monarchy at a time of great danger from Napoleon Bonaparte and Revolutionary France. Events there had shown what could happen if a disgruntled member of the royal family put himself at the head of the opposition. For this is what George's old friend the Duke of Chartres – later the regicide Duke of Orléans – had done before being arrested and guillotined. Although the Whigs were not yet Jacobins, who could say how events might turn out? For England, too, had a royal libertine with a grudge against the sovereign. Many Tories shared the king's apprehension, not least Robert Huish, who thought the Whigs would insidiously reach George, and 'seduce him from the moral standards before he had acquired any knowledge of human artifice'. One friendship in particular seemed to George III to be the dangerous prelude to England following the way of France: that of the Prince of Wales and the Whig politician Charles James Fox.

A close relationship had existed between the two men since George was twenty-one and Fox one of the best-known political figures in Europe, committed to championing the rights of the people against attrition by the monarchy. Brilliant in both conversation and political strategy, Fox was part of a Whig triumvirate that included the philosopher Edmund Burke and the playwright Richard Brinsley Sheridan – even his political enemies agreed he was the greatest talent in a British political party at the time. Fox's distinctive appearance was as sinister as his reputation, making him one of the most recognizable figures in London. Horace Walpole memorably described him as follows:

> His bristly black person and shagged breast quite open, and rarely purified by any ablutions was wrapped in a foul linen nightgown and his bushy hair dishevelled. In these cynical weeds and with epicurean good humour, did he dictate his politics – and in this school did the heir of the Crown attend his lessons and imbibe them.

Apart from his obvious abilities and eccentric character Fox had one other important qualification for being the prince's friend: he was hated by George III, who disapproved of his dissipated lifestyle as well as his radical politics. Fox was an unusual combination of vice and virtue, with a hard-won reputation for being one of the most compulsive gamblers in London. Most evenings he would leave his lodgings in St James's and stroll along to Brook's Club and take his place at the gaming-table. Fox's gambling was funded by his wealthy father, Lord Holland, a man who had suspiciously made a large fortune when acting as Paymaster General of the British Army. The relationship between Holland and son could not have differed more from that of George III and the Prince of Wales. Where the English King had been repressive and moralistic, Lord Holland was liberal and indulgent in the extreme and exercised virtually no control over his son. Once, when Charles announced his intention of wantonly smashing a watch he had been given, Lord Holland simply replied: 'Well if you must, I suppose you must.' Not only did he treat Charles as a friend and companion but he was happy to encourage him in the same dissipations that he enjoyed himself. Even in the liberal social atmosphere of 1763 it was most unusual for an aristocratic father to take a young son as companion on the Grand Tour of Europe, but

Lord Holland disdained convention. Travelling in a leisurely fashion through France, Belgium and Italy he introduced the boy to the most immoral society of the time, allowing him to drink wine freely and giving him money at Spa, Belgium, to start his gambling career. Even before he went to Eton Charles had acquired a worldly sophistication that made him the envy of his fellow pupils. It was obvious to all who met him as an adolescent that the boy was destined for a political career, not least because he would frequently leave his studies and go up to London to listen to the debates in Parliament. After Oxford Fox accompanied his father on another tour of Europe where he met Voltaire and the Prince of Wales's friend, the Duke of Chartres, also adding a passion for art to that of gambling. Now an addict of the gaming-tables, Fox would be in almost constant debt for the rest of his life. On returning to England in 1768 Lord Holland purchased his son the pocket borough of Midhurst in Sussex so launching his son's extraordinary parliamentary career. Within the next few years Lord Holland earned a bitter reward for the unconventional upbringing that he had given his son for the family fortune was steadily eroded by Fox's gambling losses, which were paid without hesitation by Lord Holland.

Although Fox had begun to destroy the wealth of the Holland family, the affectionate relationship between father and son was undiminished. Matters might have been even worse for Fox then developed a costly passion for racing that involved purchasing a string of expensive racehorses. These, in spite of his friends' gloomy predictions, proved an unexpected success, and Fox was one of the few people in society actually to make money from the sport. He proved an astute punter, too, and it was said that, unlike his friend the Prince of Wales, he won far more than he lost on the racetrack. But even his wins on the horses could not compensate for the heavy losses he suffered at the gaming-table. Most evenings he was fleeced by unscrupulous players who took advantage of his good-natured generosity. Often he would spend the whole night gambling at either Brook's or Almack's and then arrive bleary eyed at the House of Commons the following morning. One night he appeared at White's Club and played through the night and well into the next day – by the late afternoon he had lost the enormous sum of £10,000. Horace Walpole gives a vivid account of Fox's gambling habit when, on one occasion, after having spoken brilliantly in a debate at the Commons, he set off for dinner at eleven o'clock in the evening, went on to White's where he drank until seven o'clock the next morning, called in at Almack's where he won £6,000 and proceeded to set off for the races at Newmarket at three o'clock in the afternoon – this was eighteenth-century clubbing with a vengeance. On yet another occasion he and his brother lost £32,000 between them in just three days. So precarious had Fox's finances become that he was said on occasions to have been reduced to borrowing money from the waiters at Brook's. Even Lord Holland at last realized that the youthful indulgence he had encouraged in his son might well be the nemesis of the Holland family fortune. When told that Charles had decided to get married, Lord Holland replied ruefully: 'I am glad of it for then he will go to bed for at least one night.'

It is not difficult to imagine the attraction that such an energetic debauchee held for the young prince. Not only did Fox outrage convention but he did it with panache. Fox was the elder by thirteen years and made an ideal mentor for a prince determined to live his own life free of conventional restraint. They also shared much in common other than a mutual passion for gambling. Both had great charm and an easy manner that enabled them to win over all but their most dedicated opponents. Furthermore, they discovered a similar taste in women: one of the prince's first mistresses, the actress Mary Robinson, had also been one of Fox's lovers. Perhaps Fox was lazy in romantic matters for he accepted a second discarded mistress of the prince in Mrs Elizabeth Bridget Armistead. A great beauty of cockney origins, Elizabeth Armistead was always known, like Dr Johnson's Mrs Thrale, by her surname and title. She had been the mistress of Lord George Cavendish, the brother of the Duke of Devonshire, before being taken on by the Prince of Wales and finally ending up with Fox. Unlike the transient relationships that characterized London society at the time, they were married in 1795 and theirs proved to be a lasting romance, with Mrs Armistead providing the love and support Fox needed to continue functioning in spite of his wild lifestyle. There is no doubt that the prince looked upon them as two of his closest friends. He had a great fondness for Mrs Armistead, as, unlike his other discarded mistresses, she made no financial demands on him when they parted. Her eventual reward was a pension of £500 a year from George to support her after the death of Fox.

By 1784 Fox and the prince were inseparable friends, with George happy to annoy his father further by flaunting the Whig colours of blue and buff in his dress. The election that year was one of the liveliest in British parliamentary history, particularly in the Westminster constituency where the famous naval hero Admiral Lord Hood was standing against Fox. For weeks bands of rival supporters brandishing placards and banners roamed the streets fighting each other and cheering on their candidate. Glamour was provided by the beautiful Duchess of Devonshire and her friends, who famously exchanged kisses for promises to vote for Fox. When their man was finally returned, Fox supporters went in triumphant procession to Carlton House where the Prince of Wales was waiting to greet them. He wore a victor's laurel wreath and fox's brush on his hat – a display of royal bias towards a political party that has never been seen since. The following day George hosted a celebratory party for his friend followed by a grand dinner that was punctuated by frequent toasts to the 'Buff and Blue'. The prince continued his own celebration for days to come until he was arrested in Mayfair for being drunk and disorderly. As not one of his companions was able to put up the bail money, one young aristocrat summoned his tailor to do the honours. When the man arrived he was astonished to see that one of the prisoners was the Prince of Wales. When he told the watch the true identity of their prisoner, they were highly embarrassed and began to mumble apologies for having offended the heir to the throne. Clapping them on the shoulders George told them with his customary good humour and lack of pomposity:

Offended my good fellows. By no means. Thank God the laws of
this country are superior to rank; and when men from high station
forget the decorums of community, it is fit that no distinction should
be made with respect to them. It should make an Englishman proud
to see the Prince of Wales obliged to send for a tailor to bail him!

In many ways Fox resembled the French Revolutionary leader
Georges Danton, who was equally scruffy in appearance but
possessed of similar charisma and intellect combined with a
rumbustuous lifestyle. Fox's friendship with the Prince of Wales
made him even more repellent to the king. When he appeared
formally at St James's on his appointment as foreign secretary in
the Duke of Portland's government of 1783 to kiss hands and
accept office, it was noticed that 'his Majesty put back his ears like
a horse at Astley's [Circus] when the tailor he had determined to
throw was getting on him'.

For his part Fox remained unconcerned and not prepared ever
to show subservience to anyone, least of all a king. In February
1772 he resigned office in order to be free to oppose the Royal
Marriage Act – which gave the reigning sovereign control over the
marriages of other royals – that the king was determined to see
pass. Fox considered it unjust and tyrannical, but in spite of an
impassioned speech his doubts were ignored and the House
approved the bill. The power of Fox's argument had, however,
greatly enhanced his reputation as a politician of considerable skill
and intellect, which was fortunate for his actual presentation was
somewhat hampered by his naturally harsh and shrill voice. This
he took great pains to deepen and modulate, much as Margaret
Thatcher did before becoming prime minister in the 1980s. Yet no
one could doubt the force and logic of Fox's liberal arguments as
when, in February 1775, he spoke on the dispute with the American
colonies. The great historian Edward Gibbon, who witnessed the
debate, claimed that Fox had 'discovered powers for regular debate
which neither his friends hoped nor his enemies dreaded'. From
that moment Fox was recognized as the greatest Parliamentarian
of his day and destined to pursue a career unique among British

statesmen of the first rank. Perversely, his time was passed almost wholly in opposition for, except for a few months between 1782 and 1783 and again for a few months before his death in 1806, he was always out of office.

Fox's treatment evoked a great deal of sympathy from the Prince of Wales. That a man of such obvious abilities should be excluded from office only because his lifestyle offended the monarch appeared to George to be national disgrace. For George, too, felt himself excluded from playing a useful role in the nation by the narrow-mindedness and spite of his father. Constantly in his youth he appealed to be allowed to enter the army and receive the training that would allow him to command troops in battle, much as his great-grandfather George II had done. His love affair with military uniforms and decorations revealed his wistful longing to be a soldier and to take part in the great military events of his time. But George III still categorically refused to consider his repeated requests while encouraging his second son, Frederick, Duke of York, to take up a career in the British Army and eventually become its commander-in-chief. The one concession the king grudgingly made was to allow George command of a single regiment, the 10th Light Dragoons, in 1793 at a time when Louis XVI had been executed and invasion by the French had become a distinct possibility. Encouraged by this modest success George appealed to the Austrian Emperor to give him a command in the Imperial Army in the fight against Revolutionary France. When the Emperor appeared ready to agree, George III promptly vetoed the arrangement. Nor would he agree to his heir having the rapid promotion in the British Army that George's three younger brothers had already received. Thus the Prince of Wales and Charles James Fox were both forced to spend their most productive years in frustration, knowing that they were capable of making a far more positive contribution than society or, more particularly, the king would allow. Resentment and boredom led them to even more dissolute behaviour, which reinforced the king's conviction he was correct in withholding power from them.

These similarities of character made the Prince of Wales and

Fox natural allies, and as George's twenty-first birthday approached he naturally looked to Fox, then briefly a member of the Cabinet, to champion his cause in pursuit of a far more generous allowance from the Crown. It was a particularly bad time for Fox to act for the king's long-standing hatred of him was now exacerbated by the latter's scathing attacks on the king's friend, Prime Minister Lord North, over the conduct of the American War. George III did not hesitate to make his feelings about Fox very plain: 'That young man has so thoroughly cast off every principle of common honour and honesty, that he must become as contemptible as he is odious,' he informed North. The previous government had, however, agreed that when the occasion arrived the Prince of Wales should have his own establishment and a suitable sum of £100,000 to maintain it. George considered this not unreasonable but was unaware that his father had decided not to sanction it. In a letter to the prince's treasurer, Colonel George Hotham, the king informed him that he could not agree to the £100,000. This had indeed been the sum granted to his grandfather, George II, by his own father, but that monarch had a wife and nine children to support whereas the current Prince of Wales did not have a family. A far more appropriate sum, the king suggested, were the revenues from the Duchy of Cornwall, which amounted to £12,000, and a further £50,000 a year from the Crown. That, the king added primly, was £27,000 more than he had himself received on coming of age. The real reason for the king's parsimony was explained in the tart and comprehensive criticism with which he concluded the letter to Hotham:

> On the smallest reflection I must feel that I have little reason to approve of any part of his conduct for the last three years; that his neglect of every religious duty is notorious; his want of common civility to the Queen and me, not less so; besides his total disobedience of every injunction I had given and which he, in presence of his brother and the gentlemen then about them both, declared himself contented with. I must hope he will now think it behoves him to take a fresh line of conduct more worthy of his station.

This was clearly George III's long-awaited chance to revenge himself on his recalcitrant son, and he took it with determination, informing the new Prime Minister, the Duke of Portland, that giving the Prince of Wales an allowance of £100,000 would be 'a shameful squandering of public money . . . to gratify the passions of an ill-advised young man'. Although disappointed, George refused to accept his father's decision and through his friend Fox involved the government in an increasingly acrimonious dispute that soon threatened to bring it down. In despair, the Duke of Portland implored Fox to persuade the prince to see reason and accept a compromise. After much discussion a deal was proposed that Fox felt sure the king would accept as it would allow him to make concessions without losing face. Under this new arrangement the prince would accept the sum and revenues already proposed by Parliament, but there would be an additional capital grant of £60,000 to allow him to pay off his debts. 'The Prince', Fox told his colleagues in Cabinet, 'had behaved in the handsomest manner.' The real cost of the deal was the wedge it drove between the king and Portland's government – the monarch insisted on seeing the agreement as a personal defeat, devised and brought about by his son in league with the accursed Fox. George III did not have to wait long for his revenge, for the coalition, and Fox in particular, were attacked by the press for supporting the wastrel prince. When the India Bill, which imposed new controls on the East India Company, was thrown out of Parliament in November 1783, the king used it as an excuse to dismiss his ministers and be rid of Fox for ever.

With his, albeit temporary, wealth the Prince of Wales set about renovating his new establishment, Carlton House, and expressing his gratitude to Fox with his customary generosity. Yet within a few years he was again heavily in debt and borrowing money at high interest rates in Antwerp and The Hague as well as arranging a loan of £60,000 from the London banker Thomas Coutts. As the creditors gathered, brother Frederick was recruited to try to raise a loan from his own father-in-law, the King of Prussia. George appealed for his help with the arch words: 'Do you think your beau père would not do a little something in the loan way.' When Frederick's attempt came to nothing, the search for funds became desperate, with George scandalously suggesting that he might offer the promise of honours for cash, the money to be repaid when he became king. Meanwhile, his debts mounted alarmingly and he owed vast sums of money to tradesmen and friends alike, including £15,000 to his close friend and political adviser the Earl of Moira. Worst of all, he could now expect little help from either political party. The Tories under Pitt shared his father's opinion that increasing the Prince of Wales's allowance would be to condone the extravagance of a wastrel. Fox and the Whig opposition were literally powerless to assist him. Furthermore, Fox had become increasingly unpopular in the country because of his initial support of the French Revolution, which he described as 'the most stupendous glorious edifice of liberty which has been erected on the foundations of human integrity in any time of country'. Fox lived to regret his words for now the Revolution had descended into bloody terror, and even the prince, whatever personal attachment he had to Fox, could not allow himself to be too closely identified with a man who had approved a revolutionary government that had murdered its own king.

As divisive as their politics now became, George still had reason to be deeply grateful to his friend for his unshakeable support during the crisis that followed the revelation that the prince might well have secretly married Maria Fitzherbert. Standing up before Parliament Fox boldly stated that he was not present at the ceremony nor had a wedding ever taken place. He quoted from a letter the prince had sent him stating unambiguously that 'there never was any grounds for these reports . . . so malevolently circulated'. Indeed, Fox claimed that his friend had, in his presence, consistently dismissed the very idea of a secret marriage as being ridiculous nonsense. So vehement were his denials and so convincing his assertion that 'not only could it never have happened legally, but never did happen in any way whatsoever' that the House was persuaded to believe this man of known principle. For the sake of friendship Fox had put himself in a very dangerous position for even in the late eighteenth century lying to Parliament was as serious an offence at it remains today. At first it appeared that Fox's intervention had been successful, but one evening a week later he was approached at Brook's by a man named Orlando Bridgeman, who had kept watch on the door during the actual marriage ceremony in Brighton. Bridgeman said to him: 'Mr Fox I hear you have denied in the House the prince's marriage to Mrs Fitzherbert. You have been misinformed. I was at the marriage.' Disaster loomed for Fox. He had either to recant his statement and so betray his friend the prince and see the inevitable ruin of his own political career or keep his mouth firmly shut on the issue. He chose the latter. To substantiate his position he avoided the prince for a whole year, although George continued to write to him as 'my dear friend' and tried to meet him at various house parties. Perversely, Fox's denial of the marriage had enraged the Catholic widow Mrs Fitzherbert, who thought that such a public denial presented her to the public as no more than the Prince of Wales's mistress.

Faced with the dilemma of choosing between friend and mistress, George took the inevitable course of expediency and raced to Brighton post haste where he took Maria's hand in his and told her in mock outrage: 'Only conceive, Maria, what Fox did yesterday. He went down to the House and denied that you and I were man and wife! Did you ever hear of such a thing!' His words only confirmed Mrs Fitzherbert's long-established contempt for Fox as a man who had encouraged the prince's dissolute ways. Later that day she told Sir Philip Francis somewhat graphically that Fox had 'rolled her in the kennel like a street walker'. For this the prince was made to pay by Maria refusing to see him. In despair, he sent for a mutual friend, Charles Grey, and told him that Fox's denial of the marriage must be modified to placate Mrs Fitzherbert. Grey politely refused the unpleasant task and suggested that the prince ask Fox himself. This George was not prepared to do, and the poisoned chalice was finally passed to their mutual friend, the playwright and MP Richard Brinsley Sheridan.

The speech that Sheridan delivered to the House was a masterpiece of ambiguity that appeared to exonerate everyone involved. He assured the House that the Prince of Wales had always behaved honourably as was only to be expected of such a beloved and respected member of the royal family. The 'other person' involved in the matter was a lady 'on whose conduct truth could fix no just reproach and whose character claimed, and was entitled to, the truest and most general respect'. The House listened to this skilful equivocation with wry smiles, highly amused to hear Sheridan's canonization of Mrs Fitzherbert's character so soon after Fox had brought it into question. A witty cartoon by James Gillray mocked this mordant display of hypocrisy in high places and showed Mrs Fitzherbert holding a crucifix and abandoned on a rock while Fox and the prince row blithely away. The prince is claiming 'I never saw her in my life', while Fox adds 'No, never in his life, damme'. Soon Parliament and the nation lost interest in the affair, but Fox was now seen as an enemy by Maria Fitzherbert. As a reprisal for continuing his association with Fox Maria now excluded George from her bed, an action that sent him, as always in emotional crises, into a dramatic but short-lived physical decline. Eventually reconciled to his beloved Maria he was told that the price he must pay for the resumption of their relationship would be a marked diminution of his friendship with Fox. As Anthony St Leger noted, the prince's coolness towards Fox 'was much increased by Mrs Fitzherbert who would never forgive his public declaration on the subject . . . and had taken every opportunity of alienating the Prince's mind from him'. At first George obeyed Maria's command and kept his distance from his old friend, but when the king became seriously ill in the autumn of 1788 he suddenly had need of his old friend again.

George III appeared to have suffered a complete mental breakdown, plunging the country into a constitutional crisis. If the king was incapable of governing then precedent ordained that the Prince of Wales should become Regent. This was a prospect that alarmed William Pitt and the Tory government as much as it elated the Whigs. The Tories saw themselves being ejected from office and replaced by the prince's old friends led by Fox. George, however, considered it a stroke of divine providence for not only would he at last be free of his father's insidious control but he could also now play a valid role in governing the nation. Fox, who was holidaying in Italy with Mrs Armistead, was immediately sent for and took charge of the bid for the Regency, claiming that the prince had 'as clear and express a right to the position just as if the king was dead'. Pitt was unimpressed and argued that it was the business of Parliament to decide the Regency not the Prince of Wales. Once more Fox had put friendship above caution, but his enthusiasm and eloquence began to persuade many of the undecided in Parliament to back the cause of the Prince of Wales. The country now divided into two opposing factions, for or against the Prince of Wales as Regent. To show their support, groups of ladies appeared in Regency caps decorated with three feathers and bearing the prince's motto 'Ich Dien'. Excited at the prospect of a return to power, the Whigs began squabbling with each other over which political offices would be on offer in the expected coalition government. Some believed that Mrs Fitzherbert would be made a duchess and George's favourite brother, the Duke of York, be made a field marshall. Even George's uncle, the fast-ageing old reprobate the Duke of Cumberland, was expected to receive an honour of some sort, perhaps as a reward for his services to debauchery.

The announcement of a full Regency appeared a mere formality when Parliament finally began debating the issue on 17 December 1789. But to the prince's intense chagrin and in spite of Fox's best efforts the opposition was defeated and the House voted for a greatly restricted Regency. George would now be unable either to create peerages or grant pensions, offices or honours to his supporters. Worse news followed. A report came from Kew that the king's condition had improved and he was making an unexpected recovery. A few days later George and Frederick went down to see their father and were astonished to find him almost completely recovered. Returning to London, they spent the evening at Brook's where they told the members that in their opinion the king was still off his head. Their words were reported to the palace and greatly distressed the queen, who accused her sons of the most shocking disloyalty.

News of the princes' indiscretion spread through London

society, and when the two brothers attended a concert at Windsor a week later to celebrate the king's recovery they found the room, on the queen's orders, had been decorated with Tory colours and regalia. No doubt the public shared her distaste for her sons' behaviour, for on the way to the opera together a few weeks later their carriage was surrounded by a mob shouting 'God save the king' and 'Pitt for ever'. Outraged, George threw open the carriage door and bellowed back 'Fox for ever', at which a man attempted to drag him out. Frederick came to the rescue and struck the assailant over the head with his stick before ordering the coachman to drive on with the doors still flapping wide open. Yet the real victory remained with Pitt and the king himself – from then on the prince's carriage was more often greeted with catcalls than with cheers and Fox was frequently hissed and booed in public.

The friendship between prince and politician now cooled, although they remained firm if more distant friends in the following years. When William Pitt died in 1806 at the age of just forty-six the way was clear for a more broad-based administration to take power. This grandly named Ministry of All Talents, led by the new prime minister Lord Grenville, included not only Fox as foreign secretary but the Prince of Wales's other long-standing friends William Windham and the Earl of Moira. Observers of the political scene, including Lord Melville, considered that the power in the land had passed from St James's to Carlton House, as the prince soon had his Cabinet agreeing to his own list of new honours and appointments. This was the situation that the prince had always wished for, but it came too late for Fox for within a year he was dead and Grenville's ministry collapsed.

When Nelson had died in 1805 after his great victory at Trafalgar, George claimed that he had 'loved him as a friend' in spite of having hypocritically criticized his involvement with Lady Hamilton. His reaction to the death of Fox was, however, infinitely more genuine and heartfelt. When the news reached him George was staying with the Marquess of Stafford at Trentham. He immediately collapsed in floods of tears that his fellow guests found heart rending. Unable to speak to anyone but his hostess Lady Stafford, George went into a decline, eating very little and claiming that he was unable to sleep. Looking pale and drawn, he put on black mourning clothes and wore them constantly throughout the following months. A fellow guest at Trentham, Lord Fitzwilliam, described to a friend how badly the prince had taken the loss of his old friend: 'He has lost all appetite and even for wine.' Three days later George wrote the following to Fox's nephew, the new Lord Holland:

> The loss of such a man, such a friend, to myself in particular, is so incalculable, and such a stab that I candidly acknowledge to you that I have neither resolution nor spirits sufficient to stand up against it, and the only wish I now feel remaining is that of retirement entirely from all my political career, for in losing Fox, we lose everything.

4

FOLLOWERS OF FASHION

TODAY it is difficult to imagine the importance that dress and fashion played in the life of aristocratic society in the late eighteenth century. A man could be, and was, judged by his appearance alone. A 'dandy' with sufficient means and a large wardrobe could make a career and earn almost universal respect just from the way he dressed. As defined by Thomas Carlyle, the fashionable dandy was 'a man whose trade, office and existence consists in the wearing of clothes. Every faculty of his soul, spirit, purse and person is heroically consecrated to this one object.'

This cult of dress was particularly important in France where flamboyant clothes in any number of colours had evolved for both men and women throughout the century. Yet even in the heyday of the *ancien régime* there were some among the French aristocracy who, like George's friend the Duke of Chartres, abandoned French ornamentation and colour in favour of the more simple 'English look'. These were the clothes of a typical country gentleman, inspired by open-air activities such as riding, shooting, fishing and hunting. As such they displayed a practicality as well as a distinctive style. This same transition from impractical colour to sober but stylish utility was made by the Prince of Wales. When making his first appearance in Parliament in 1784 he could well have been at the Court of Versailles, turning up in a gold-embroidered black velvet coat lined with pink satin with pink-heeled shoes and hair carefully coiffured. By 1800 he had changed his look completely in favour of natural, unpowdered hair and well-cut coats in plain colours worn above simple black or brown boots ornamented by a single tassel.

Since childhood George had taken a great interest in his dress, and throughout his life was to spend vast sums with his tailors, shirt-makers and cobblers, never buying single items but ordering in multiples of whatever took his fancy. As he aged, his obsession with clothes, rather than waning, increased in intensity perhaps as recompense for his increasing weight gain and unhealthy appearance. Denied an army career, he again found compensation in his obsession with military costume, even devising a uniform of red, blue and gold for the staff and servants at Windsor Castle. This reminded many visitors of those worn at Frederick the Great's court in Berlin. When his flamboyant appearance was criticized by his father as wanton extravagance, George, in defiance, responded by promptly increasing his tailors' bills. By the end of his life he had accumulated an immense collection of coats, suits, waistcoats and shirts, boots and breeches, gloves and hats, walking sticks and wigs of all sorts. When the Duke of Wellington went through George's possessions after his death he found a collection of over three hundred riding whips, 'canes without number, every sort of uniform, the costumes of all the orders in Europe, splendid furs, pelisses, etc.' George's fascination with clothes continued to the end of his life, and there were a dozen pairs of new corduroy riding breeches ordered long after he could ever have mounted a horse. The cost of this indulgence was enormous, and by 1793 the prince's tailors' bills, largely unpaid, amounted to a colossal £30,000, equivalent to well over a million pounds today. No detail and accessory escaped him, and, magpie-like, as the historian Steven Parissien has noted, 'his eye could always be drawn to bright, gaudy objects whether ruby rings, ormolu clocks or gilded mouldings'.

Some of the prince's earliest letters, particularly to his closest friend at the time, his brother Frederick, show this obsession with dress. One written in 1781 when Frederick was in Hanover promises to keep the exile in the latest London fashion:

by the next messenger I will send you two uniforms at least, with the dress and undress of my hunting uniform. It is called so and is universally admired throughout London . . . If there are any other cloaths of any sort or kind besides . . . I will take care of it.

In return Frederick collected and sent his brother items of German military uniform that he knew would please him. Often George would provide a list of desired items for Frederick to find that sometimes included complete uniforms 'and particularly one of Zieten's Hussars'. His other brothers were also recruited to the cause, with the Duke of Cumberland urged to send George the sketches of the latest designs for the new uniforms of certain Hanoverian regiments and William, Duke of Clarence, ordered to send him the uniform details of a new regiment, the Royal Spelthorne Militia. This fascination with dress made the Prince of Wales a natural associate of the most famous dandies of the time, all of whom placed a similar importance upon physical appearance, refined language and leisurely hobbies. Some historians have seen this form of exhibitionism as a protest against the rise of egalitarian principles and a nostalgic adherence to the historical and traditional values that were threatened by the changes taking place as a result of the Industrial Revolution.

Dandyism had been long established in England in the form of 'the Macaroni', one of the more colourful sights of eighteenth-century London. These were young men of good family who, like Fox, had made the Grand Tour to Italy and returned as followers of fashion and with an assumed cynical attitude to life. The Italian word *maccherone*, a boorish fool, perfectly described the appearance and manners of such a foppish young man as George Russell, the fourth Duke of Bedford, whose overelaborate manners and contrived appearance had earned him the title of Prince of Maccaronies. Yet, by middle age Russell's responsibilities as a Gentleman of the Bedchamber for George III had necessitated a more muted appearance and less elaborate posturing. Fashion being notoriously unpredictable, by the time the Prince of Wales left his father's confines at Kew, the Macaroni had been replaced by the less fatuous dandy. A dandy was a man who used his clothes to demonstrate a search for perfection without flamboyance, although Thomas Carlyle held the dandy in contempt as merely 'a man whose trade, office, and existence consist in the wearing of Clothes'. What the fashionable man also expressed through his appearance was a rejection of the puritanical virtues of sobriety and modesty of dress, and which had dominated England in the previous century under the Commonwealth, in favour of rebellious extravagance and relaxed morals. If George III represented the puritan tradition, then his eldest son would inevitably opt for that of the libertine. This was a form of rebellion literally using kid gloves, expressed in an elaborate dress code, long-drawn-out toilettes, lavish dinner parties and time wasted in both the gambling club and on the racecourse. By associating with these men of fashion George could enrage his father but escape retribution by claiming that he was doing no more than hundreds of other aristocratic young Englishmen.

Among the leaders of this group was William, Lord Alvanley, a man said by the diarist Captain Gronow to have rivalled even the playwright Richard Brinsley Sheridan as a wit. While many of the dandies were of limited intelligence and experience, Alvanley was disarmingly intelligent and had travelled widely. Good natured and easy going, he delivered his laconic comments on life with a distinctive lisp. He was equally at home in French and Russian society as he was at the English court. Often he would accompany the Prince of Wales in the hunting field or to the races at Newmarket. Once at a hunt, when riding with a man named Gunter, the wealthy owner of a London tearoom famous for its sweets and ices, his companion announced that he was nervous about his high-spirited mount. 'Oh, my lord, I can't hold him, he is so hot,' said the agitated confectioner. 'Ice him, Gunter,' replied Alvanley; 'ice him.'

In an age when society dinners lasted for hours, Alvanley's, like those of his good friend the prince at Carlton House, were among the best in London, although intimate by the standards of the time. Customarily they consisted of eight guests, and an apricot tart was invariably served whatever the season. In spite of his languid manner, Lord Alvanley was capable of strong opinions and maintained a particular dislike of the Irish nationalist leader Daniel O'Connell. In 1835 this culminated in Alvanley challenging him to a duel. O'Connell's son Morgan took up the challenge, and the combatants met at Chalk Farm near London. Shots were exchanged, honour satisfied, and both men walked away unscathed. On their way home in a hackney coach, Alvanley remarked to one of his seconds: 'What a clumsy fellow O'Connell must be, to miss such a fat fellow as I am. He ought to practise at a haystack to get his hand in.' When the carriage arrived at Alvanley's door he gave the coachman a sovereign. The man was grateful but protested that it was too generous for 'only having taken your lordship to Wimbledon'. 'No, my good man,' Alvanley replied, 'I give it to you, not for taking me, but for bringing me back alive.'

Like the prince, Alvanley was a member of both White's and Waiter's Clubs. What he also shared with the prince was an almost total disregard for expenditure and living far beyond his means – the wealth accumulated by his father was dissipated, and the family estates had to be sold off to pay his debts. When he died in 1849 he was considered a relic of the Regency but still the undisputed wit of the age. As Captain Gronow wrote:

> He was awarded the reputation, good or bad, of all the witticisms in the clubs after the abdication of the throne of dandyism by Brummell who, before that time, was always quoted as the sayer of good things.

Not all of the prince's fashionable friends were such wastrels. One of the most able was Frederick Gerald Byng, a politician known as Poodle Byng because of his unruly and distinctive hairstyle. Byng was one of a group of dandies that often sat with Beau Brummell in the bow window at White's Club passing sardonic comments on the dress of passers-by. In fact, it was Brummell who had given Byng his sobriquet because of the latter's habit of letting his light-coloured hair curl around his forehead. Byng delighted in his nickname and even purchased a live poodle as his contribution to the joke. Once, when driving with the dog beside him in his curricle in Hyde Park, he met Brummell in his carriage. Leaning over the carriage door Brummell hailed him with the words: 'Ah, how d' ye do, Byng? A family vehicle, I see.' In spite of his frivolous attitude, Byng took his role as a Member of Parliament with great seriousness. He represented the Middlesex constituency for over fifty-six years as a Whig, and at the age of eighty-one addressed his electors in a valedictory speech saying that as the oldest member of either House he rejoiced in having seen that all the great and liberal measures advocated by his old colleague Charles James Fox had been accomplished. His most amusing parliamentary experience had been his appointment as escort to the King and Queen of the Sandwich Islands when they visited London in 1824. That the king's name was thought to mean 'dog of dogs' and that he was being shown around by Poodle Byng was considered a great joke at the time. Unfortunately, King Kamehameha II caught measles and died at Osborne's Hotel before his visit to the city had been completed.

More typical of the men of fashion was Edward Hughes Ball, known as Golden Ball. A particularly handsome young man, he had been left a fortune of £40,000 by a rich uncle and proceeded to spend it as swiftly as possible. Known about London by his distinctive chocolate-coloured coach, Ball spent vast sums of money on dress and is credited with inventing the simple black cravat for evening wear. Far less effete than other dandies, he shared the Prince of Wales's keen interest in pretty actresses. One evening in 1823 George arrived at the King's Theatre to see Mercandotti, a beautiful sixteen-year-old Spanish dancer who was the toast of London. As the performance was about to begin, the manager suddenly appeared on stage and announced with regret that Mercandotti had disappeared. The next morning it transpired that she had run off and married Golden Ball. As the novelist Harrison Ainsworth succinctly put it: 'The damsel is gone, and no wonder at all that, bred to the dance, she is gone to a Ball.'

When the Duchess of York died in 1820 Ball still had enough

money to purchase her house, Oatlands, from Frederick, Duke of York. But Ball's incessant gambling and extravagance eventually reduced him to penury and he ended his days in Paris, hiding from his creditors. The diarist Captain Gronow thought him the greatest gambler of the age, so addicted that he would even play at pitch and toss rather than be without his favourite excitement. Ball told Gronow that he had lost considerable sums at battledore and once at shuttlecock, playing it after dinner with Lord Petersham with such intensity that they continued all night and were found the next morning by Ball's valet lying fast asleep on the ground.

As Ball had provided society with the black cravat so another friend of the Prince of Wales, Viscount Petersham, gave it two articles of his own design: the Harrington hat and the Petersham overcoat. His style so impressed George that he ordered an overcoat in the Petersham style for each day of the week. Also the owner of a chocolate-brown coach, Viscount Petersham aspired to be as stylish as Beau Brummell himself, copying his famous lisp and never appearing in public before six in evening. George was said not only to have emulated Petersham's clothes but also his snuff-taking – Petersham had 365 snuffboxes, a different one for each day of the year – and his obsession with tea drinking. In a society where wine was king, Petersham chose to be a connoisseur of fine tea, and his sitting-room contained dozens of canisters of many different flavours and varieties.

While Ball and Petersham were among the most handsome of George's rakish friends, the unfortunate Sir Lumley Skeffington was one of the least prepossessing in appearance. A thin, pallid little man with sharp features and rouged cheeks, he was always doused in exotic scents that gave him the aroma of a perfume shop. It was said of him by his friend Lady Spencer Stanhope that 'his dress was so exaggerated as to render his lack of beauty the more marked'. Known always as Skiffy, Skeffington, in spite of his poor looks, was one of the leading dandies of the day and, like Petersham, always wore highly expensive garments that he had designed himself. So acute was his good taste that George often consulted him before ordering a new coat or breeches. Skiffy was also a talented playwright and a friend of Percy Shelley since their schooldays together at Eton. He became immortalized by another great friend, Lord Byron, in his satire *English Bards and Scotch Reviews*, which contains the words: 'Sure great Skeffington must claim our praise, for skirtless coats, and skeletons of plays.' When his drama *The Sleeping Beauty* was produced at the Theatre Royal, Covent Garden, it was a great success and widely praised. But Skiffy's wild extravagance soon consumed the royalties from the play and led to him serving time in the debtors' prison. On release he emerged dressed in all his finery and intent on retaking his place in fashionable society. On being asked who this splendidly dressed individual was, Lord Alvanley commented caustically: 'It is a second edition of *The Sleeping Beauty*, bound in calf; richly gilt and illustrated by many cuts.' Now a sad figure on the edge of society, Skeffington was described by Lady Spencer Stanhope as a victim of the passage of time:

> The blackness of his false ringlets never varied, the brilliant rouge of his cheeks, or the strange costume which he had worn during the heyday of his existence, and to which he clung after it had been obsolete for half a century . . .

A similar description at that time might have been given of Skiffy's old friend the Prince of Wales. By now King George IV, he remained a recluse, wearing a brown wig and with his face similarly rouged.

As fashionable as these men had once appeared, none had the same impact on the Prince of Wales's tastes as did George Bryan 'Beau' Brummell, the greatest dandy of the age. Sixteen years younger than the prince, Brummell's elegance, wit and over-weening self-confidence had made his reputation even before he left Eton where the gold buckle he wore in his white stock betrayed the first sign of dandyism. Relatively poor by the standards of the aristocracy, he made his way via Oriel College, Oxford, into the prince's own regiment, the 10th Dragoons. Here his impudence, supplemented by an originality of dress and amusing conversation, proved irresistible to the royal colonel of the best-dressed but worst-behaved regiment in the British Army. Within days the prince and the dandy had become the closest of companions, with the prince being instructed by Brummell on how to open a snuffbox expertly with one hand. George found the Beau's wit as irresistible as the stories that were told about him, such as when asked how he had caught a cold Brummell replied that he had gone to Pietri's Hotel and been shown into a room where a damp stranger was sitting. For a period George was almost besotted with Brummell, who had suddenly resigned from the regiment when it was posted to Manchester, declaring that such 'foreign service' would be too depressing for him to bear. Rather than being affronted by the resignation, George declared that he admired the young man's cheek and the relationship became even closer.

Brummell now began his true career, that of doing virtually nothing but with enormous style. With what was left of his inheritance, Brummell bought a large house in Mayfair and began filling it with beautiful objects, including the finest and best-cut clothes of the day. Bright colours had no part in the Brummell wardrobe, and his coats were invariably of blue, black or brown. One of the first sartorial minimalists, he preferred clean lines in their cut and instructed his tailors to hide the pockets inside the tail-flaps. The result was a distinctive but seemingly effortless elegance that was deeply admired by a circle of close friends. In spite of his obsession with clothes, Brummell was no empty-headed dandy for, as one observer remarked: 'He had wit as well as humour and drollery and the most perfect coolness and self-possession.'

Brummell's humour was as admired as his dress sense and so disarmingly bold that he began to play the role of court jester to the prince. Only Brummell was able to say the most outrageous and provocative things to him without giving offence. His house in Chapel Street, with its excellent furniture and a library that contained the works of eminent authors of every period and of every country, reflected his personal taste much as Carlton House did that of the Prince of Wales. His canes, his snuffboxes, his Sèvres china, were all exquisite; his horses and carriage conspicuous for their excellence.

Capable of transforming the mundane into the dramatic, his morning toilette became recognized as one of the most admired performances in London and was described in great detail by his friend and fellow dandy Thomas Raikes. Those privileged enough to attend, including the Prince of Wales, gathered at his house in Chapel Street to await the arrival of the Beau from his bedroom. The door of the dressing-room would open, and a naked Brummell would enter and begin the meticulous task of dressing. As with his coats, simplicity was the keynote of his other clothes, with buff doeskin breeches, waistcoat, starched linen shirt and white cravat and black leather Hessian boots with the soles polished, perhaps dangerously, to the same bright sheen as the uppers. In the evening he invariably wore trousers, a fashion newly arrived from Germany. Often the drama of the dressing-room would continue all day so that the prince would send his carriage away and stay on for dinner with the Beau. What also made him so different from the majority of his fashionable contemporaries was a fanatical commitment to personal hygiene. Unusually for the times, he bathed every day and was always scrupulously clean shaven and with carefully brushed teeth. Even his laundry was sent outside the city to be dried in the fresh country air away from the smuts of London. As he changed his shirt three times a day, his laundry bills were considerable. The climax of the Brummell toilette was the tying of the cravat, a long and complex process that assumed the proportions of a religious rite. A satirical verse of the time mocked the exactitude required to make this simple piece of cloth the most envied cravat in London: 'My neckcloth of course, forms my principal care. For by that we criterions of elegance swear, And costs me, each morning, some hours of flurry, To make it appear to be tied in a hurry.'

So powerful an arbiter of taste did George Brummell become that he was able to dispense his criticisms with impunity, as once when walking with the Duke of Bedford along Pall Mall. The duke asked him if he approved the cut of his new coat. After examining the garment with ill-concealed disdain Brummell looked up at the duke and murmured laconically: 'My dear Bedford, do you call this thing a coat?'

With his haughty arrogance Brummell inevitably made enemies among his social superiors, who considered he had become far too big for his elegant Hessian boots. Even the prince had to play a secondary role when this fashionable arriviste held court, and a mutual friend, Captain Jesse, tells of an incident when Brummell was staying at Belvoir Castle. So similar were they in dress that the crowd mistook Brummell for the prince and cheered him loudly. When told of this George fell ominously silent. A more light-hearted anecdote during Brummell's stay at Belvoir shows a self-obsession that verged on arrogance. One evening he left a ball early and retired to bed. Suddenly the ringing of a powerful fire-alarm bell, followed by Brummell, who appeared on the balcony overlooking the dance floor, brought the dance to a standstill. He said: 'I beg your pardon, ladies and gentlemen but there is no hot water in my room.'

As long he remained the inseparable companion of the Prince of Wales, Brummell had little to fear from society. But this very success had clouded his judgement, and he made the fatal mistake of beginning to mock both the prince and Maria Fitzherbert. Always conscious of his increasing bulk, the prince was shocked to learn that Brummell had referred to him as a Ben and to Maria as Benina – a reference to a massively built porter known as Big Ben who worked at Carlton House. He was also said to have summoned Maria Fitzherbert's carriage one evening by pointedly referring to her as Mistress Fitzherbert rather than Mrs Colonel McMahon, the prince's secretary, also reported that the Beau had foolishly said of his royal friend when the relationship appeared over: 'I made the Prince of Wales what he is, and I can unmake him.' No matter how intimate a friend Brummell had become, this was intolerable behaviour, and it was now only a matter of time before the prince turned on the dandy.

One evening in 1811 while dining at Carlton House, Brummell became drunker than usual, and as the party sat in the drawing-room after the meal he decided to summon a servant. Instead of ringing the bell himself he leant over to the prince and said loudly: 'Wales, ring the bell.' Considering the past intimacy between them, and that George had often sacrificed his dignity to the other's amusement, there was nothing extraordinary in this. But this time the room fell silent, and saying nothing the prince did as he was asked, but when the servant arrived he said quietly: 'Mr Brummell's carriage!' Brummell was never invited to Carlton House again.

Two years later and still smarting at being ignored by the prince, Brummell, together with Lord Alvanley, Henry Pierrepoint and Henry Mildmay, organized a ball at the Argyle Rooms. Although pointedly not invited, the prince announced his intention to attend anyway. As George entered the room he bowed to each of his three hosts but ignored Brummell and turned back to talk to Alvanley. Smarting at so public a cut Brummell said loudly: 'Ah Alvanley, who is your fat friend?' George never spoke to Brummell again.

Time was running out for Beau Brummell in other ways, too, for his creditors were now determined to recover their money. The outcome was inevitable. One evening he went to the opera as usual, but when he left he drove not to his London house but to Dover where he boarded the packet boat for France, never to return. In Calais, beyond the reach of creditors, he rented a modest house and took up residence there. His few remaining effects were sold off after his departure, including his china, some drawings, a double-barrelled and a Manton shotgun that had never been used, as well his furniture, linen and wine cellar. The revenue from the sale made barely a dent in the vast sum he owed to London tradesmen let alone the money he had borrowed from friends.

Living on a pittance in France, Brummell was forced to raise money in any manner he could. One story reveals his humiliating attempt to bring himself to George's attention again. Apparently the prince and the Beau had in their days of amity intended to exchange snuffboxes, and George had commissioned one from a jeweller that would bear his portrait on the lid. But after the scene at the Argyle Rooms he had cancelled the order even though Brummell had completed his and had sent it to him. From Calais the Beau wrote to a friend in London asking him to remind the prince, now king, of their agreement and suggesting that, given the changed circumstances of their friendship, he might wish to return Brummell's box. The king's reply was to dismiss the request as complete nonsense but added that perhaps 'the poor devil' was just looking for £100, in which case he would have it sent to him.

Trapped in Calais by his own folly, Brummell became part of the group of English debtor *émigrés* who waited on the quayside each day for the arrival of boats from England. As it docked they would try to cadge some money from their fellow countrymen on their way to Paris. In 1822 George himself arrived in Calais *en route* to Hanover. Among the crowd lining the dock stood the forlorn figure of his erstwhile bosom friend Beau Brummell. When Brummell stepped forward and attempted to speak George brushed past him with barely an acknowledgement. Climbing briskly aboard their carriages the royal party set off at full speed for Brussels, leaving Brummell to spend the following weeks writing begging letters to his few remaining friends in England. At length George must have relented a little for he sanctioned Brummell's being given the post of British consul at the Norman town of Caen. This was almost a sinecure, requiring discretion rather than hard work. Again Brummell acted foolishly, drawing attention to himself by writing to the foreign secretary, Lord Palmerston, stating that there were no duties attached to the post and recommending its abolition. This act of financial suicide is partly explained by a supposed desire to be appointed to some more active and lucrative consulate, but in this he was mistaken. The consulate at Caen was abolished in accordance with his own suggestion, and Brummell was plunged into poverty again, a state in which he remained until his death a decade later in the Caen lunatic asylum.

Of all the friendships that George engaged in throughout his life, that with Brummell certainly became the most acrimonious. It is easy to see why the Beau needed the fellowship and patronage of the prince to make his way into the top echelon of English society but less easy to see why the prince needed Brummell. He already enjoyed the company of such smart and witty men as Lords Alvanley and Petersham, who could provide all the sartorial advice that he needed – and there were enough sycophants in his circle to provide the approval, too. There has been some speculation that the attraction may have been sexual and that the prince developed an almost schoolboy-like crush on the younger, prettier man. Certainly Brummell's sexuality may have been ambiguous for he was decidedly effeminate and reserved his affections for his pet dogs. There is no existing evidence, however, of any homosexual liaisons, although there are many accounts of him dismissing the idea of marriage even though women found him a delightful asset as a guest. Morbidly obsessed with his deteriorating appearance – by 1800 his hair was so sparse that he always wore a wig – and his increasing weight, the prince found in Beau Brummell the Adonis that he would have liked to have been.

The Beau's sharp wit and ruthless dismissals of the pretentiousness of others also appealed to a man whose position as heir to the throne denied him the freedom to attack cant and pretension as openly he might have wished. There is no doubt that George found the Beau's bitterly sharp tongue and utter disregard for accepted standards attractive for he was the social rebel that George would have liked to have been. But admiration was destined to turn to envy and then to disdain as Brummell increasingly flouted the intimacy that had developed between them, particularly because of his scathing remarks about Maria Fitzherbert, the only woman whom George ever truly loved. There was also the need on George's part to behave more seriously as his ascent to the throne approached, and Brummell's style-obsessed approach to life challenged this. Perhaps, as Steven Parissien has speculated, George, in the manner of Shakespeare's Prince Hal, finally came to see Brummell as his Falstaff, an ephemeral lord of misrule who had to be rejected before the prince could fully become his own man and the ruler of Britain.

5

ARTISTIC FRIENDS

THERE was an uncanny similarity between the demise of the prince's friendship with George Bryan Brummell and the termination of his relationship with the first of his many artistic friends, the miniaturist Richard Cosway. Both men came to presume too much from their association with the heir to the throne and began behaving with complacent arrogance towards him. In Cosway's case the friendship ended abruptly one day in 1808. The prince had sent a message asking Cosway to come urgently to Carlton House and give an opinion on some paintings that George was proposing to buy. Cosway sent back a note claiming that he was too busy that day to attend. Amenable as ever, the prince called for his own carriage, had the paintings loaded aboard and drove round to Cosway's house. At the door he was met by a servant who informed him that his master was otherwise engaged and could not receive him. Such rudeness was insufferable, and from that moment Cosway never received another commission from Carlton House nor did the prince ever speak to him again.

This abrupt end to the friendship was in complete contrast to their first meeting, when George had been shown round the Royal Academy by an eager-to-please Cosway. Dressed in an elaborate dove-grey-and-silver embroidered court dress complete with sword and hat, the diminutive Academician showered his guest with obsequious compliments as he strutted before him in his scarlet-heeled shoes, constantly bowing and smiling. When the prince returned to his carriage at the end of his visit and was surrounded by a cheering crowd, Cosway scurried along after him so desperately that he managed to trip over his own sword and fell sprawling in the mud. 'Just as I anticipated, ye gods!' exclaimed George to his companions in the carriage. Meanwhile, the embarrassed Cosway was lifted like a child up into the arms of a burly Academy porter and carried inside as the mob roared with laughter.

Richard Cosway was the artistic phenomenon of the time; a tiny dandyish rake known to the satirists as Tiny Cosmetic but possessed of a brilliant talent. At the age of twelve he had been sent to London to study art with William Shipley, the founder of the Royal Society of Arts. Cosway's ability to handle meticulous detail in his work led to him being swiftly elected to membership at the prestigious Royal Academy. As a painter he gained the reputation of being the most successful miniaturist of his generation. At a time before photography had been invented, the miniature was the only means of capturing an intimate portrait. As such they were used as fashionable gifts among the aristocracy. Cosway was the acknowledged master of the genre, much of his success being down to his innovative technique of painting in watercolour rather than in oils, which brought a finesse to the picture when used on an ivory base. This delicacy of technique contrasted strongly with his appearance for he was a small ugly man with the reputation of a libidinous monkey.

The Prince of Wales met him soon after leaving the confinement of Kew, at a time when he appeared to be seeking the company of older men, such as his uncles, as compensation for his father's coldness. Cosway proved an ideal mentor for he was twenty years older than George, a man of the world with a wide knowledge of European art as well as having the added attraction of being married to a beautiful and gifted wife. He also had one other impeachable qualification for friendship with the prince: he was heartily disliked by King George III. Always flamboyantly dressed and possessed of a conceited self-confidence, Cosway was much derided in cartoons but envied by fellow painters for his sharp financial acumen. Impressed by his unusual combination of ability and poise, George thought him an ideal adviser on all artistic matters and appointed Cosway as his first and only *Primarius Pictor*, or Principal Painter, in 1785, with responsibility for advising him on the purchase of the paintings that would decorate Carlton House.

Cosway's tendency to arrogance was tempered in those early years by the presence of his wife Maria, who had grown up in Florence where her father, having spotted an excellent business opportunity, had kept an inn patronized by the English aristocracy on the Grand Tour. Her father had great ambitions for his artistically talented daughter and had sent her to London where she met Richard Cosway, who saw in her physical beauty all that was lacking in himself. Theirs may well have been an arranged marriage for Cosway settled the considerable sum of £2,800 on his bride when they were married at the fashionable St George's Church in Hanover Square in January 1781. Setting up home in the very smart Schomberg House in Pall Mall, the Cosways became one of the most sought-after couples in London society.

Their early patrons, such as Georgiana, Duchess of Devonshire, were as impressive as their new smart address. The Cosway's reputation as a gilded couple spread to France where, visiting the painter Jacques-Louis David in Paris five years later, they were introduced to the American Minister in Paris, Thomas Jefferson. While Richard Cosway was involved in painting a portrait of the Duke of Chartres' children – a highly lucrative commission obtained for him by his new friend the Prince of Wales – Maria flirted with Jefferson. The American statesman had fallen in love with her, becoming so entranced that he delayed his return to America for a month. When the Cosways themselves left for London in October 1786, Jefferson was devastated and wrote Maria a letter that became known as the 'Head and Heart Letter', in which he describes his dilemma in the form of a debate between his reason and his emotions, coming to the sad conclusion that 'the art of life is the art of avoiding pain'. That both Cosways had impressed a man famous for his sound judgement of art shows why Richard and Maria became such close friends of the prince. Jefferson described them as 'possessing good

sense, good humour, honest hearts, honest manners, and emi-
nence in a lovely art of engravings'. Now an accomplished painter
herself, Maria Cosway also exhibited at the Royal Academy as
well as displaying her equally impressive musical talent as a composer and singer by performing at home in the presence of such
luminaries as Horace Walpole, Gouverneur Morris and James
Boswell. The constant presence of the Prince of Wales at
Schomberg House soon led to gossip that it was Maria's beauty
rather than her talent that was the attraction, and there was speculation that George may well have had a short-lived affair with
her.

Cosway's value to the Prince of Wales was not only as a successful painter. He was also as an astute adviser on collecting other
artists' work. An inventory taken a year before his death reveals
his own house crowded with paintings of all sorts, including Old
Master drawings and over seven thousand prints. So large was
Cosway's collection and so important his connections that he was
able, two months before the fall of the Bastille in 1789, to pass on
to George four magnificent tapestries to decorate Carlton House,
having just bought them from Louis XVI. There is no doubt that
his magpie capacity to acquire works of art served to encourage
the Prince of Wales to start his own collection.

With Cosway's departure from his service, George needed
immediate help in choosing more paintings to complete his collection at Carlton House. He found it in another extrovert character,
Walsh Porter, a highly excitable and nervous man capable of an
embarrassing sycophancy that exceeded even that of Richard
Cosway. Typical of Porter's gushing style was a report to his royal
master on his latest purchases for Carlton House:

> I do flatter myself I have succeeded in culling a small but rare assem-
> blage . . . and this I have done Sir, *solely* with a view of endeavouring
> silently to accomplish what I conceived to be the *wish* of yr Rl Hss of
> making that apartment refined and *classical* as possible.

Porter was a fellow bon viveur and frequently entertained the prince at his own house, the famous Craven Cottage, in Fulham. Although of modest proportions, this cottage *orné* had a dramatic and theatrical interior, with each room decorated in the style of a different historical period, including Gothic, Egyptian and Tudor rooms. The entrance hall was bizarrely constructed in the manner of a robber's cave, with huge rocks on either side of the staircase, and the dining-room was done out as a smaller-scale replica of the ruins of Tintern Abbey. This amusing disregard for architectural convention greatly appealed to the prince, who was equally impressed by Porter's gay flamboyance and interest in music – Porter had written and composed a comic opera called *The Chimney Corner* that was a great commercial success. The friendship with Porter, as well as the adventurous interiors of Craven Cottage, inspired George to begin the Gothic dining-room at Carlton House and later the Chinese interior of the Royal Pavilion at Brighton.

Their friendship ended not in a dispute but by Walsh Porter's sudden death in 1809. After this the prince turned to a very different character to advise on his art collection, the sardonic aristocrat the Earl of Yarmouth, heir to the Marquess of Hertford and son of one of George's later mistresses, Lady Hertford. Yarmouth has been caustically described by the art historian John Ingamells as 'a wayward son, a wretched husband, a feckless Irish landlord, a Tory autocrat abusive of reform and an example . . . of undisguised debauchery'. These were all excellent qualifications for friendship with the Prince of Wales, even if he had not possessed an excellent taste in art. The proof of Yarmouth's incomparable judgement can be still be seen in the sheer quality of the paintings he acquired for the Wallace Collection at the Hertfords' London house in Manchester Square. The money to pay for it had come largely from his marriage to one of the wealthiest heiresses of the day, Maria Fagniani, the putative daughter of the prince's friend Old Q. Yarmouth and his new bride had been in Paris in 1803 when the Peace of Amiens suddenly broke down. Both were arrested and imprisoned at Verdun for three years until the prince persuaded Fox, then foreign secretary, to negotiate with Napoleon for their release. When they returned to England, George used his concern for Yarmouth as an excuse to further ingratiate himself with the young man's mother.

Many of the pictures that Yarmouth acquired either for himself or for his royal patron had once been the property of the French aristocracy and had been seized by the new Republican government in Paris. Works of a Catholic or religious nature were, in the English tradition, generally ignored by Yarmouth in favour of those by Rembrandt and other Dutch painters of the seventeenth century. Like Beau Brummell, Yarmouth was significantly younger than the Prince of Wales, who found that 'his judgement and his discrimination is really quite wonderful and he is indeed in point of talent very superior to all the young men of the rising generation'. Ironically, Yarmouth's first success on behalf of his patron was acquiring bargains for him at the sale of the late Walsh Porter's collection, which raised the enormous sum over £30,000. So highly did George come to value their friendship that Yarmouth was given his own room at Carlton House, made Vice-Chamberlain of the prince's household, Warden of the Stannaries – a lucrative sinecure – and a member of the Privy Council. Yet the ties of common interest and taste that bound them together could not survive the acrimonious break-up of the relationship between George and Yarmouth's mother in 1819.

For George, much of the appeal of Cosway, Porter and Yarmouth had been that, as well as being artistic mavericks, they were not beholden to George III for patronage, unlike the painter Thomas Gainsborough or, to a lesser extent, Sir Joshua Reynolds. Gainsborough in particular was the king's favourite, and he commissioned many works from him, particularly a series of his formal, full-length portraits. Although never consistently patronized by the Prince of Wales, Gainsborough did receive the odd commission, including portraits of his first significant mistress, Mary Robinson, and his hunting companion Anthony St Leger. When Gainsborough died in 1788, George III transferred his favours to the American-born painter of historical subjects Benjamin West. The very fact that his father favoured West by making him Surveyor of the King's Pictures was enough to exclude West totally from George's patronage. Nor did West's known friendship with the prince's much despised old tutor, Dr Hurd, exactly endear him to the occupant of Carlton House. So it was perhaps inevitable that when George III fell ill in 1810 the prince would cancel West's royal pension and fail to collect or pay for West's large religious canvasses his father had ordered for the Royal Chapel at Windsor Castle.

As Sir Joshua Reynolds, the other great painter of the age, became heartily disliked by George III, his son was predictably drawn to him. What had made Reynolds unpopular at court was his friendship with Charles James Fox and his series of portraits of leading Whigs. Reynolds had also annoyed the king by his reluctance to accept the presidency of the new Royal Academy, one of the king's favourite projects. When it became known that Reynolds was heavily involved with the Prince of Wales in the decoration of Carlton House, the king ended any remaining patronage and churlishly dismissed his work as 'coarse and unfinished'. This royal hostility guaranteed a warm friendship with the heir to the throne and a whole series of new commissions flowed from Carlton House that included portraits of many of the prince's closest friends, such as his brother Frederick, Duke of York, Lord Moira, the Duke of Chartres and Maria Fitzherbert. In fact, George continued to purchase Reynolds's works long after the artist's death in 1792 and gave them pride of place at Carlton House, much to the embarrassment of visiting Tory ministers.

George's natural affability was always apparent in his dealings with his artists, and he always treated them with consideration while demonstrating a perceptive knowledge of their work. The miniaturist Henry Bone, whose intimate portraits of the prince's closest friends decorated his bedroom at Carlton House, said touchingly of him: 'Were I a rich man I would rather work for the prince for nothing than for many another for money.'

A similar admiration of their royal patron was shown by the various painters of sporting scenes George employed. This interest in sporting art confirms what a hard decision it must have

been for him to abandon his involvement in horse racing after the
Chiffney scandal for he considered his best horse picture to be
that of Escape painted by Sawrey Gilpin. George also patronized
the greatest of all English animal painters, George Stubbs, who
produced the memorable portrait of George's old friend Lady
Lade on horseback. His unusual loyalty to a friend can also be
seen in his decision to continue employing the artist James Ward
long after he had fallen out of favour with other aristocratic
patrons. Again, when another painter, William Beechey, was
abruptly dismissed by George III, the prince stepped in and offered
him both commissions and a friendship that became intimate
enough for the prince to once borrow £390 from his own artist!
Beechey eventually produced the prince's favourite portrait – of
himself in military uniform and striking a particularly martial pose
that had the added benefit of annoying George III. This pattern of
patronage persisted, and when the king abandoned another
painter, John Hoppner, the prince immediately adopted him, too,
making Hoppner his Principal Portrait Painter in 1793. Again, a
warm friendship developed between them as witnessed by the landscape painter and diarist Joseph Farington at a Royal Academy
dinner in 1807. When the elderly Hoppner apologized for his
clumsiness at the table, the prince 'put his hands to Hoppner's
cheeks and patting them said, "Oh! you have constitution enough
to do anything".' Farington witnessed a similar familiarity displayed by the prince to another artist, William Owen, and
admired George's 'easy and familiar' manner. When the sculptor
James Ward went to stay at Windsor in 1824 he found himself
walking along with George's arm round his shoulder and being
told that at Windsor he should 'do here, if you please, just as you
would if you were at home'.

A more intimate friendship was reserved for the ageing but still
beautiful painter Elisabeth Vigée Le Brun, who was in exile in
London after fleeing Revolutionary France. Le Brun had captured,
in a series of portraits, the last years of Louis XVI at Versailles and,
in particular, the images of Queen Marie Antoinette and her ladies.
Not least of these beautiful paintings was one of Le Brun,

showing her dressed in the casual English style of dress that she had personally introduced to the French court. The fact that Le Brun had been so intimately connected with the doomed Bourbon royal family fascinated the prince, who became a regular guest at the modest dinner parties at her little rented house in Maddox Street. As he told her: 'I flit about from one soirée to the next, but at you I stay put.' Predictably, Le Brun was equally charmed by the prince, whom she described in her memoirs as wearing a wig 'very artistically disposed, the hair parted on the forehead like the *Apollo Belvedere*'s, and this suited him to perfection'. She was particularly grateful to him for making sure that she was excluded from the restrictions governing the movement of French *émigrés* at the time so enabling her to 'travel over the interior of the kingdom staying wherever I wanted . . . The Prince of Wales put the seal on his obligingness by bringing me the paper himself'. In return, she painted a portrait of him that was dismissed as crude and badly finished by her jealous rivals for the prince's patronage. Of this, she noted:

> Several English painters became enraged against me on hearing that I had begun this picture and that the Prince allowed me all the time I asked to finish it, for they had long and vainly been waiting for the same concession. I was aware that the queen mother said her son was making love to me, and that he often came to lunch at my house. Never did the Prince of Wales enter my door in the forenoon except for his sittings.

In later years, as George's tastes became more conservative, his favourite artists were Sir Thomas Lawrence and Sir David Wilkie. Lawrence, the unchallenged master portraitist of the time, was famous for being able to depict his sitters with convincing flattery, as can be seen in his famous portrait of the Duke of Wellington in scarlet uniform, in which the craggy-featured duke is transformed into the noblest of warriors. The relationship was helped by a genuine mutual admiration between artist and patron, as the prince began regularly commissioning Lawrence and making him his Principal Portrait Painter in Ordinary. Lawrence's greatest asset to George was his undoubted skill in being able to portray the increasingly fat and decrepit prince in the most flattering of lights. Often the portraits were of the prince in military uniform and wearing the decorations that he had so assiduously collected from all over Europe. As the writer William Hazlitt disingenuously observed:

> Sir Thomas Lawrence had with the magic of the pencil recreated the Prince Regent as a well-fleshed Adonis of thirty-three . . . and we could not but derive a high degree of good natured pleasure from imagining to ourselves the transports with which his Royal Highness must have welcomed this improved version of himself.

Theirs was a friendship of mutual need: George needed Lawrence to portray him in a heroic light, and the artist needed the consistent patronage of the future sovereign of England. Too busy to marry, Lawrence lived for his work but managed to retain an exceptionally generous nature both as artist and man. With his royal patron's approval Lawrence was elected President of the Royal Academy in 1820, and George himself presented him with his gold chain and medallion of office. The following year Lawrence, who had devised the visual presentation of George IV's coronation, asked for the unusual distinction, as a mere painter, of being allowed to march in the ceremonial procession from Westminster Abbey. This was willingly given.

This close association with the Prince of Wales gave Lawrence the power to command the highest prices of any painter then working in Britain. Moreover, unlike many of his rivals, Lawrence was paid promptly by George for every work completed. His earnings from royal patronage alone amounted to over £25,000 in just five years. Yet Lawrence, even with his prodigious productivity, failed to complete every work commissioned by George and died in 1830. This perceived favouritism for Lawrence enraged many of his rivals, including the historical painter Benjamin Haydon. The ambitious Haydon became so jealous of Lawrence that he dismissed his work as merely patronizing and bereft of true artistic merit. But Lawrence's heroic style was appropriate to the times and captured the public imagination in a manner unmatched by any of his contemporaries. When he died, six months before George himself, Lawrence's body lay in state in St Paul's Cathedral before a funeral that brought thousands of Londoners on to the streets in tribute.

George had remained close to the end, their friendship even having survived, decades earlier, one of the most infamous scandals of the age when Lawrence was suspected of having been seduced by George's estranged wife, Caroline of Brunswick. Summoned by Caroline to her house at Blackheath to paint her portrait, Lawrence was alleged, in evidence given to the so-called Delicate Investigation into Caroline's behaviour that was set up prior to the royal divorce, to have been seduced by her. It appeared a similar fate had been reserved for other visitors to Montague House, including Admiral Sir Sidney Smith and the rising star of the Tory Party George Canning, for, as her footmen Roberts told the shocked Investigation, his mistress 'was very fond of fucking'. It was alleged that when Caroline was sitting for Lawrence one evening after her ladies had gone to bed, she he got up and led him off to her infamous Blue Room, from where suspicious noises could be heard from behind the locked doors. Whatever the truth of the allegation, it did not damage the relationship between Lawrence and the prince, who continued to shower the painter with commissions and to treat him in the friendliest manner.

George's relaxed attitude to those he considered friends, even if they were of a considerably lower social order, was noted with approval by Joseph Farington. He claimed that when Lawrence was with the prince 'he did not keep him standing but desired Him to sit down which of course He did and they continued to converse together'.

While Thomas Lawrence satisfied George's appetite for heroic depictions of himself, David Wilkie provided the genre paintings that seemed to otherwise attract him in his later years. These were a far cry from the dignified canvases of Gainsborough and

Reynolds, bearing such homespun titles as *The Penny Wedding* and *Blind Man's Buff.* The bucolic sentimentality expressed in Wilkie's work seemed appropriate to George's own increasing melancholy, referring as they did to a fast-vanishing England as the countryside was consumed by the growing Industrial Revolution. As Steven Parissien has pointed out, George's remodelling of the Royal Lodge at Windsor, with its modest thatched roof and rustic embellishments, showed how much his artistic tastes had changed from the grandeur of Carlton House and extravagance of the Brighton Pavilion. As with Lawrence, George formed a close friendship with Wilkie, encouraging a similar relaxed intimacy that came from his respect for the artist's work. The sculptor Francis Chantrey thought that 'the King's kindness to Wilkie was beautiful'. When George died in 1830 Wilkie was genuinely bereaved and wrote: 'I have lost the greatest friend I have ever met with . . . whose gracious generosity has done much for me than I deserved.'

Chantrey himself was one of George's favourite sculptors and was given many commissions, including a bust when George became king in 1820. Again George treated Chantrey much as he had Thomas Lawrence and David Wilkie and was described by Chantrey's biographer as having 'evinced an affability towards him which he often mentioned with pleasure'. On the first occasion that he sat for him, George put Chantrey at ease with the words: 'Now Mr Chantrey I insist on your laying aside everything like restraint . . . do here just as you would if you were at home.' Then holding up his wig, he added: 'Now Mr Chantrey which way will it be? With the wig or without it?'

6

SHERIDAN'S WIT

MUCH of Richard Brinsley Sheridan's drive and inspiration derived from the miserable time he had endured at Harrow School where he was mocked as an outsider and known dismissively 'the player's son' because his father had been an actor-manager in Ireland. The humiliation he suffered gave him a determination to succeed at all costs, which, combined with his brilliant wit and powerful intellect, enabled him to enter society on his own terms. Rather than waiting humbly to be invited to the great aristocratic salons he sent invitations to its members instead, asking them to come to his house. With the added advantage of having a talented and beautiful wife, Sheridan soon conquered London, holding soirées of his own and receiving invitations to the Duchess of Devonshire's parties where he first encountered the young Prince of Wales. George was, in Sheridan's words, 'then in the seventeenth year of his age, in the splendour of his youth and the manliness of his beauty'. Sheridan told his son Tom how the prince was always surrounded by flatterers and beautiful women keen to be acknowledged by this paragon of royal youth. Yet there was something sincere about the prince, Sheridan believed, that 'in his easy address and gaiety of manners won you to his side'. That first evening both Sheridans were introduced to him by Georgiana, the Duchess of Devonshire, with Charles James Fox standing beside her holding her arm. Bowing to Elizabeth Sheridan, George told her he was as great an admirer of her singing as he was of her beauty. Sheridan and the prince then spent the rest of the evening together drinking champagne and chatting like long-lost friends with that 'delicate open-hearted freedom which cast away the distinction of rank'. A few days later they met again at another of Georgiana's dinner parties and became so bonded by mutual attraction that they remained close friends for years to come.

Sheridan had met the sixteen-year-old Elizabeth Linley at Bath in 1770 where she was living with her father, the composer Thomas Linley. Father and daughter gave concerts together at the Assembly Rooms there, attracting her many admirers, among them a certain Major Matthews, who was determined to press his attentions on the young girl. To save her from a fate worse than death, Sheridan unhesitatingly put himself forward as her protector, devising a plan that involved spiriting her away from Bath and taking her off to a most unlikely refuge at a convent in France. During the journey he confessed that he loved her himself and they were secretly married at Calais. Returning from what was really a secret elopement, Sheridan found a furious Major Matthews waiting to exact his revenge. A duel to settle the matter was arranged, but neither combatant could agree on the choice of ground in Hyde Park so the entire party retired to a nearby pub where an inconclusive fight took place in which neither man was injured. After that, both men agreed that honour was satisfied and Sheridan returned to Bath. The whole town had followed events with keen interest and some amusement, particularly as Mr Linley now decided that his daughter should have nothing more to do with the troublesome Sheridan.

Eventually they were all reconciled, and Richard and Elizabeth moved to London where, with no income or capital other than a few thousand pounds brought by his wife, they took a house in Orchard Street and furnished it 'in the most costly style'. Then, between 1775 and 1779 Sheridan, who was later considered to be the greatest comic playwright of the age, produced a series of masterpieces, commencing with *The Rivals*. This alone brought him enough money to buy the Theatre Royal in Drury Lane as well as to begin a political career in 1780 as the Member for Stafford. In Parliament his patron was the Duke of Devonshire and his allegiance wholly committed to Charles James Fox and the Whigs.

Always the centre of controversy, Sheridan was said to owe his election to having bribed the burgesses of Stafford with five guineas each for the honour of representing them. He was also said to have cannily provided free dinners and ale even to those who did not have a vote. There must have been truth in such allegations for he used his first speech in Parliament to defend himself eloquently against accusations of bribery and corruption. Although the most celebrated dramatist of the day, Sheridan, perhaps as another consequence of his early humiliation, thought politics a far more suitable occupation for a gentleman.

George greatly admired Sheridan's wit and never took offence even when described by him as being 'too much a ladies' man to be the man of any lady'. Typical of Sheridan's cheek was his stratagem to become a member of Brook's Club. Discovering that his membership was being constantly blackballed by one member, the snobbish George Selwyn, Sheridan and the prince devised a plot together. When an election was next held, Selwyn was summoned to a drawing-room by the Prince of Wales and there held in conversation for an hour until a waiter entered the room and rubbed his chin as a prearranged signal that the vote had been taken. Sheridan was duly elected a member of Brook's. Prince and playwright enjoyed such pranks so much that even when in Brighton with Maria Fitzherbert George could not do without his amusing companion and insisted that Sheridan join them whenever possible. Sheridan found the Pavilion delightful, except that each visit meant enduring the discomfort of the powerful heating system so disliked by all the prince's guests. Sweltering in the dining-room one evening Sheridan asked George Hanger how he felt. 'Hot, hot, hot as hell,' Hanger replied. 'That is quite right,' replied Sheridan, 'for in this world we should prepare for that we know we will endure in the next.'

With his incomparable mind and ability with words Sheridan was the first person the prince turned to for advice in any emergency. Such a crisis occurred one evening when Maria Fitzherbert appeared in a royal box at a theatre as the royal family were watching a play. Queen Charlotte was scandalized to see her and immediately wrote to her son condemning the presence of 'a certain person'. Sheridan was urgently summoned from Brook's to help draft a reply and quickly perceived a way of turning the tables on the queen. 'Ask her who she means by a certain person,' Sheridan advised. 'Her Majesty will hesitate to commit a name to writing. Besides it would be very impolitic of your Royal Highness to know to whom Her Majesty alludes.' George did as he was bid, and the queen, realizing she had been outwitted, spoke no more of the matter.

Meanwhile, Sheridan's political career was flourishing after he had seized his great opportunity in the impeachment of Warren Hastings, the ex-Governor-General of India charged with corruption. His speeches in the proceedings were by common agreement among the finest ever delivered in that generation of great orators. The first was on 7 February 1787, when the charges brought against Hastings were debated. Sheridan spoke without pause for more than five hours, moving the House into such a state of passion that the session had to be adjourned to allow the atmosphere to cool.

Sheridan was again on hand when George, now desperately short of money to pay his enormous debts, appealed to his Whig friends in April 1787 to raise the matter in the House. The first to speak was Alderman Newnham, who asked the government if it proposed 'to bring forward any proposition to rescue the Prince of Wales from his present very embarrassed situation'. Pitt refused to be drawn, but another Tory member made a provocative speech suggesting that the prince's debts should be considered in the light of 'a question which went immediately to affect our constitution in Church and State'. This, as the whole House realized, was an allusion to the prince's rumoured secret marriage to the Catholic Maria Fitzherbert. When Newnham persisted, Pitt threatened to reveal 'circumstances which he should otherwise think it his duty to conceal'. Immediately Sheridan sprang to the prince's defence and called Pitt's bluff by insisting that the Whigs would not withdraw Newnham's motion so causing the prime minister to state that the matters he alluded to concerned only money and not 'any extraneous circumstances'. That night the prince congratulated Sheridan on his bold performance, but both realized that a further explanation would have to be made, and Sheridan was dispatched to Brighton to deal with Mrs Fitzherbert's increasing unease. Using his customary charm he persuaded her to maintain her silence, for everyone's sake. But Fox's declaration to Parliament a few days later that the rumour of a marriage between the prince and a certain person had 'not the smallest degree of foundation' infuriated Maria. The one most in danger because of his constitutional position from all this was the Prince of Wales and he implored Sheridan for help. Only a man of Sheridan's inventiveness and cheek could devise an explanation that would satisfy the House and mollify Mrs Fitzherbert. 'Sheridan', said the prince in desperation, 'must say something.'

So on 4 May 1788 Richard Brinsley Sheridan stood up and began the most important speech of his life, on which the very future of the throne of Britain might well depend. Using his incomparable mastery of language he wove a spell of ambiguity and equivocation in a performance that was a masterpiece of diplomacy. Without mentioning Mrs Fitzherbert by name he urged his listeners to share his own feelings for a person 'on whose conduct truth could offer no just reproach and whose character claimed and was entitled to the truest and most general respect'. By using the language of gallantry Sheridan persuaded his listeners that they should judge the issue as gentlemen rather than as politicians. This unexpected appeal to the emotions rather than to reason offered Pitt and the government an excuse to escape from having to call Fox, and by implication the prince, a liar and so plunging the nation into a serious constitutional crisis. None of this mollified Maria Fitzherbert, however, for she had already blamed Fox for having openly denied before God that she was married to the prince. For a time she showed her displeasure with Sheridan, too, and persuaded George that if he wanted to maintain his intimacy with her he should see somewhat less of his old friend.

Yet two years later the friendship appeared to be fully restored, with Sheridan occupying a role in the prince's life similar to that which George Brummell once held. Like Brummell, he was so confident of the friendship that sometimes he did not hesitate to criticize George's behaviour in public. Sheridan's wife Elizabeth recalled after his death that at a ball in the summer of 1787 the prince had become almost offensively drunk. When others appealed to him to intervene, Sheridan went up to George and pushed aside the bottle in front of him with the words '*You shall not* drink any more.' At this the prince looked up at him and said: 'Sheridan I love you better than anyone but *shall not* is what I cannot put up with.'

That same year their friendship was again tested during the Regency Crisis, the constitutional emergency that marked George III's first decline into insanity. The prospect was now imminent that the heir to the throne might have to be made Regent. If this occurred then George would at last enjoy the income he so desperately needed. The incentive for his Whig friends to champion his cause was the mouthwatering prospect of so many government offices at their disposal. They agreed among themselves that the Duke of Portland should be prime minister, Fox the secretary of state and Sheridan would get the highly lucrative post of Treasury of the Navy. When negotiations dragged on, the Whigs began bickering among themselves, Portland declaring that he would not have Sheridan in his Cabinet because, as the Duchess of Devonshire put it, of 'his sly game'. Portland, like some other party members, was suspicious of Sheridan's commitment to the party, believing that he was more concerned with the Prince of Wales's interests than theirs. Sheridan's duplicity seemed confirmed when, having been evicted by bailiffs from his own house, he moved immediately with his wife into Mrs Fitzherbert's London home. The squabbling Whigs were now lambasted by the press, which demanded that if George was made Regent then he should dismiss the lot of them, particularly Richard Brinsley Sheridan, that 'needy adventurer ready to bring his ability to the best market'. In response, Sheridan masterminded a public-relations campaign on behalf of his royal patron that portrayed George in a glowing light as 'the first young man in Great Britain'. He also used his charm and diplomatic skills to end the bickering in the Whig party as Parliament prepared to vote on the powers to be allowed the Regent if the king failed to recover. When the vote finally came, the Whigs were soundly defeated by sixty-four votes, and the prince was told by Pitt that even if made Regent he would have only limited powers without the authority to distribute pensions, offices or honours to his cronies. Just as the Regency Bill was finally passed, fate struck royal hopes a final blow when it was announced that King George III was fast recovering from his illness.

The possessor of many vices, Sheridan had one important virtue that made him almost unique among the prince's circle of close friends – he was not a gambler. He did, however, drink to excess, and this weakness would bring about his downfall. As John Wilson Croker succinctly put it, Sheridan was 'a self-immolated victim of his own lamentable and shameful weaknesses'. This persistent drunkenness was to rob him of his political career and divorce him from the company of his friends. While most of them, including the Prince of Wales himself, were notoriously heavy drinkers, their indulgence remained under control while Sheridan's did not. Byron describes having to take a drunken Sheridan home after dinner one evening and trying to negotiate a spiral staircase:

> which had certainly been constructed before the discovery of fermented liquors and to which no legs, however crooked, could possibly accommodate themselves. We deposited him safe at home where his man evidently used to the business, waited to receive him in the hall.

Yet even in these degraded circumstances Byron could still say of him: 'Poor fellow, his very dregs are better than the first sprightly runnings of others.' Regardless of his increasing drunkenness Sheridan was always a welcome guest at the Pavilion, often with George's encouragement, acting the part of the Lord of Misrule. Even at the age of fifty-five Sheridan continued to enter into whatever fun was going on as if still a young boy. Creevey recalls him rushing into the drawing-room at the Pavilion disguised as a law officer to arrest the dowager Lady Sefton for playing some unlawful card game. On another occasion when a séance was in course and the whole dining-room in complete darkness, Sheridan crept in and sat down heavily on the lap of a visiting Russian dignitary, a Madame Gerobtzoff, who screamed loudly enough to wake the whole of Brighton. The prince was naturally delighted with Sheridan's buffoonery but chose to ignore the harm that heavy drinking was doing to his friend. Even when Sheridan complained that he was ill from drinking and took to his bed the prince would have none of it, handing a bottle of claret and a glass to Creevey and sending him up to Sheridan's bedroom with the words: 'Now Creevey, go to his bedside and tell him I'll drink a glass of wine with him, and if he refuses, I admit he must be damned bad indeed.' Sheridan refused to touch the wine, and Creevey returned to the prince, telling him that poor old Sheridan must really be ill. But at two o'clock in the morning, while everybody was engaged in dancing, Sheridan appeared at the door as if from the grave, smartly dressed and with powdered hair. He then asked Creevey to join him for a late supper in the kitchen where he entertained the servants by telling them that if he was the prince then they should all have much better accommodation. As Creevey reports, they all rushed to wait upon him as he 'ate away and drank a bottle of claret in a minute, returned to the ballroom, and when I left it between three and four he was still dancing'.

Such a lifestyle of excess was unsustainable, and Sheridan eventually paid a heavy price for it. The first casualty as he descended into serious alcoholism was his political career. When he inevitably lost the seat of Stafford he blamed everyone but himself. George refused to condone this self-deception when Sheridan appealed for sympathy, telling him without equivocation that it was Sheridan's own indolence and indecision that had caused the loss. Desperate to get back into Parliament, Sheridan sought the aid of Lord Moira, who interceded on his behalf with their mutual friend, and George agreed to help. There was an offer of a seat from the Duke of Norfolk, but George advised his friend not to accept it as he would then have to vote as the duke directed – not a happy prospect for a politically free spirit such as Sheridan. Instead, the prince offered to put up £3,000 himself to buy Sheridan a seat at Wootton Bassett in Wiltshire from a young man who was retiring from the House. Knowing Sheridan's chaotic financial circumstances, George ordered that the money be held by a solicitor rather than be handed directly to Sheridan. 'We knew him too well for that,' he remarked too rue-fully to Lord Moira. The prince's caution was fully justified for when his secretary, Colonel John McMahon, was summoned to Sheridan's house at the unlikely hour of eight o'clock in the morning, he found him ready packed and with carriage apparently waiting to take him to Wootton Bassett. Impressed by his keen-ness, McMahon then released the money to the solicitors and the prince awaited news of Sheridan's acquisition of the seat. Yet a few days later, while riding in Oxford Street, George noticed someone he thought was Sheridan in the distance but 'the person, whoever he was, turned into Poland Street . . . as if to avoid me'. Mys-terious sightings of Sheridan continued, and McMahon, now desperately concerned about the prince's £3,000, called on the soli-citor, who told him he knew nothing of Wootton Bassett but that Mr Sheridan had instructed him to use the £3,000 to pay off his most pressing debts, including the solicitor's own bill. This was deliberate fraud on an old friend, and, although a sign of Sheridan's growing desperation and lack of judgement, it marked the end of what had been a warm and close relationship. Having paid, as a debt of honour, another £3,000 to the owner of the seat, George later wrote sadly but objectively:

> I never saw Sheridan, to speak to after, not that it was much worse in principle than other things of his, nor that I had given orders to exclude him, but it was felt by Sheridan himself to be so gross a violation of confidence – such a want of respect and such a series of lies and fraud, that he did not venture to approach me, and in fact, he never came near me again.

Sheridan did make one last attempt to redeem himself and requested a meeting with John McMahon to explain his actions, at which Sheridan went to great pains to absolve himself of any responsibility for the fraud and to put all the blame on others. As the prince wrote: 'McMahon listened to all this but with no good-will towards Sheridan and came immediately to report it to me, but after that Sheridan never came near either of us.'

Sheridan's decline was, as Lord Byron recognized, a tragedy for parliamentary debate, as he was undoubtedly one of the brightest stars of the House. His incisive wit and dismissal of cant made him stand out even in an age of great debaters. The power of his contributions still impress, with an apposite relevance to today, as when he warned the British people that:

> the love of ease that luxury brings along with it, the selfish and compromising spirit in which the members of a polished society countenance each other and which reverses the principles of patriotism by sacrificing public interests to private ones, and the repression of enthusiasm by fastidiousness and ridicule, these are among the causes that undermine a people . . . and the period in which their rights are best understood may be that in which they most easily surrender them.

There was also a personal tragedy for Sheridan in the loss of the genuine friendship with the Prince of Wales for the two men had much in common. Sheridan's compulsion to ruffle feathers and his ability to mock the more ridiculous aspects of English conservatism greatly appealed to George, who, confined by the straightjacket of his role as heir to the throne, could never speak with the freedom that Sheridan enjoyed. Both men were flirtatious and gregarious, but Sheridan's iconoclasm, although it made him a great comic dramatist, also made him suspicious of society. Sheridan's downfall was a warning to his friend of the dangers of addictive drunkenness – a path that George might well have followed had he not been surrounded by attendants and politicians to keep him on course.

Now in desperate financial circumstances, Sheridan appeared to have been deserted by his erstwhile friends, but the diarist Croker claimed that it was Sheridan who abandoned them by choosing to hide himself away from society. Finally, when George was told of his old friend's desperate situation, he remarked: 'I said that his illness and want made me forget his faults and that he must be taken care of.' The prince then immediately sent him £500, although he said that he set no limit to the sum nor imposed any conditions on how it was to be used. The money was taken to him by a mutual friend named Vaughan, who found Sheridan and his wife both in bed and apparently dying from disease and malnutrition. The greatest playwright of the age was living in filthy conditions and had not moved from his bed for a week. Vaughan ordered that the house be cleaned and food provided, but two days later he told Colonel McMahon that Sheridan had sent back the money with the excuse that he did not need it after all as some of Mrs Sheridan's friends had come forward with a gift. Vaughan had no idea what the truth was but insisted to McMahon that 'three days ago I was enabled with His Royal Highnesses [*sic*] bounty to relieve him and her from the lowest state of misery and debasement in which I have ever seen human beings'. Perhaps the episode reflects Sheridan's stubborn pride and his lifelong refusal to accept charity or favours from anyone, even a prince. When told of Sheridan's death, George took to his room in grief for the loss of one of the most intimate friends of his youth. Although they had had their falling out, he maintained an affection and respect for the feckless reprobate for, as he told the Irish poet Thomas Moore, Sheridan's first biographer:

He was a great man, Mr Moore, but in the simplicity of his nature he never knew his own greatness. He had an abounding confidence in every man; and although his pen indicated a knowledge of human nature, yet that knowledge was confined to his pen alone, for in all his acts he rendered himself the dupe of the fool and the designing knave.

Sheridan had wanted to be buried next to the great Parliamentarian Charles James Fox, as he did not want to be remembered by posterity as merely a writer of plays. But his wishes were disregarded, and he was, fortunately, placed in Poets' Corner at Westminster Abbey, appropriately beside the great actor David Garrick. A fitting epitaph was written by Lord Byron, who said of him:

> The life of such a man may be made more amusing than if he had been a Wilberforce [a known teetotaller] ... compare him with the coalitioner Fox, and the pensioner Burke as a man of principle ... Without means, without connexion, without character he beat them all.

A far different version was told by Moore in his *Life of Sheridan*, which appeared in 1825. Moore, once a close friend of the prince but now a critic, hinted that it was Vaughan himself who had given the money to Sheridan and not George. The insinuation that the prince had ignored the plight of such an old friend was deeply wounding, and when John Wilson Croker visited Windsor that November he found George in a resentful mood. With Moore's book open in front of him the king launched into a heated defence of his actions towards Sheridan, which lasted an hour, insisting that he had constantly offered Sheridan asylum in Carlton House to save him from his creditors and that he had given him £4,000 'as soon as he knew that it would be of essential service'. Urged by George to put his case to the public, Croker agreed to review Moore's biography in the *Quarterly* magazine where he attacked the author and revealed just how much Sheridan had received from the Privy Purse. In the next edition of the book Moore diplomatically inserted a statement that was tantamount to a retraction 'disclaiming all idea of imputing a want of generosity in pecuniary matters, to the illustrious personage concerned'.

7

THE ARCHITECTS

I F the Palace of Versailles is testimony to the grandeur of Louis XIV and the dominance of French architecture in the seventeenth century, then the Brighton Pavilion is the memorial to the idiosyncrasies of King George IV in the late eighteenth. Yet the exotic design of the Pavilion reveals only half the story for George's passion for building had begun with the remodelling of Carlton House in London where his fascination with innovation and experimentation were first displayed. When the renovation began in 1783 Carlton House was an eclectic building in a traditional manner but without any coherent style or distinguishing features. Working over the next twenty years with five of the leading British architects of the age, George was to transform it into one of the most discussed palaces in Europe. This task would involve him in a series of working friendships with the most important British architects of the time and demonstrate his unusual capacity to work with skilled professionals. In this George was unique for no other British prince has ever been so closely involved, and to such an extent, in architectural projects before or since.

When the Prince of Wales was given Carlton House in 1782 he also inherited the services of the Royal Architect and Surveyor General, Sir William Chambers. This was the man credited with introducing the chinoiserie style of decoration into Britain and who had taught George III the rudiments of architectural drawing. Chambers had the great disadvantages for George of being both an architectural conservative and a man fully committed to his father. Certainly, the young Prince of Wales would have preferred to use the services of the more adventurous Adam brothers, 'whose boyish conceits and trifling complicated ornaments' may have been more appealing than those of the elderly Chambers. Yet, dependent on his father's goodwill for the state funds needed to renovate Carlton House, George had little choice but to commission him to begin the renovation. From the start Chambers assumed a master-and-pupil relationship that was deeply resented by the prince. As one of the busiest architects of the day, Chambers was also busy working on commissions in England and Ireland for aristocratic patrons and appears not to have devoted his full attention to the Carlton House project. The long delays that resulted soon provided George with the opportunity and the excuse to transfer the work to an architect of his own choice, the neoclassicist Henry Holland.

Working with great energy, Holland produced what at the time was seen as an innovative realization of French classicism in a building described by Horace Walpole as 'a chaste palace of august simplicity'. As the historian Steven Parissien has pointed out, Holland and his patron were responsible for a building that marked the beginning of the Regency style in England. Holland was delighted to be able to work in an informal and productive manner with the prince, knowing that he had a sympathetic patron and what appeared to be an almost inexhaustible budget. Significantly, Henry Holland came from a humble background. His father had been a bricklayer, and he did not assume the air of artistic superiority that Sir William Chambers had displayed. This made it all the easier for the prince to deal with him in the friendly manner that he always assumed when involved with so-called social inferiors. Work progressed well but soon patron and architect had gone through the £60,000 budget provided by the king. Ignoring the mounting costs, George continued to allow Holland free reign to spend virtually unchecked. All that mattered as far as George was concerned was to achieve the desired aesthetic results regardless of expense, a pure if dangerous policy to pursue. As a result of this quest for perfection, only the finest craftsmen were employed and all the high-quality hand-picked fittings were imported from the Continent. Throughout the project George was a constant presence at Carlton House, and Holland never hesitated to involve him in even the smallest detail. As a consequence, the great marble fireplaces seemed to visitors to be constantly on the move from one room to another and regularly placed *in situ* for the prince to give his opinion. While Holland produced a neoclassical façade for the exterior, the interiors were far more adventurous and deeply influenced by contemporary French design. The result was, according to one later critic, 'the most perfect and refined Anglo-French interior ever realized in England'. Yet the friendship and positive working relationship between George and Henry Holland was not to last, and it ended in 1802, not over any stylistic disagreement but over a financial dispute between them over a piece of land in Devon that led to Holland taking offence and breaking off all contact with the prince.

The quarrel appeared to influence George's opinions on the merits of what Holland had really achieved at Carlton House, and he now turned to his old friend Walsh Porter, creator of Craven Cottage, to eradicate much of what Holland had produced. The choice of Porter was significant because the prince clearly had need of personal reassurance, and with the sycophantic Porter this was guaranteed. The fact that Porter was more picture dealer than architect appears not to have mattered to George at a time when personal loyalty appeared more important than professional qualifications. Over the following years George and Porter together destroyed all that Holland had achieved, replacing it, according to Joseph Farington by 'substituting and finishing in a most expensive and motley taste'. This was a case of old friends working together in a relaxed manner and completely atypical of the traditional relationship between royal patron and architectural adviser. Porter had the incomparable advantage of not only being self-confident but good company, too – virtues always appreciated by the Prince of Wales. Therefore it was only natural, as the collector Francis Bourgeois stated, that Porter's company 'was much cherished by the Prince of

Wales at the expense of material achievement'. So George set about, as Farington acidly put it, 'pulling Carlton House to pieces under the direction of a gentleman called an *amateur architect*'. George's tolerance of his friend must have been exceptional for everyone else involved in the project was shocked both by Porter's arrogance and his technical ignorance. Nor would this self-assertive little man tolerate any criticism of his designs or of his failure to provide estimates for the work. When, in 1805, he was asked for precise details of the colossal expenditure involved he was unable to comply but shifted any possible blame on to his patron by claiming that he had not 'added or branched out into a single thing that was not planned by the Prince himself'. With an architectural friend like this it is little wonder that the prince soon made enemies in a government shocked by the soaring expenditure at Carlton House.

The importance to George of the Carlton House renovation cannot be overestimated. It was as if the two great frustrations of his own life – his father's overbearing control and the denial of a fulfilling military career – could be exorcized by architectural achievement. With the help of Porter's bold approach and the creation of interiors that were non-conformist in design and colour he would make a positive statement about himself to English society. Cleverly, Porter devised an Admiral's Room and a Military Tent Room to appease his patron's thwarted martial ambitions. There was also Porter's use of bold and assertive colours in the new Chinese dining-room, a symphony of red, gold and black, and in the music room where sky-blue walls clashed violently with the orange-hued carpet and Holland's remaining scagliola columns with their silver capitals and the lavender cornice. At the heart of this swirling mêlée of colour was the Plate Closet, a room devised by Porter to display the prince's Aladdin's Cave collection of gold and silver plates and ornaments. The final result, according to the novelist Robert Plumer Ward, stood comparison with the splendour of Versailles or St Petersburg, although on a much smaller scale. Even when Porter died in 1809 George continued to change the decoration of the rooms at Carlton House as if he could never make up his mind what really pleased him –

rather as his changes of mistress reflected some innate doubt and uncertainty about his own judgement of women.

Whatever the reservation over the costs, Carlton House became the design sensation of the day, and here, as later at the Brighton Pavilion, George was able to indulge his talent for entertaining in style. A series of sumptuous breakfasts, balls and fêtes were held, culminating on 19 June 1811 in a celebration of his Regency. Two thousand representatives of the nobility and gentry of Britain and Europe sat down to dinner at a supper table over two hundred feet in length bisected by a stream of real water flowing down the middle. The following day the prince ill-advisedly opened the house to the public. Thousands arrived to gape in awe at this architectural spectacle, but in the jostling crowd many spectators were injured and hundreds of shoes lost. The correspondent of the *Morning Chronicle* witnessed the chaos:

> The number of stray shoes . . . was so great that they filled a large tub, from which the shoeless ladies were invited to select their property. About a dozen females were so completely disrobed in the squeeze, they were obliged to send home for clothes . . . and one lady was so completely disencumbered of all dress, a female domestic, in kind compassion, wrapped her up in an apron.

Yet, grand as it was, Carlton House soon proved too small for entertaining on the scale that the prince demanded, and even after the constant changes and refurbishments it was no more than an inflated mansion rather than the spacious palace he really desired. With Walsh Porter gone there was no one bold or courageous enough to produce yet another dramatic and costly renovation. Gradually George lost interest in the building and turned his attentions to the prospect of the Brighton Pavilion, leaving Carlton House to fall into neglect until its demolition in 1826. By then it was a near ruin and was described by the Italian sculptor Antonio Canova as being 'blackened with dust and soot like an ugly barn'. George had by this time moved on to new projects and new architects, among them James Wyatt, who did attempt to save the crumbling fabric of Carlton House. As the cost of Wyatt's work spiralled out of control, however, the task was abandoned. In other respects Wyatt appeared an excellent replacement for Porter, and he and the prince struck up a good friendship and a promising relationship until James Wyatt's sudden death in a carriage accident in 1813. When news of his father's death reached London, Wyatt's son Philip tried desperately to retain George's patronage for himself. Knowing the close relationship that existed between his father and the prince, he drove down to the Brighton Pavilion to tell him personally the sad news and insisted on being admitted to George's bedroom although it was now three o'clock in the morning. The prince, according to Philip's dramatic account of the event, immediately burst into tears, although he did remain calm enough to sensibly deny Philip's request that he be immediately given his father's architectural positions. Instead, the lucrative position of Prince of Wales's main architect passed to the little-known but highly talented John Nash.

Like his predecessors Walsh Porter and Richard Cosway, Nash had realized early in his career that adopting an urbane and sophisticated manner and moving in the right social circles was just as important for success as having innate talent. In Nash's case there may have been another reason for his friendship with the prince, as it was rumoured that his much younger second wife, Mary Anne Bradley, had at one time been one of George's mistresses. As with Richard Cosway and the Royal Academicians, Nash's friendship with the prince and his grand lifestyle aroused the envy and resentment of many of his professional colleagues. One of them, Richard Finch, felt he had much in common with his patron, dismissing him, perhaps enviously, as 'a great coxcomb. He is very fond of women . . . attempted even Mrs Parke, his wife's sister. He lives in Dover Street, has a charming place on the Isle of Wight and drives four horses.' Nash's intimacy with George led to another unsubstantiated rumour that one of Nash's pupils, James Pennethorne, was in reality the prince's natural son. It is more likely, however, that Nash's rise to fame and fortune as royal architect had far more to do with careful planning for instead of approaching George directly Nash had become friendly with the prince's artistic adviser Lord Yarmouth as well as his current secretary Benjamin Bloomfield. By so ingratiating himself with these important doorkeepers to the prince, Nash was finally able to approach George himself and gain the position as architect to the Department of Woods and Forests.

One of his first tasks was the creation of the beautiful terraces that surround Regent's Park in London. Strangely, these elegant buildings in stucco and cast iron were dismissed at the time as meretricious, with the writer Maria Edgeworth claiming to be 'shocked by the new town built in Regents Park' and indignant at 'plaister statues and horrid useless domes and pediments crowded with mock sculpture figures which damp and smoke must destroy in a season or two'. Ironically, the Nash Terraces proved an outstanding contribution to London and perhaps the most lasting testament to the creative friendship between the prince and his architects. While George's relationship with his previous designers had always been affable, only Nash was allowed more intimate contact with the prince's private life by acting as his personal representative in the negotiations with Solicitor General Sir Samuel Romilly concerning the settlement with Caroline, Princess of Wales. He even had the authority, according to Steven Parissien, to offer Romilly – on George's behalf – the post of Lord Chancellor in return for a favourable outcome to the negotiations.

As the prince's new principal architect, John Nash had inevitably been asked to contribute to the never-ending and outrageously expensive renovations at Carlton House. One of Nash's most notable additions was a new Gothic dining-room, which alone cost £9,000, but much of his involvement concerned the toning down of the garish colours that Walsh Porter had imposed. Now crimson, blue and white became the dominant theme, and these tones would later dominate at the refurbished Windsor Castle and Buckingham Palace. When, after 1810, George largely lost interest in Carlton House – finding its location too public to satisfy his increasingly reclusive temperament – his attention turned wholeheartedly to the Brighton Pavilion. At the time it remained a small but extremely elegant building, a seaside retreat created for the prince and completed by Henry Holland in 1795. All of George's subsequent architects had contributed to the building, and it had gained an enormous stables as their patron's tastes became evermore exotic and focused on Indian and Chinese design. Now as Regent, George had easier access to the funds required, and Nash was asked to carry out a full and fundamental programme of building works that would transform the Pavilion into the exotic edifice that exists today. Yet even the extra funds available did not go far in realizing Nash's grandiose and costly schemes, and the government was forced in 1816 to intervene and to ask the prince to temporarily suspend all activities there. This he quietly ignored, and the following year work discretely began again.

The Brighton Pavilion now became a folly in every sense. Nash transformed Holland's modest classical building into an oriental fantasy that today serves as the best-known and most fitting memorial to one of the most controversial of British monarchs. With its eclectic oriental style and pastiche decoration that makes only a passing reference to true Eastern architecture, the Brighton Pavilion remains one of the most unusual buildings in Britain. Given the limited building technology of the time, it is hard to imagine anything that would have shocked and fascinated late Georgian Britain more. Decorated both internally and externally in various oriental styles, it also contained the latest modern domestic technology, including gas lighting and central heating. To the dismay of George's many friends, the latter was invariably turned on full regardless of season. Visitors more familiar with draughty English country houses sweltered in the heat of the vast dining-room where 'the inmates are nearly baked or encrusted'. To the amazement of his companions, the prince always appeared cool and relaxed in spite of the insufferable heat. Always obsessed with personal hygiene, as his unfortunate wife Queen Caroline found to her cost, George had taken a personal interest in the plumbing arrangements, too. With Nash he designed an ingenious pipe system that conducted seawater via a boiler directly to his own bathrooms, of which were no less than five, ranging from a vast plunge bath lined with veined marble to a modest douche bath. Hundreds of workmen were involved in these projects, but only a few were entrusted with constructing the notorious secret tunnel to the stables that had, according to the diarist Charles Greville, cost more than £3,000.

Although the king expressed himself wholly delighted with Nash's completed Pavilion, most of his friends shared John Wilson Croker's opinion that it was 'an absurd waste of money, and will be a ruin in half a century or sooner' – a prediction that almost came true. When George boasted to Princess Lieven, the Austrian Ambassador's wife, that the chandeliers alone had cost nearly £11,000 she was shocked by the wanton extravagance. She wrote:

> I do not believe that, since the days of Heliogabalus, there has been such magnificence and such luxury. There is something effeminate in it, which is disgusting. One spends the evening half-lying on cushions; the lights are dazzling; there are perfumes, music, liqueurs . . . to light the three rooms, used when the family is alone, costs 150 guineas an evening.

In the economic depression that followed the Napoleonic Wars, the Pavilion attracted savage criticism as an example of almost obscene extravagance, and the London cartoonists mocked it mercilessly. To them it was a godsend, but to the prince it became an architectural albatross hung around his neck so that whenever he was ridiculed over some new misdemeanour this oriental folly was shown accusingly in the background.

The last collaboration between the prince and Nash was the conversion of the Royal Lodge at Windsor to a small palace, and the renovation of the vast and decrepit Windsor Castle itself. In 1812 Nash had given the Lodge, at that time little more than a large cottage, a makeover and had also renovated nearby Cumberland Lodge in order to provide overspill accommodation for royal guests. Nash's initial work had again been costly to the nation, with a conservatory resulting in a bill for £2,429 and new furniture a staggering £17,000. But cost had never proved a deterrent to a man who had already lavished vast sums on Carlton House and the Brighton Pavilion.

At this point George changed architects and replaced Nash with the equally urbane but less inspiring Sir Jeffry Wyatville. He came with the strongest recommendation from Georgiana, Duchess of Devonshire, who was delighted with the work he had done on her new mansion at Endsleigh in Devon. The last of George's architectural friends, Wyatville was described as 'a busy bustling vain little man' who once had been simply Jeffry Wyatt but, after he was awarded the commission to renovate Windsor Castle in 1823, had decided to aggrandize his name. To distinguish himself from more humble members of the Wyatt family from Derbyshire, he informed the king that he was proposing to change it to the more Frenchified Wyatville. When he asked for his permission for the name change, the king seemed baffled and simply replied: 'Vile or mutton, call yourself what you like.'

By now the king was used to dealing with pretentious architects, and he struck up another close friendship with Wyatville, who managed his relationship with his sovereign with commendable diplomacy. To celebrate George's birthday in 1824 he gave all the workmen employed at Windsor five shillings to buy a good dinner in the town, then planned to have them line up on the towers and walls of the castle to cheer as the king arrived. Caution prevailed, however, as by this time many of the men were drunk, and Wyatville feared some might fall, so he assembled them on the lawns below instead. Once again the estimates given bore little relation to the actual cost of work, as Wyatville radically rebuilt the exteriors and created wholly new interiors. By the end of the decade the renovation of Windsor Castle had cost well over half a million pounds, compared with the original estimate of little more than one thousand. At every stage Wyatville was careful to involve George in approving the work and handled his friendship with the king with a diplomacy that pleased his royal master. Purists were shocked by the results, particularly by Wyatville's use of mock portcullis and imitation mortar joints in his freestone blocks, yet admirers of the Gothic revival such as Sir Walter Scott thought them splendid innovations. Among the critics of the renovated castle were George's mother, who thought the rooms too cramped, and the diarist Charles Greville, who considered the project 'poor value for the enormous sums expended' and that it could not compare to Versailles or any other of the great French palaces. Lord Dudley's more mundane criticism was that the interior was so bitterly cold in winter that even the food arrived cold on the table. But George was delighted with Wyatville's concept, particularly the gilded woodwork and plaster and the heavy brocades that hung on the walls.

Even the cost of the renovation at the more modest Windsor Lodge had soared, provoking embarrassing questions in Parliament. The minister concerned, Lord Londonderry, attempted to explain to indignant members that the word 'cottage' was a misnomer, as the Lodge was not really a modest thatched house but 'a very comfortable residence for a family' and the only one the prince could make use of when he went to Windsor. By 1826 the Duke of Wellington must have come to regret encouraging George to move to Windsor in the first place, as work on both projects had already cost the nation well over a million pounds. In completing the Lodge, Wyatville had used every trick of the new historicism – including Tudor chimneys, Gothic windows and stuccoed walls – to complement the original medieval framework. Purists such as the young Augustus Pugin thought the result an eclectic mess that had resulted in little more than a 'thatched palace'. In spite of the criticism, George was delighted with the Lodge and particularly its proximity to Virginia Water. Here he was to ask Wyatville to build him his last architectural project, a classical temple on the banks of the lake using columns and statues found in a courtyard at the British Museum and other statues found on a captured French frigate. In the last years of his reign George would delight in bringing his friends each afternoon to fish and boat on the lake.

Throughout the years George had remained firm friends with John Nash, and in 1828 attempted to reward him for a long and positive working association that had even survived the scandal of the overspending at Brighton and Windsor. He told the prime minister, the Duke of Wellington, that he wished to make Nash a baronet, but Wellington refused the request, pointing out that after the colossal expenditure on architecture that Nash was associated with it would be seen as a near insult to the public. The king protested, saying that Nash was being 'most infamously used', but the duke stood firm. Nash's true reward may well be his association with the most famous open space in one of the world's great cities, Trafalgar Square in London. Built to Nash's original design, it was to become one of the highlights of any tourist's visit to London. Ironically, the two pillars supporting the portico of the National Gallery on the north side of the square also act as a memorial to Nash and his royal patron for they are all that remain of Carlton House.

8

A REMARKABLE HOST

NOTHING gave the Prince of Wales greater pleasure than entertaining his friends, first at Carlton House and later at the Brighton Pavilion. As a host he was incomparable, providing fine food and wine and encouraging relaxed and stimulating conversation.

For George, Carlton House represented the material evidence of his final escape from parental control and from the parsimony of the Dutch House at Kew. Here his personal tastes could be indulged and guests welcomed as friends, although it never provided the setting for 'bacchanalian orgies' nor did it more resemble 'the interior of a Turkish seraglio than the home of a British Prince' as claimed by Robert Huish. Carlton House did, however, become a magnet that attracted the most interesting members of London society. Those invited were struck by their host's almost obsessive fascination with interior design and the strange and innovative arrangement of the rooms. Each time they came to dinner, regular visitors would find that the prince had yet again altered either the arrangement of the furniture or the curtains and sometimes both. Lady Spencer told her brother that 'he changes the furniture so very often that one can scarcely find time to catch a glimpse at each transient arrangement before it is all turned off for some other'. No expense was spared on the furnishing, and even the aristocratic Lady Spencer, well used to living in a grand house, was impressed by the sheer opulence of Carlton House and by the obvious cost involved. 'I can only tell you,' she continued to her brother, 'the lustre in one of the rooms of glass and ormulu, looking like a shower of diamonds, cost between *two and three thousand pounds*. I write the number at full length, that you mayn't fancy I have put in a cipher too many.'

The quality of the interior was matched by the prince's own natural charm, which qualified him for the title of the most urbane host in London. What impressed guests most was the quality of the conversation at the dinner table, which far surpassed the social gossip that characterized the typical English country house at the time. With friends such as the philosopher Edmund Burke, the playwright Richard Brinsley Sheridan and the great Charles James Fox he could provide both wit and provocative ideas to entertain his guests all evening. Most surprising of all was the prince's own erudition for, unlike most members of the British royal family since, he was able to discuss literature and even quote passages from Homer or Virgil by heart. Unfortunately, as Lord Erskine pointed out, regular guests became used to hearing the same sections repeated over and again. Aesthetes such as William Beckford, the builder of Fonthill Abbey, the greatest folly of the age, found his company a delight and wrote a breathless account of being entertained by the prince one evening at Carlton House:

> Jewels as in duty bound, sparkled on every side. The prince, brighter than sunshine, cast a brilliant gleam wherever he moved. I never saw him in a livelier or kindlier mood, more graceful, more insinuating. To me in particular he was graciousness personified.

When entertaining his brothers George was far more down to earth and less concerned with discussing philosophy than in downing vast quantities of alcohol with them. His personal preference was for sickly maraschino cherry brandy, while brother Frederick preferred drinking up to six bottles of claret before dinner. William restricted himself to a pint of sweet sherry. In spite of George's indulgent reputation, Frederick was undoubtedly the heavier drinker, yet he suffered less from the effects of excess than did his elder brother, who was constantly warned by doctors he was damaging his constitution. Rumours of this light-hearted debauchery inevitably provoked criticism from the more puritanical members of society, and the fact that it often took place on a Sunday was even more shocking. The biographer Robert Huish, combining pomposity with intolerance, condemned 'these Circean scenes which would have merited castigation on any night, much more so on the Sabbath'. In reality there was only an occasional episode of foolish drunken behaviour from the prince such as falling over on the dance floor or getting sick at the end of the evening.

Whatever his personal problems, George remained a magnificent host at the many balls and receptions held at Carlton House. Still a handsome and imposing figure, he would walk confidently among his guests, as Sir Nathaniel Wraxall put it: 'Louis XIV himself could scarcely have eclipsed the son of George III on a ballroom or when doing the honours of his palace surrounded by the pomp and attributes of luxury and royal state.' To his older, more staid friends, particularly the politicians, his witty conversation and excellent memory made him a delightful companion. The Irish MP John Wilson Croker claimed never to have met his equal 'for a combination of personal imitation with the power of exhibiting the character of those he was mocking'. The Tory Duke of Wellington agreed with this assessment, even though he was well aware of George's failings in other directions. The duke considered that the prince had 'the most extraordinary talent for imitating the manner, gestures, and even the voice of other people, so much so that he could give you the exact idea of anyone, however unlike they were to himself'. At the other end of the political spectrum, the radical Henry Brougham was equally impressed with George's conversational skills and thought him 'a very clever person'. Even a quiet and sober academic such as the musicologist Charles Burney, the father of the writer Fanny Burney, was captivated by his friendliness and erudition, finding that in spite of his notorious dissipation George retained 'a good knowledge of books in general, discrimination of character as well as original humour'. At their first meeting at Carlton House, he told Fanny, the prince took him aside and talked exclusively about music for almost half an hour, displaying, as he put it, 'as much wit as Charles II with much more learning'. Burney was convinced that the prince would have made an excellent music critic for there was no one to whom he enjoyed talking about music more than 'this most captivating Prince'.

George's talents as a host on a grand scale were spectacularly demonstrated in the entertainments he devised at Carlton House to celebrate his elevation to the Regency in 1789. His friend, the poet Tom Moore, wrote:

> Nothing was ever half so magnificent an assemblage of beauty, splendour and profuse magnificence . . . women out blazing each other in the richness of the dress . . . I really sat in the Prince's room after supper silently looking at the spectacle . . . the Prince spoke to me as he always does with the cordial familiarity of an old acquaintance.

Equally impressive was the polished service provided that day by the prince's staff so that the two hundred guests were served quickly and efficiently with a wonderful array of foods and fruits accompanied by iced champagne. All of George's friends and family were present, with the exception of fifteen-year-old Princess Charlotte, whose pleas to attend had been ignored, and his mother and sisters, who thought it an inappropriate celebration at a time when the new Regent's father was so desperately ill.

When George moved to the Brighton Pavilion his stylish entertainment went with him, and he was now able to entertain friends in a far more spacious setting, again dismissed by Huish as 'a nondescript monster in architecture having no beginning middle or end'. Now the responsibility of dealing with his guests was shared with Maria Fitzherbert in her new role as hostess at the Pavilion. In the autumn of 1805 Whig politician Thomas Creevey, while walking with his family along the seafront, encountered the prince, who invited him to dinner a few days later. Creevey passed an enjoyable evening and got on so well with his host that he became a regular guest, dining at the Pavilion two or three times a week. As close neighbours the Creeveys were on nightly standby to make up the numbers at dinner if more important guests failed to arrive. Their invitation would often not arrive until the evening, giving them little time to dress and scurry round to their punctilious and often drunken host at the Pavilion. After a while Creevey began to find these last-minute summonses deeply annoying and commented in his diary that 'to be sent for half an hour before dinner, or perhaps in the middle of one's own, was a little too humiliating to be very agreeable'. After one such occasion he wrote:

> Oh, this wicked Pavillion! We were there till ½ past one this morning, and it has kept me in bed with the headache till 12 to-day . . . The invitation did not come to us till 9 o'clock: we went in Lord Thurlow's carriage, and were in fear of being too late; but the prince did not come out of the dining-room till 11.

Their efforts may well not have been justified by the quality of the meal for, according to Lady Holland, writing as early as December 1824, the household budget had been drastically reduced. 'The good cooks are dismissed; and the dinner is supplied for each guest at so much par tete, which certainly is a miserable way for any decent house.'

As the prince's closest neighbour, Thomas Creevey was well qualified to give a detailed description of the evening routine at the Pavilion and particularly of George's conduct towards his guests:

> We used to dine pretty punctually at six, the average number being about sixteen . . . Mrs Fitzherbert always dined there she was a great card-player, and played every night. The Prince never touched a card, but was occupied in talking to his guests, and very much in listening to and giving directions to the band. At 12 o'clock punctually the band stopped, and sandwiches and wine and water handed about, and shortly after the Prince made a bow and we all dispersed.

On some evenings George provided more active after-dinner entertainment for his friends by producing an airgun and inviting them to shoot at a target placed at the end of the room. A skilful shot himself, he caused mild controversy by encouraging ladies to take part in the contest, too. Although Creevey excused himself and his wife on grounds of their short-sightedness, others were bolder but often with unpredictable results. He noted: 'Lady Downshire hit a fiddler in the dining-room, Miss Johnstone a door and Bloomfield the ceiling.' During his many evenings at the Pavilion, Creevey saw little evidence of the prince's reputed heavy drinking, noting in his diary: 'I never saw him the least drunk but once.' This newly discovered sobriety was certainly the result of Maria Fitzherbert's constant presence and her insistence that George behave as a proper husband should. This meant resisting the influence of the many notorious drunks who were regular guests. One stratagem she suggested when the Duke of Norfolk, a noted imbiber, was present, was that the prince should excuse himself after dinner and leave the table, saying that important state papers had just arrived from London and that he must deal with them at once. Norfolk would then be left to drink to his heart's content with the Duke of Clarence or whoever else happened to be present that evening.

By the time the Duke of Wellington became a regular guest, the atmosphere at the Pavilion had changed considerably since the amusing evenings described by Creevey. What had not altered was George's amiable demand that his friends must come whenever summoned. These invitations, Wellington complained, always arrived when he was already committed to some other social engagement. Yet he was loath to refuse for when he once declined a royal invitation because it clashed with the annual shoot at his house, Stratfield Saye, George's mistress at the time, Lady Conyngham, flew into a rage, thumping the table and complaining that Wellington treated him in the most impertinent manner. The duke considered that even the discomfort of a routine meeting of the Privy Council scheduled for the following day in London would be more appealing than remaining at the Pavilion, but when he asked the king for permission to return to town George, racked by the pain of gout, shouted out 'damn the Council' and ordered the duke to stay put at Brighton. The ageing hero of Waterloo was therefore forced to spend the rest of the week incongruously lying around on cushions with the other guests, playing patience and talking chit chat.

Wellington, who had little time for gossip, found his visits to the Pavilion a tedious experience, saying that the whole house was overheated, the lights were dazzling and the rooms reeked of scent. This was far too enervating for such an active man, although he continued to enjoy George's company in spite the assumed bonhomie that George, now the king, adopted whenever the duke was present. This may well have been the result of the hero worship he felt for him as a man who had fulfilled all the military ambitions he had once had for himself. As a result of a conversation at dinner one evening Wellington agreed to accompany George on his long-held ambition to visit the field of Waterloo during the royal visit to Hanover in 1822. Having listened dozens of times at the Pavilion to Wellington's own account of the conflict, he was familiar with every minute detail. Now accompanied by the great man himself George drove slowly around the battle site before getting down from his carriage and wandering about on foot in the pouring rain. As the duke, walking beside him, yet again recounted the events of that day the king appeared to poke determinedly about in the mud with his walking stick. The cause of his wandering attention was soon revealed when he abandoned the duke altogether and went off alone in search of the Marquis of Anglesea's leg. This had been famously struck off by a cannon ball at the height of the battle as Lord Anglesea sat on his horse beside the duke. When George at last found the stone that marked its final resting place, he waved his stick triumphantly in the air before, ever the sentimentalist, sitting down and bursting into tears.

Another guest, the diarist Charles Greville, had become as disenchanted with life at the Pavilion as Wellington. He, too, thought the splendour that had once amused now bored him, that the food was now frequently served up cold, and he loathed the 'bowing, smiling sycophants that infested the place'. His royal host often seemed increasingly bored with his own guests, preferring to sit quietly playing patience before leading the company into dinner. Gone were the boisterous companions who thronged the Pavilion in earlier days, and now a far more sedate class of guest such as the Creeveys sat down to dinner.

Perhaps the growing boredom at the Pavilion explains George's decision to move to the Royal Lodge at Windsor, a good thirty miles from London and therefore safer than any London palace. The idea was suggested one evening at dinner by Wellington, who added that if the king agreed he was confident that he could persuade the government to spend money on improving both the castle and the Royal Lodge in Windsor Great Park. The government would allow the king complete artistic control of the project, the public would again foot the bill and for the first time in his life George would be able to try his hand at landscape gardening. George thought it an admirable suggestion and accepted at once, soon becoming more interested in the modest Royal Lodge than in the vast and decrepit castle itself. The Lodge, little more than a large cottage at the time, had been given a thorough makeover by the architect John Nash, who at the same time had renovated the nearby Cumberland Lodge so that it could provide overspill accommodation for royal guests at the Lodge. The result disappointed many, and the only feature that all visitors praised was the new conservatory – 'a lovely Greenhouse' – where George would join them in listening to his German band in the evenings.

9

THE SECRETARIES

THROUGHOUT his adult life as prince, Regent and king, George relied implicitly on the services of a personal household comptroller, or secretary, to act as a diplomatic buffer between himself and either the Crown or Parliament. Given the intimate knowledge of the prince's financial and personal affairs that the post required, such a person inevitably became a close friend and a keeper of intimate secrets. To those brave or foolhardy enough to take on the role it invariably proved a thankless task, as each in turn struggled to reconcile the prince's extravagance with his responsibilities towards the government. There was also the problem of juggling the prince's complicated emotional life as well as having to buy off the increasingly hostile attention of the media of the day. Considering all these difficulties, the office of Secretary to the Prince of Wales, later King George IV, must have been one of the most difficult positions in the realm. George's wild spending on houses, clothes and paintings provoked hostility from his father, indignation from the government and constant demands from tradesmen that they be paid what they were owed. Furthermore, there were demanding mistresses to deal with and irate husbands who needed placating. If this was not enough for any man, then George required an almost total commitment to himself and an understanding of his many foibles that made the task even more complicated. What the role required was a man who was a convincing apologist and skilful accountant adept at getting his master out of whatever trouble he was in from one month to the next.

The first to attempt the near-impossible task was Lieutenant-Colonel Gerald Lake, a veteran army officer who, in 1780, was almost twenty years older than the eighteen-year-old prince. They had known each other for several years, as Lake had been one of the tutors at Kew, and a mutual respect had developed between them. As the prince was still under financial constraints laid down by his father, Lake had none of the problems that were to drive his successors to distraction. Both George and his brother Frederick had formed a close attachment to the man who, in many ways, acted as second father to them. For his part Lake was quite happy to provide the young princes with sound advice based upon his own wide experience of life. Like Markham, his style of teaching was to encourage rather than criticize, and his pupils responded well to being treated in this positive manner. Even George III approved of Lake's influence on his sons, and when he took up the official role of Prince of Wales's Secretary the king wrote that he considered him a 'pleasing exception' to the usual assembly of reprobates who already comprised the majority of the prince's friends.

Clearly, both royal brothers enjoyed the company of a man of the world who had fought in Germany with his regiment and who could enthuse them with tales of daring and adventure. It was certainly Lake who encouraged George's own early military aspirations that were to be so damagingly thwarted by his father. This practical soldier made an excellent and sound first adviser to George and might well have managed to curtail his extravagance more effectively than subsequent secretaries had he remained in the post. But when the war with the American colonies broke out just a year after his appointment, an officer of Lake's experience was urgently needed, and he was ordered by the War Office to return to the army. When told of his impending departure, both royal brothers were devastated, particularly as Frederick had himself recently been sent to Hanover by his father. George wrote emotionally to his brother after Lake had gone:

Our parting, as you may suppose, was a very severe trial for us both, especially as we had received so great a shock in our late separation from you. You know how much I love him and therefore will easily conceive what a loss he is to me at the present moment.

Even when campaigning in America, Lake found the time to send George letters containing sound advice and praising his good sense 'of which no one had a greater share'. Lake prophetically warned his young friend to avoid becoming the dupe of any political party – advice that George soon ignored when openly attaching himself to Charles James Fox and the Whigs – and to stop writing letters to 'a certain sort of lady'. Where George III had offered only criticism, Lake continued to provide the prince with sound and fatherly advice, praise and reassurance. Above all, he gave him a perceptive warning about the many hangers-on that were already gathering around the heir to the throne:

> Allow me to say it is more so for you, as the retired and private education unavoidably chalked out for a Prince has prevented you from knowing so much of them as young men who have reaped the benefit of a public school in general do at your age ... I am sorry to say that too many there are in this world who, to gain your favour, will acquiesce and encourage you in doing things that they themselves perhaps would be the first to condemn, and when they find the world disapproving your conduct, will lay the blame entirely upon yourself.

Lake's advice was all the more appropriate as it was couched in more positive terms than anything George had ever received from his own father. When – after many more years of military service in Ireland where he helped put down the Rising of 1798 – Lake was sent to India, George made sure that he was appointed commander-in-chief of the army. Eventually Lake left the army and returned to England to begin a political career, knowing that he would always have the support of the Prince of Wales. Their friendship continued undiminished, and when George visited the now Viscount Lake on his deathbed in 1808 he was so moved by grief that he fainted and was 'not restored until a quantity of cold water was sprinkled over his face'.

Less affection was shown to Colonel George Hotham, who took over Lake's unofficial role as moral adviser to the prince but who, as his treasurer, had the daunting task of dealing with the already horrific debts that had accumulated in the four years following the prince's majority. When Hotham assessed the prince's finances in 1784 he was aghast to find that his royal master's extravagance had run up a colossal sum of over £300,000, much of it owed to London tradesmen. When, in desperation, one of his London jewellers, Grays, threatened to sue for their money, Hotham complained to the prince that 'it is with grief and vexation that I now see you Royal Highness . . . totally in the hands, and at the mercy of your builder, your upholsterer, your jeweller and your tailor'. When Hotham gave up the unequal task of attempting to control the prince's rampant spending, he was followed in swift succession by Sir John Lade and Captain Jack Payne. Both were appointed at George's insistence but were totally unsuited to the role, being masters of excess themselves. Lade, the drunken horseman, could not have been a worse choice, and Payne, a successful naval officer and MP, was a notorious gambler with a reputation in the London gambling-houses for not paying his debts. This counted for little with the Prince of Wales, who considered Lade such a close friend that he provided him with his own room at the Brighton Pavilion. Predictably, neither man lasted long in the post, and both soon resigned under pressure from George III.

The next incumbent of the thankless task was another soldier but a far more wily character than any of his predecessors. Colonel John McMahon was a fascinating and controversial figure, who became suspiciously close to the prince. One of his qualifications was that he was Irish. By the time he was twenty George had acquired many Irish friends, among them Richard Brinsley Sheridan and George Hanger, whose easygoing attitude to life matched his own. Hanger had long passed out of George's intimate circle when the prince's political adviser, the Whig peer Lord Moira, suggested to him in 1804 that one of his own retired officers, Colonel John McMahon, would make an excellent royal secretary.

Born the illegitimate son of Lord Leitrim's butler in Ireland,

McMahon had used his natural resourcefulness to escape the poverty of rural Ireland for Dublin where he opened an oyster shop. After providing himself with a decent education he decided on a military career and enlisted in the British Army at the time of the War of American Independence. By good fortune he had chosen the regiment commanded by Lord Moira, who, in an act of considerable generosity, purchased a commission for him in his own regiment. Whatever his military abilities, McMahon soon discovered that he possessed a unique talent as a 'fixer' for his dissolute colonel. Backed by Moira's considerable wealth, he would procure locally anything his master required, from good wine to accommodating women – a role he would later fulfil for the Prince of Wales. Soon Moira had him providing the same services for fellow officers, and McMahon's remarkable success in this vital area of campaign life ensured his rapid promotion. Acting as a procurer for his superiors in America proved so profitable that when the war ended and the army returned McMahon arrived back with a full purse and a ready-made career. Maintaining the useful contacts he had made in the army, this short, red-faced bustling man became the Member of Parliament for Aldeburgh while continuing his profitable career as discrete procurer-in-chief to the aristocracy. Soon he had accumulated enough money to marry one of his own attractive protégées and settle her in rural comfort at Richmond in Surrey. It was this lady, according to the scandal sheets, who would enable McMahon to take his final step up the ladder of society.

One day, it was alleged, 'a certain illustrious individual' was riding with Lord Moira near Richmond when he noticed a dark, mysterious beauty at a cottage window. When the prince pointed her out, Moira claimed to recognize her as the wife of his old friend John McMahon, adding that he was sure she would be only too delighted to meet the prince. Without further ado, the story continues, they called at the house, and the lady found George so charming that she invited him to drop by at any time. The prince took her at her word, but whenever he called he found McMahon invariably away on business, leaving his wife to entertain her royal guest alone in a manner she thought appropriate. Again, there must have been an element of truth in this story for the public was soon made aware of the prince's amatory excursions to Bushey Park. A cartoon, *Princely Predilections* by George Cruikshank, appeared, depicting George and Mrs McMahon romping together in rural bliss. The story was given further credence when McMahon, on the prince's personal direction, was, for no good military reason, suddenly promoted first to Brevet Major and then to Lieutenant-Colonel, a commission that could be sold on for thousands of pounds. These appeared to be handsome rewards for McMahon's generosity with his wife's favours and his own well-mannered discretion.

Such a resourceful man could go far in the prince's service and McMahon was promptly offered a minor post that he filled with 'diligence and affability'. Then, to the discomfort of the prince's more established advisers, George offered him the important and highly sensitive position of royal secretary. McMahon accepted, relishing the challenge, and with energy and efficiency set about relieving his master of most of the tedious bureaucratic duties that George found so irksome. Behind the scenes McMahon used his unrivalled experience as a procurer of exceptional talent to add even more colour to the prince's private life. One of his many clandestine activities was to smuggle a royal mistress, Lady Hertford, in and out of the Brighton Pavilion through a secret passageway. Even the energetic McMahon soon found himself fully employed by the prince's varied and energetic sex life. He would have to pay off an angry, cuckolded husband one day then hurry down to Fleet Street to bribe a cartoonist into suppressing yet another scurrilous cartoon the next.

George IV's first biographer, Robert Huish – a precursor of the moral rectitude that was to to characterize the reign of the prince's niece Queen Victoria – discovered factual evidence of McMahon's nefarious activities. He quotes a highly compromising letter written by McMahon to his royal master in which the secretary states he is 'ever alive to obtaining possession of any object which may contribute to your royal pleasure', and claims to have picked up two attractive young girls while travelling through Wiltshire in a public coach. When a local clergyman and his daughters got on at Marlborough, McMahon was struck by their beauty, considering them ideal fodder for his master. The letter describes their 'apparent simplicity and ignorance of the world', making it clear that, with his help, the unfortunate girls could soon 'be brought to comply with the wishes of your Royal Highness'. The first step, McMahon suggested, was to inveigle them to London by offering their father a lucrative living at a parish in the city. The prince thought this an excellent scheme and told McMahon to proceed with the plan at once.

A few weeks later the unwary girls, according to Huish, duly arrived, and McMahon persuaded their father to allow them to lodge with his old friend, a certain Mrs Duff, in the ominous sounding Fops Alley. Unknown to their ingenuous father, Mrs Duff was a fashionable demi-rep whose box at the opera was always full of such notorious libertines as the prince's own chaplain at Carlton House, the Reverend Knight. After a few weeks of careful grooming by Mrs Duff, the girls were taken by McMahon to the house of a Mrs Hamilton where both he and the prince, in the guise of a 'Colonel Fox', seduced them. Huish ends this sad story with a bitter condemnation of the moral depravity of McMahon and the prince. 'The heart sinks', he writes, 'at such cold-blooded, systematic destruction of female innocence.'

Adventures like these made McMahon the custodian of George's most intimate secrets that, as a hazard against fortune, he carefully and systematically documented. Yet he appears to have been even more intimately involved with the prince than many contemporaries suspected for McMahon not only procured attractive *ingénues* for his master but also kept a lookout for older society ladies with compliant husbands. Such men would be prepared to turn a blind eye to their wife's infidelity in return for the lucrative reward of a royal appointment. This was the path already taken by both the Earl of Jersey and the Marquis of Hertford, who clearly condoned their wives' activities with the prince and received prestigious appointments in the royal household in recognition.

McMahon's duties may well have included playing a much more active role himself for he appears to have at times assumed the role of 'woman tester' for the prince, personally checking out amenable women before passing them on to his master. This would have involved having a brief liaison with the lady so as to ascertain her suitability but above all to test her discretion and perhaps that of her husband, too. It seems likely that George's last mistress, Lady Conyngham, was 'checked out' in this manner by John McMahon. The author of an anonymous book, *The Secrets of the Castle,* has no doubt that this was the case and that this lady and McMahon were indeed lovers before she embarked on her affair with the prince. The colonel, it claims, paid her such 'assiduous attention' that one Sunday they were 'found by the fond husband . . . preparing to be particularly intimate'. Henry Conyngham was said to have been so outraged that he challenged McMahon to a duel and only withdrew the challenge when the secretary 'offered a purse in lieu of a bullet to the noble lord'. This aggressive defence of his wife's honour does seem uncharacteristic of Lord Conyngham's behaviour, particularly as the author goes on to suggest that when McMahon recommended her to his master 'the lady did not hold out long . . . priding herself on the conquest she had made. Her first connection with the Prince produced her a present of £1,000 and her husband received something equal to £600.'

Involvement in such activities could not have made McMahon any less than the most intimate of friends, knowing as he did George's closest and most potentially embarrassing secrets. True to character, McMahon used this knowledge to make sure that he gained financial rewards commensurate with his discretion. In 1812 George had him appointed to the lucrative post of Paymaster of Widows' Pensions as well as Auditor of the Duchy of Cornwall. The Colonel was now his master's principal trouble-shooter, adept at dealing with embarrassing revelations and satirical attacks by the press. A typical problem dealt with by McMahon was when a publication known simply as *The Book* was published in 1807. It detailed the evidence contained in the Honourable Spencer Perceval's Delicate Investigation that had taken place prior to George's divorce action against Caroline of Brunswick. The account not only revealed Caroline's embarrassing behaviour but deeply compromised George, too. Although Spencer Perceval, the chancellor of the exchequer, managed to burn most of the copies personally, some were known to remain in private hands. In order to recover them, McMahon bribed a London bookseller, W. Lindsell, to advertise for copies in *The Times*, offering a handsome reward for any such copies 'of a CERTAIN BOOK printed by Mr Edwards in 1807'. The writer and journalist claimed that just five copies were recovered, at a the huge cost of £3,300. Never slow to seek a reward for his services, four years later McMahon persuaded George to ask Spencer Perceval, now prime minister, to ask that his friend and secretary be appointed to the vacant Lord-Lieutenancy of Derbyshire that was customarily in the gift of the Duke of Devonshire. But this proved a gift too far and was refused by Perceval after an intervention by the highly indignant duke.

When McMahon resigned in 1817 his place as secretary was taken by Sir Benjamin Bloomfield, yet another ex-soldier with a gift for discretion and diplomacy. So able a negotiator was Bloomfield that he was once sent as Minister Plenipotentiary on a secret mission to Sweden on behalf of the government. His friendship with George became as close as that with McMahon had been, and he was equally involved in trying to stem the flood of criticism of his master that continued to appear in the newspapers and print shops of London. His task was made no easier by his master's flamboyant and self-indulgent lifestyle, which continued both to irritate and fascinate the public. In the year 1820 alone, over eight hundred scurrilous cartoons featuring the new king appeared. George was as much distressed by their extent as he was by their content. In a vain attempt to curtail the flow, he ordered Bloomfield to use the secret-service fund to suppress them. Using a go-between, one Josh Calkin, Bloomfield went furtively about London attempting to stem the flood of ridicule. During the period from 1819 to 1822 he handed over more than £2,600 of taxpayers' money to bribe cartoonists not to publish their work. The best-known publisher, J.L. Marks, received £35 for withdrawing one particularly vitriolic cartoon followed by another £500 for destroying dozens more. Marks admitted that these secret payments not only provided him with a lucrative second income but also saved him the cost of printing ink and paper. The most acerbic cartoonist of all, the great George Cruikshank, received a further £100 from Bloomfield for promising 'not to caricature His Majesty in any immoral situation'. Cruikshank then ingeniously devised a more subtle way of making his point by showing the king as a penitent sinner dressed in a white sheet.

Such clandestine activities took their toll on Bloomfield, too, as he became increasingly critical of his royal master in a manner that proved intolerable, even though it came from a close friend. It was now apparent to the government that the current royal secretary had proved no more successful than his predecessors in curbing his master's extravagance. In 1821 embarrassing questions about the king's lifestyle were being asked in Parliament, and the prime minister, Lord Liverpool, had came under increasing pressure from his ministers to intervene in the king's financial affairs. Summoned to a private meeting by Lord Liverpool, Bloomfield gave him a solemn assurance that he would do all in his power to curb George's wild spending. A new financial regime was introduced into the royal household based upon the novel concept of accountability. From that point on every area of expenditure was closely scrutinized and rigid economies ordered by Bloomfield, desperate to honour his promise to the government while retaining his friendship with the king.

Under constant harrying and questioning from Bloomfield, George began to wilt, becoming increasingly fretful at the prospect of having to justify every aspect of his expenditure to his penny-pinching secretary. George began to lose the amiability that had always been apparent when dealing with his aides. Now he frequently lost his temper with his secretary and was once seen grabbing him by the collar and giving him 'a good hearty shake'. Such treatment alienated Bloomfield in turn, and in March 1822 he complained bitterly to the Tory politician Charles Arbuthnot that the king no longer shook hands or even spoke when he entered the room. He also claimed that, to his great embarrassment, he had even been shockingly abused by the king in front of one of the royal cooks. Nevertheless, Bloomfield was so persistent in his task of curtailing the household expenditure that the king's current mistress, Lady Conyngham, finally decided that Benjamin Bloomfield must be driven from the royal household forthwith. As with every conflict at Brighton or Windsor, it soon became public knowledge that she was determined to get rid of the royal secretary at any cost. There was even a rumour that she wanted the post of secretary herself to add to her current title of Lady Stewardess. But those closer to events at court life dismissed such gossip out of hand, considering that Lady Conyngham and Sir Bloomfield had too much in common ever to really fall out. This same idea had now occurred to the satirists, who depicted their mutual dependency to that of a pair of thieving servants conspiring to fleece their master in his own house:

> Ben Bloomfield and the fat old cook
> Herself a perfect larder
> A simple jig together took
> The tune was Shave the Barber

When George set off on 10 August 1822 for Scotland there was a new face in his entourage, that of the well-known society doctor Sir William Knighton. Now the rising star of George's entourage, Knighton was given the cabin next to his own, while Bloomfield, increasingly out of favour, was relegated to a more distant one. There other reasons for Elizabeth Conyngham wanting to see the back of Benjamin Bloomfield. Not only had he originally been recommended for his post by her despised predecessor Lady Hertford but he had also, against her clearly stated wishes, insisted on maintaining a warm friendship with the Hertford family. Lady Conyngham was concerned that, like Lord Hertford, a previous intimate official of the king's, Bloomfield might be carrying tales to the enemy. While remaining 'very civil' to his face and refusing to criticize him too harshly in front of the king, she now took every opportunity to undermine him subtly behind his back. One effective stratagem was to encourage her son, Lord Francis, to offer to help the king with some of the secretarial tasks that Bloomfield currently performed. As the resentful secretary told Charles Greville that December: 'Francis goes to the King every morning, usually breakfasts with him, and receives all his orders.' Bloomfield had no doubts that, in spite of her continuing smiles, the royal mistress was responsible for this. She was, he told Greville, secretly scheming his ultimate downfall and disgrace. As proof, Bloomfield offered the startling claim that he had been told as much by a certain Frenchman, whose ex-mistress was now the lover of Lord Francis Conyngham. This woman had heard Lord Francis openly boasting of his mother's power over the king, of all the jewels that he had given her and of how she intended to get rid of the main witness, Sir Benjamin Bloomfield. This story soon became so well known in society that even a foreign visitor to England, Captain Gronow, refers to it in his diaries, adding the twist that Elizabeth's jewels really belonged to the Crown and that, as Bloomfield was the only one to know the truth, he had to be removed.

As part of the strategy to replace Bloomfield with a more amenable Keeper of the Royal Purse, Lady Conyngham had begun grooming a suitable replacement, the egregious society physician and gynaecologist Sir William Knighton. One of Knighton's first and most clandestine duties had been to conduct Elizabeth in a hired carriage to Carlton House without the knowledge of Sir Benjamin. Under her subtle and insidious pressure, Bloomfield's self-confidence began to wilt. He began to lose his grip on affairs and, in turn, the confidence of the king. When his salary was abruptly stopped by royal command, Bloomfield knew his departure was imminent. In desperation he began lobbying his political cronies at Westminster and openly blaming Machiavellian scheming for his threatened downfall. His natural audience should have been the Whig opposition, but they were unimpressed by his complaints of royal betrayal for Lady Conyngham's brother was a member of their own party. He was the irreproachably respectable William Denison, and he told a different story. His sister, he said, had revealed in confidence that the real reason for wanting Bloomfield removed was a strange event that had occurred in Dublin a few weeks before the royal visit of 1821. Bloomfield had gone ahead to supervise the final arrangements and had decided, one evening, to visit a local theatre. In an attempt to impress someone he believed was an important representative of the king, the manager of the theatre ordered the national anthem be played as Bloomfield entered his box. The audience, believing that a member of the royal family had joined them, stood up and joined in a rousing chorus of 'God Save the King'. Unwisely tempted by this unexpected adulation, Bloomfield stepped forward, smiled and bowed royally to the audience. When told of this hilarious event, the king's usual sense of humour failed him, and he told friends that he took Bloomfield's behaviour as a personal affront, holding him personally responsible for this inexcusable 'insult'. As a result Bloomfield was immediately excluded from the glass-walled sitting-room at the Brighton Pavilion known as the Magic Lantern where the king met his intimates every day.

Yet another, more credible, explanation for Bloomfield's demise was given by the courtier Sir William Freemantle, who, in a letter to the Duke of Buckingham, claimed that an unannounced audit of the previous year's coronation expenses revealed, in the spring of 1822, that a large sum of money was unaccounted for. When Bloomfield was questioned he admitted that the deficit resulted from a large purchase of diamonds that he had made, as he put it, 'by order of the King'. It appeared that George had blithely added some personal gifts to the coronation expenses, much as a salesman might add a purchase from the hotel shop to his bill. In spite of his predicament, the king was adamant that Bloomfield should have held his tongue. This awkward revelation served to confirm George's growing conviction that Bloomfield was losing his touch for in the past he could always have been relied on to bury such compromising evidence beyond fear of detection. What particularly appalled the king was that Bloomfield had implicated him in the affair, although it is difficult to see what else the wretched man could have done other than to confess to stealing the money himself. The destination of the diamonds was no mystery to William Freemantle, who was certain that they had ended up adorning the neck of the royal mistress. It was a sorry business, resulting, thought Freemantle, 'from an intrigue in the party now governing at the Pavilion'.

Again, in the mysterious passage of scandal from court to cartoonist, a print by J.L. Marks appeared, putting the blame for the whole sordid affair entirely on the king and his crafty mistress. Obligingly, Marks sent a proof copy of this across to Carlton House before running it off in volume. The king was horrified and immediately sent Bloomfield down to Fleet Street for the last time to deal with Marks. This was to be the last such secret payment for when the sanctimonious Sir William Knighton became royal secretary he ordered that the practice cease. Bloomfield handed over £45 to stop the publication, and Marks, having surreptitiously printed off a few copies for reference, destroyed the plate in front of him. No evidence existed that the money was ever drawn nor was any receipt given by the publisher. Given Bloomfield's shady past dealings, it would not be surprising if some of these bribes, as rumoured, did find their way into his own pocket. Indeed, in the year before his dismissal Bloomfield, realizing that his lucrative position would soon be gone, was rumoured to have spent over £100,000 on buying property in Ireland.

Benjamin Bloomfield was a man who knew many secrets. Whatever speculation he may have been involved with was less important to the king and his mistress than his potential for exposing their own secrets. The king was therefore greatly relieved when his ministers agreed to his insistence that Bloomfield must be induced to go, and go quietly. In return for his acquiescence he would be rewarded with a generous settlement. With Sir William Knighton's assistance, the king wrote to Lord Liverpool, asking him to abolish the post of Private Secretary. This, he thought, would make Bloomfield's departure appear as a political rather than a royal decision so providing the face-saving stratagem that Bloomfield desired. Lord Liverpool then informed Bloomfield of the Cabinet's decision, taking great pains to exonerate the king from any blame in the matter. He assured him that it was not from 'any preference to any other individual, nor from want of any personal confidence' that his office was to be abolished. As compensation he was offered the Governorship of Ceylon or, if he preferred, his current salary for life and, at the king's suggestion, the Order of the Bath. Bloomfield thought he merited far more than these and insisted that he should, at least, be given an English peerage. When the king was told of this demand he flew into a rage and threatened to do to Bloomfield what he done to his late wife, the hated Queen Caroline, and make sure that he was ostracized and driven out of society.

Eventually Bloomfield, ever the pragmatist, came to an agreement with his master. Although he refused the offer of Ceylon, he agreed to accept the Order of the Bath, a sinecure worth £650 a year and the Governorship of Fort Charles in Jamaica that he would later exchange for the post of Minister at Stockholm. This royal largesse appalled those such as Thomas Creevey, who had always despised Bloomfield and considered him little better than a common footman, 'having made himself a fortune by palpable cheating and robbery in every department'. Although constantly suspected of sharp practice, Bloomfield had, none the less, been a popular character, and his demise was attributed by the press entirely on the baleful influence of others. When invited to Brighton to receive the Order of the Bath from the king's own hand, he excused himself, preferring not to face his hated nemesis again.

Bloomfield now accepted his fate with equanimity and, having been a libertine all his life, unexpectedly embraced Christianity as an apparently devout convert to Methodism. Soon, passers-by were amused to see on the door of his London house in Portman Square a large, white placard bearing the words 'At Prayer'.

10

ENTERTAINING CHILDREN

DISMISSED by many of his biographers as a selfish spend-thrift with little regard for the concerns of others, George consistently displayed a most unusual and even touching capacity for generosity and friendship with children. Never having been indulged as a child himself, he compensated in later life by showering gifts on his friends' children at Christmas and on their birthdays. Proof of this generosity is contained in his household accounts, which reveal the enormous number of toys purchased on his behalf. Among the papers are bills for dolls, lead soldiers, games, miniature farmyards, doll's houses, rocking horses and playthings of every sort.

One notable recipient was Queen Victoria, who, in spite of condemning her late uncle's morals, always praised his kindness towards her. 'He always took notice of me,' Victoria wrote in middle age, and she always referred to him in the most affectionate terms. She recalled visiting him when seven years old at the Royal Lodge in Windsor. As she curtsied to him, he said: 'Give me your little paw,' and gently took her hand in his before lifting her on to his knee so that she could give him a kiss on the cheek. She remembered vividly that his face was covered in rouge and that he wore an old-fashioned wig. As she left he gave her a present, a miniature of himself set in diamonds, which was gently pinned to her dress. The next day they met again as the king's carriage passed by when she was walking with her mother in Windsor Great Park. George ordered his coachman to stop and said to her mother: 'Pop her in!' The little girl was lifted up into his arms and the carriage drove on. Victoria was delighted by the adventure, but her mother was left a little shocked by this royal 'kidnapping' of her little daughter.

This empathy with the young had been established long before he played with the young Victoria on the banks of his ornamental lake at Virginia Water. During his own childhood he was callously separated from his brothers and sisters by his dominant father but managed to retain a warm sympathy for all of them. The only reason that Frederick was his favourite brother was that they were virtually incarcerated together and had formed a natural bond of friendship in adversity. His sisters, in particular, missed the presence of their eldest brother when young, and held him in the highest esteem throughout their lives. To one, Princess Elizabeth, he was 'all heart . . . a more generous creature never existed and had his talents been properly called out he would have been very different from what he was'. Yet while her brothers were able eventually to escape their father's tyranny, Elizabeth and her four sisters never could. Handsome, extremely well educated and accomplished, they were condemned to a miserable life by being kept too long from marrying by George III and repressed by their mother, who insisted that they live in a state of mourning and refrain from all pleasures when their father went mad. In spite of his genuine concern for his sisters, George was powerless to oppose his parents' dictatorial control over them until he finally became king in 1820 – by then, they were too old to be saved.

Their plight was amusingly, if poignantly, expressed by the youngest sister, Princess Sophia, who, in December 1811, wrote to George hoping that she and the other 'four old cats' were not causing him difficulty with his ministers:

How good you are to us which, however imperfectly expressed, I feel most deeply. Poor old wretches as we are, a dead weight upon you, old lumber to the country, like old clothes, I wonder you don't vote for putting us in a sack and drowning us in the Thames . . . Ever your unalterably attached, Sophy.

At the head of the letter is the mock address 'The Nunnery, Windsor Castle'.

When, in 1800, another sister, the pretty Princess Amelia, the king's favourite child, fell in love with General Charles Fitzroy, one of her father's equerries, she appealed for her brother's help to marry and escape from Windsor. Her mother dismissed the match as an impossibility, woundingly referring to her daughter's one romance as 'this unpleasant business'. George III agreed with his wife and told Amelia of his implacable opposition so ensuring that poor Amelia would remain firmly under the queen's control. The prince was furious with his parents and deeply sympathized with his unfortunate sister, yet considered himself incapable – while his father was still king – of challenging George III's right to determine the fate of his daughters. As a practical token of his feelings, he agreed to lend her £4,000. Those who were aware of the details of this sad affair did not blame the prince, knowing that he was powerless to prevent his father's harsh action. Lady Holland thought he had had behaved throughout 'with the greatest tenderness ... with the utmost circumspection and decorum'. But his failure to rescue his sister began to haunt the prince, and even three years after her premature death in 1810 he would burst into tears whenever her name was mentioned.

Outside his family George displayed an equal sense of care and affection for the children of friends. One of his favourites, and a frequent visitor to the Brighton Pavilion, was a little girl named Sarah, a relative of the courtier Sir Philip Francis, who was often seen sitting on the prince's knee and eating sugar plums. Behaviour such as this today would be treated with suspicion, although, given George's obsession with matronly women, it was completely innocent. Recalling those happy days at the Pavilion, Sarah wrote in middle age of how much she had looked forward to visiting the prince, whose talents she thought 'truly extraordinary and delightful' and for whom she had 'extreme admiration for all his amiable qualities, fascinating manners and uncommon accomplishments'.

Perhaps the best-known of these childish friendships was with Mary Seymour. Minney, as she was always known, was the youngest daughter of Lady Horatia and Lord Hugh Seymour, the latter

The devoted brothers: George and Frederick with their mother Queen Charlotte at Kew Palace. Later they would share their childhoods away from their siblings, and their affection for one another formed at this time lasted for the rest of their lives. *Print from a painting by Johann Zoffany, 1765*

Reconciliation: This picture is a figment of the artist's imagination, as throughout his youth Prince George was on bad terms with his highly critical father. Only by developing a broad circle of friends did he compensate for the lack of parental affection. *Print by James Gillray, 1804*

The beau: The stylish George 'Beau' Brummell became the main arbiter of the prince's tastes. However, his fatal arrogance eventually destroyed the friendship and led to the destruction of his social standing and eventual exile. *Contemporary print*

The wily Colonel: Colonel John McMahon graduated from being George's secretary to his friend. The keeper of the prince's most intimate secrets, McMahon later used this knowledge to great personal advantage. *Painting by Sir Thomas Lawrence*

The Royal Confessor: Sir William Knighton was the prince's last secretary.
Wholly dependent on Knighton's advice and support, George became
increasingly distanced from the colourful friends of his youth. *Mezzotint by
S. Cousins, after a portrait by Sir Thomas Lawrence, c.1830*

The horror in the mirror: George sees his greatest enemy reflected. His marriage to Queen Caroline was a disaster from the start, but his rejection of her cost him friends and led to public resentment of his actions towards her. *Print by James Gillray, 1820*

Ca ira !

A DEMOCRAT,—or—REASON & PHILOSOPHY.

Fox the Jacobin: George's friend Charles James Fox's early sympathy with the principles of the French Revolution earned him public condemnation. The most important political figure of the age, he became and remained an intimate of the prince. *Print by James Gillray, 1792*

The frustrated soldier: His father's insistence that Prince George should not have a military career led to years of frustration and further increased the acrimony between father and son. Here he is shown in uniform but with peacock feathers and a corkscrew in place of a watch fob. *Print by George Cruikshank, 1819*

Woman of the people: Georgiana, Duchess of Devonshire, a close if not intimate friend of the Prince of Wales. Here shown canvassing for Charles James Fox and the Whig Party in the famous General Election of 1784. *Print published by William Holland, 1784*

The wizard of the north: Sir Walter Scott made the tricky graduation
from being George's favourite novelist to his firm friend, and their
mutual admiration ensured a lasting relationship. Scott organized
George's successful, if slightly ludicrous, visit to Scotland in 1822.
Print after a portrait by Charles Leslie, 1824

The bosom pals: George enjoyed the company of such friends as the playwright Richard Sheridan, the philosopher Edmund Burke, the politician Charles James Fox, Georgiana, Duchess of Devonshire, and the dissolute sportsmen Sir John Lade and Colonel George Hanger, all of whom appear here. *Print published by William Holland, 1786*

The friends below stairs: George was the most socially democratic of monarchs, enjoying the company of people from every social class. He was particularly kind and benevolent to his servants. *Anonymous print*

The man of the people: The prince's dissolute lifestyle made him friends as well as enemies. In his early years he was admired for shrugging off convention and indulging his love of gambling, sport and mistresses. *Print by George Cruikshank, 1819*

The tragic princess: Princess Charlotte Augusta was George's only child by the hated Queen Caroline. He never managed to establish the close relationship with his daughter that he enjoyed with other children. She died in childbirth at the age of just twenty-one. *Mezzotint by Richard Golding after a portrait by Sir Thomas Lawrence, c. 1822*

The incomparable Sheridan: The greatest comic dramatist of the age, Richard Brinsley Sheridan was also a formidable political orator and a loyal friend to Prince George. His early death from alcoholism left a gap in the prince's affections that was never again filled. *Painting by John Hoppner 1790*

Louis Philippe Joseph, Duke of Chartres and Duke of Orléans: The French aristocrat admired George's lifestyle and love of horse- racing. He joined the Jacobin faction that executed his cousin, Louis XVI – taking the revolutionary name Philippe Égalité – but despite his support for the Revolution he was guillotined during the Reign of Terror. *Print by Philibert Louis Debucourt,*

The Emperor triumphant: Although the defeated Napoleon called George 'the most powerful, the most constant and the most generous of my foes', George saw Napoleon as having all that he lacked himself: a brilliant military career, supreme political influence and an importance that would outlive the age. *Print by George Cruikshank, 1815*

His greatest enemy: George used an official green bag – customarily used for conveying legal documents – to present evidence of Queen Caroline's immoral conduct during what became known as the Delicate Investigation into her behaviour. However, this satirical caricature suggests that Britain's most notorious adulterer was, perhaps, no less guilty.
Print by George Cruikshank, 1820

ROYAL HOBBY'S, or The Hertfordshire Cock-horse!

The cock-horse: George's mistress, Lady Hertford, was just one of the many that tried to influence him to gain patronage for her own family. Her son, Lord Yarmouth, became George's close friend and astute adviser on art.
Print by George Cruikshank, 1819

The COURT at Brighton à la Chinese !!

The Great Joss: George is here likened to an oriental potentate. He was mocked for the extravagance of the Brighton Pavilion and Carlton House where he entertained his friends with great generosity. His mistress Lady Hertford is making the sign of the cuckold over her husband's head. *Print by George Cruikshank, 1826*

The Tory monarch: Having been a confirmed Whig in his youth, George became increasingly conservative as he aged. Where Fox had once been a close friend, now the Tory Duke of Wellington became his most trusted adviser. Here the duke and George's ministers look on as the king – in the guise of Jonathan Swift's King of Brobdingnag – 'extinguishes' the Lilliputian Queen Caroline and her entourage. *Print by George Cruikshank, 1821*

having been Master of the Robes and Keeper of the Privy Purse to George III. As both Seymours were close friends of Maria Fitzherbert, Lord Hugh had resigned his royal positions in support of her when George abandoned Maria in order to marry Caroline of Brunswick in 1795. Lord Hugh then took his ailing wife to the West Indies in the hope that she would recover her health, leaving the infant Minney in Maria Fitzherbert's care. Sadly, both parents died the following year, leaving the little girl with Maria in spite of her father's will stipulating that she should now go to the joint legal guardianship of her aunt, the Countess of Euston, and her uncle, Lord Henry Seymour. While recognizing the love and attention that Maria had provided, the new guardians demanded that she give up custody of the child to another aunt, Lady Waldegrave. When, in August 1802, Maria wrote to Lady Waldegrave asking if she might continue caring for Minny until she was eleven, her offer was declined. Lady Waldegrave's argument was that if the situation was not altered, Minney's affections would remain with Maria and not with her own family. Secondly, as Mrs Fitzherbert was a Roman Catholic, Minney would not be raised in the Protestant and moral tradition of her father and the Seymour family. These words were taken by Maria to be a thinly veiled condemnation of her own religion and of the Prince of Wales's character. Although secretly married to the prince, Maria was, in the eyes of the world, the mistress of a married man who, with his dissolute lifestyle, would be unable to provide the child with the appropriate moral upbringing.

Realizing that the loss of Minney was now a distinct possibility, Maria Fitzherbert became inconsolable, threatening that if all else failed she was quite prepared to run off to Europe with the child and live in exile. As she told another relative of Minney's, Lord Robert Seymour:

> She is now past four years old. I am perfectly certain no person can feel for her as I do ... The child was placed with me by both parents in confidence that I should treat it as my own. This confidence I accepted and had occasion to renew the promise to her poor mother while she was sinking fast into the grave.

Maria also claimed that Minney's mother had specifically implored her help by saying: 'You are more her mother than I.' The Prince of Wales had also been summoned to Lady Horatia's deathbed where she had repeated her request that Mrs Fitzherbert should have charge of her child. Maria claimed that George was deeply moved by the dying mother's plea and had personally promised Lady Horatia that he 'would himself be her friend and her protector through life'. This seems an unusual commitment for the heir to the throne to make, but it has been suggested by some biographers that George might have agreed with Maria that, as they were unable to openly marry or have children of their own, Minney would be their symbolic love child in much the same way as his friend the Duke of Chartres had done with his mistress, Madame de Genlis, and Pamela, the little English girl she adopted. If Minney could have chosen her own future, there is no doubt that she would have opted to stay with her 'Mama', as she called Maria Fitzherbert. She also, with amusing precocity, addressed the Prince of Wales as 'Prinny', and the diarist Mrs Calvert once heard her say to him, with her arms around his neck: 'Prinny, won't you fight for me? You won't let them take me away from you.'

The Minney affair was already becoming a *cause célèbre* in English society when in June 1803 Maria filed an action in Chancery contesting the claims of the Eustons and Lord Henry Seymour. When the court ruled against her, Maria immediately lodged an appeal so that the dispute eventually had to be decided in the House of Lords. With the aristocracy evenly divided, George began frantically canvassing peers on Maria's behalf, in some cases even hinting that he was Minney's natural father. When the anti-Catholic politician Spencer Perceval strongly objected to his behaviour, George dismissed the intervention with 'the most offensive abuse and an oath that cannot be recited, that he felt he could jump on him and stamp out his life with his feet'. Finally, only eight peers, including his brother the Duke of Gloucester, held out against him. On learning that the Marquis of Hertford and his wife had offered to be the legal guardians of their granddaughter and were happy to leave her with Mrs

Fitzherbert, the Lords approved the arrangement without a vote. The prince's dogged and emotional determination to retain the little girl convinced many that she really was his and Maria's own daughter. Others thought the emergence of the Hertfords as honest brokers had more to do with Lady Hertford's aspirations to be the prince's new mistress than with a genuine interest in the welfare of a grandchild. Nevertheless, Maria had got her way, and Minney continued to live with her and enjoy a family life in which the prince played a vital role. The intimacy between the middle-aged prince and a lively young girl produced a fascinating correspondence between them. What these letters reveal is a man able to relate intuitively to children and capable of conversing with them about their own little concerns and interests. Many of Minney's letters are adorned with hearts and crosses at the bottom to represent love and kisses and always contain a thanks for making her so happy. A typical letter to the prince is preserved in the archives at the Royal Pavilion:

My dear Prinny,
How kind you were to remember my birthday, and send me such a beautiful present; I have placed it in a very conspicuous situation, and it is very much admired, pray accept my grateful thanks for it. I must not omit thanking you, for the piece of paper, I found inclosed [sic] in Colonel McMahon's letter, it is very acceptable, as sometimes I am rather an extravagant personage. I ride almost every day, and Adonis is as great a favourite as ever, dear little Sancho, is rather neglected, for I fancy myself almost to [sic] idle on him. I hope my dear Prinny that you enjoy good health, and that you will ever believe me to remain
  Your most grateful and affectionate. MINNEY

Another shows the hard-headed realist that the twelve-year-old Minney had now become for, after thanking him for the present, she adds: 'I soon poked the ten-pound note out of the essence box and was very delighted with it. What a naughty personage you are dear Prinny to send me such new years gifts.'

A perceptive witness of their friendship was George Keppel, a young playmate of Minney's, who wrote how fond the prince and Minney were of each other. Keppel described George as 'a merry good-humoured man, tall and fat with laughing eyes, pouting lips and a turned up nose'. What fascinated Keppel most was the prince's wig, 'which in my innocence I believed to be his own hair ... Round his throat was a huge white neckcloth of many folds out of which his chin seemed to be always struggling to emerge.' Whenever the prince sat down, Keppel recalled, Minney would always jump up on his knee, sitting on his leather pantaloons with her small feet dangling down beside his Hessian boots. Sometimes Keppel was invited to join her on the spare knee as they all jabbered away together. This was a delightful tableau of the heir to the throne behaving like a favourite uncle towards two excited children.

Minney's brother, George Seymour, recalled in old age how well the prince had honoured his promise to Minney's dying mother to protect and provide for her. Such was his generosity that each year he had sent her an expensive birthday present, while at other times he showered her with gold charms, almanacs, cakes, scent, bracelets, earrings and money. On her twenty-first birthday he wrote, telling her that when her parents died he had secretly invested a small fortune of £10,000 for her benefit. Now he 'was happy to find the interest had so increased that it was now worth nearly £20,000' and he was enclosing a draft on Messrs Coutts Bank in her favour for that amount. This investment made Minney a desirable heiress in her own right and Maria suspicious of anyone who showed an interest in her. Such a man was the Honourable George Dawson, a young officer with the reputation of a rake but who had returned a hero from the battlefield of Waterloo. Once again, Maria Fitzherbert battled to save Minney – in 1822 the young woman had now fallen completely in love with Dawson. With the support of the Seymours, Maria persuaded Frederick, Duke of York, to have Dawson posted to the West Indies while Minney was sent off on a tour of Europe. But, remembering how close they had always been, Minney outflanked her guardians by cleverly writing directly to George, now king, asking him to 'recollect how much happiness or misery' still lay in his hands and appealing for him to persuade Maria to allow her to marry Dawson. The inevitable result was that the king supported her case and Maria was eventually pacified when Dawson agreed that his wife's dowry should be set aside for their children. The news that Dawson's aunt had settled an estate on the newlyweds worth £2,000 a year helped further to reconcile Maria to the marriage and prompted her own decision to purchase a commission in the Guards for Dawson and to fund his later career as an Irish MP.

This generosity and genuine concern for children was a side of George IV not widely known in his lifetime and contrasts strongly with his public image as a selfish, uncaring debauchee. His empathy with small children and the capacity to form close but innocent friendships with them is unique in any British monarch. No other sovereign even comes close to his success, which makes his failure to maintain a wholly positive relationship with his only daughter, Princess Charlotte, all the more poignant. At the age of eight Charlotte appeared an attractive little child with blonde hair, blue eyes and an excitable disposition that totally captivated her grandfather George III, who thought her 'a perfect little creature'. Whenever he saw little Charlotte running towards him, according to his daughter Princess Elizabeth, the old king went into 'extacys of joy'. Queen Charlotte also adored her and thought she behaved like a little angel in the royal presence. Even a more objective observer such as the Earl of Minto lavished praise on her as 'really one of the finest and pleasantest children I ever saw . . . I wish my girls were so accomplished.' The Prince of Wales also told his friends that he 'doted upon her', although he was already wary of the dangers of her being exposed to the baleful influences 'from a certain quarter'. To this end he warned her governess Lady Elgin that the 'bad examples' emanating from Blackheath, where his estranged wife was living, must not be allowed to corrupt Charlotte.

Yet even the highly moral Lady Elgin was unable to contain the increasingly temperamental nature of the child as she approached adolescence. Trivial events either filled her with delight or plunged her into despair. Such an occasion occurred in the presence of a tutor, Mr Watson, when Lady Elgin inadvertently unpinned a watch from her dress. Charlotte exploded in a temper tantrum, screaming and shouting and accusing her governess of deliberate cruelty towards her. When Watson told the prince what he had witnessed, George was in despair, convinced that in spite of his warnings his estranged wife was somehow influencing his daughter's behaviour. His suspicions that Queen Caroline was interfering appeared confirmed when King George III, who had persuaded the prince to allow his daughter to live at Windsor, contacted Charlotte's mother and suggested they should all meet at Kew. George, appalled at the prospect of a closer relationship between his daughter and her hated mother, insisted that the child's activities be more tightly controlled and that she should spend part of the year close to him at Warwick House in London. Even in an age of lax morals, at least among the aristocracy, Caroline's behaviour was shocking, and it is easy to understand the prince's fears for his daughter. Caroline boasted that she could 'have a bed-fellow whenever I like' and encouraged her friend Lady Douglas to 'amuse herself with Prince William of Gloucester' as well as announcing that she would attend the birth of Lady Douglas's next child by coming along with a bottle of port and a tambourine to entertain the baby. Many thought her insane, including Sir Walter Scott, who had altered his opinion of the queen and now lamented his royal friend's misfortune in ever having married this 'Bedlam Bitch'.

Meanwhile, Princess Charlotte was becoming a far less appealing child. While Minney Seymour, George Keppel and their other friends were gentle youngsters, Charlotte had become hot tempered, rude and acquisitive, with a very high opinion of herself. George Keppel's grandmother, Lady de Clifford, who happened to be one of the tutors given the responsibility of instructing the young princess, was shocked by her rudeness. Once, when Charlotte rushed into the room without closing the door behind her, Lady de Clifford reprimanded her bad manners with the words 'My dear Princess, that is not civil, you should always shut the door after you', Charlotte snapped back rudely 'Not I, indeed. If you want the door shut, ring the bell' before flouncing out again. Such insolent behaviour would have deeply offended her father, whose own deportment had earned him the soubriquet of First Gentleman of Europe. Charlotte's rudeness was compounded by further wild and sometimes aggressive behaviour, as when she snatched the wig off the head of Bishop Fisher, her supposed spiritual guardian, for criticizing her and threw it on the fire. On another occasion she struck a female servant, and the same Bishop asked her why she had not followed his advice and prayed when she felt a fit of rage coming on. 'I did my Lord Bishop,' she replied 'or I should almost have killed her.' Whenever other children, such as George Keppel, came to play she rushed about the house ahead of them, opening doors and leading them into her father's private rooms where she pulled the covers off the beds. On one occasion she behaved even more violently, leading her companions into the garden and pushing them into the stinging nettles. Her general antisocial demeanour distressed even the tolerant Bishop Fisher, who sadly noted that 'her nose requiring to be wiped, she did not apply her handkerchief but wiped it with her sleeve as vulgar people do'. Such coarse behaviour would have been shocking to her highly fastidious father as he struggled to relate to what must have seemed to him more an alien from a distant planet than his own daughter.

But to George the explanation was simple: Charlotte had wholly inherited her mother's character rather than his own. Conceived in haste soon after the wedding on probably the only occasion that he was intimate with her mother, Charlotte was a constant reminder of that disastrous marriage. The only reason the prince had agreed to marry Caroline of Brunswick in the first place was a rare and ill-advised attempt to please his father. George had been led to believe that if he would agree to marry and settle down with a suitable German princess then his father would make a substantial contribution to reducing his son's colossal debts. Misled as to both the character and appearance of his intended bride, George was appalled when confronted by the reality. Not only was Caroline short, fat, coarse and unattractive but she was also dirty and malodorous, as he discovered to his horror on their first night together. A separation was inevitable, and in 1799 Caroline finally moved into her own residence at Montague House, Blackheath. Until Charlotte's birth in January 1796 Caroline had divided her time between Carlton House and the Brighton Pavilion, but she received little more than frigid courtesy from her husband. After years of incessant bickering over finances and the upbringing of Princess Charlotte, Caroline left England and embarked with an Italian lover on a bizarre progress through Europe. Her outrageous behaviour abroad clearly shamed and embarrassed her husband, but in a perverse way it caught the imagination of the public, which became fascinated by every salacious detail. With Caroline anything seemed possible, so that a country clergyman living in Devonshire was capable of noting in his diary that he had just heard that 'the Princess of Wales has been brought to bed of a fine boy in the harem of the Bey of Algiers'.

Even before her departure for Europe, George considered his wife incapable of bringing up their daughter in a decent and responsible manner. As Cornelia Knight, friend and lady-in-waiting to George's daughter, later recalled:

> He talked to me a long while against the Princess of Wales, and the little regard she had shown for Princess Charlotte when a child . . . whereas he used continually to watch beside her cradle.

When evidence of his wife's bad influence became obvious, he did all in his power to stop Charlotte living with her mother. His attempt to control Charlotte's upbringing and education was not only uncharacteristic of his usual easygoing amiability it was also a disturbing echo of the tyrannical rule imposed on him by his own father. Fear turned into an obsession, and he wrote constantly to Bishop Fisher, criticizing the supposed freedom allowed his daughter. Given her mother's licentious character he was particularly concerned that Charlotte, even at the age of eleven, 'should never be left alone with any of her masters . . . I repeat to your Lordship that no man is to be of my daughter's private society.' Predictably her father's censorious attitude did little to endear his daughter to him, although she routinely told him of her devotion: 'I assure you, my dear papa. I will struggle to get the better of my lessons and of all my learning and do everything I can to please you.'

For someone who delighted in the company of children, George would have liked to have spent more time with Charlotte, but she was a constant physical reminder of his detested wife. His greatest fear was that she would eventually take her mother's side in the continuing matrimonial dispute. Even his own mother, Queen Charlotte, urged him to spend more time with the girl:

> From the bottom of my heart do I wish that she should connect with her filial duty and sincere friendship for you which may be gained by seeing a little more of her and by making her look upon you as the source of every amusement and pleasure granted to her.

The irony was that a man who had so much time to play with and amuse other children could not form a true friendship with one of his own. Circumstances had made Charlotte a pawn in the battle between her parents. At the age of just sixteen, in 1812, she fell in love with an army officer, Charles Hesse. Her mother eagerly encouraged the affair, knowing that it would enrage her estranged husband. Charlotte later confirmed as much to her father, telling him that her mother had locked Hesse and herself in a room together, saying: 'I leave you to amuse yourselves.' More dangerously, as Charlotte confessed to her father on Christmas Day 1814, her mother had retained copies of the intimate letters that passed between herself and Hesse and could at any moment make them public. Having learnt that Caroline had then appointed Hesse as her equerry in Brunswick, Charlotte broke off all contact with him, now convinced of his insincerity: 'God knows what would have become of me if he had not behaved with so much respect to me,' Charlotte told her father.

'My dear child, it is Providence alone that has saved you,' he replied.

As the sole heir to the British throne it was important that Charlotte make a marriage that reflected the importance of her position. Having rejected the suggestion that she marry the Prince of Orange, Charlotte's choice was the handsome Prince Leopold of Saxe-Coburg-Saalfeld. On this matter, if on nothing else, both her parents were united in favour. Charlotte excitedly told her friend Margaret Mercer Elphinstone that her father had told her:

> It would be my own fault if I was not happy, as from the little he had seen and could say of him, he thought he had every qualification to make a woman happy . . . With the Queen he is wonderfully in favour.

Whatever the quarrels and disagreements of the past, Charlotte's delight at her engagement restored the friendly relationship with her father. On 1 May 1816 Charlotte and Leopold were married and settled down in what appeared domestic bliss at Claremont in Surrey. The following year she was found to be pregnant, and there seemed every prospect of a safe delivery when she went into labour on 3 November. Tragically it was not to be, and after the birth of a stillborn child Charlotte herself suffered a severe haemorrhage and died. The loss of the young princess produced a wave of national grieving never seen before, and her secular canonization was marked by a dramatic statue, paid for by public subscription, expressing the nation's sorrow.

When told of his daughter's critical condition, George, who had been at a house party with the Hertfords at Sudbourne in Suffolk, summoned his carriage and drove at full speed to London. Although he already knew that the child was dead, he had every reason to believe Charlotte would survive, and so decided to stay the night at Carlton House before visiting her the next morning. But in the early hours the household was woken and told that Princess Charlotte was also dead. At this terrible news George was seen to strike his head with both hands and fall forward into the arms of the Duke of York. Five days later, when taken to see the embalmed bodies of his daughter and his grandson, he was overcome with a grief that was 'impossible to describe', and his shock was 'so intense as to excite great apprehension and alarm'. Having regained the affections of his daughter he had by a stroke of fate lost her again and appeared incapable of dealing with the grief. The loss even led to a restoration of his relationship with his mother, Queen Charlotte, who shared his grief, telling him that he had done everything in his power to make his daughter happy in her relationship with Leopold. But he remained inconsolable, keeping to his room and going to bed as early as eight o'clock in the evening yet still unable to sleep.

In a postscript to the tragic event, he did his best to absolve Charlotte's doctor Sir Richard Croft of any blame for her death by thanking him publicly for the 'zealous care and indefatigable attention manifested by Sir Richard' to his beloved daughter. However, Croft, the object of an almost nationwide campaign of attack for not using the latest surgical instruments available, was unable to withstand the universal calumny and shot himself the following year.

The loss of Charlotte remained the most tragic event of George's life, as his own health continued to decline. His bereavement was made all the more poignant when his last mistress Lady Conyngham moved into the Brighton Pavilion with her family. Her daughters, Elizabeth and Maria, were a sad reminder of the lost Princess Charlotte, yet their presence gave him a last opportunity to experience the normal family life that he had never been able to enjoy. In the last decade of his life, the Conynghams became his own ready-made surrogate family, giving him his first real experience of domestic contentment. George found that he liked them enormously and enjoyed playing the role of an affectionate uncle or even a second father to them. Their presence in his household allowed him to show the open affection that he had been denied with Charlotte when she became the object of an emotional tug-of-war between himself and his wife. He was also able to recreate with Maria, the younger of the two Conyngham girls, the enjoyable relationship he had once had with Minney Seymour. Once again he shared a delightful correspondence that revealed his instinctive understanding of a child's mind and demonstrated the ability to communicate with the young in his own special way. In George's letters, Maria is always referred to as his 'Darling Ri', and his correspondence is unusually affectionate and paternal. As he tells Maria in one letter:

> You are ever in my thoughts. Believe me, my sweet child, when I tell you that not only a day does not pass without my thinking of you but that you are constantly before me in my imagination and thoughts and you cannot imagine what a relief it is to me: in the midst of the many painful and anxious moments to which I am doomed, when your little self darts before my eyes.

His fatherly concern appears delightful, if almost comic, at times as when he writes inviting her to join them all at Windsor. In another letter he writes:

> Dearest Mater mentioned to me . . . that you complained of being tormented to the greatest degree with chilblains. I instantly sent off to our little friend Barrett at Brighton for his lotion . . . I need not say how much I have missed you and how long I have wished to see you . . . and it is therefore with a delight I have not words to express that I announce to you that upon the arrival of a Knight Errant, who will suddenly arrive, seize upon you, and as suddenly convey to the old Castle at Windsor when you may be sure, my beloved child, you will be received with open arms by its old Possessor.

Once, when Maria was away from Windsor, he writes telling her of the 'pretty pranks' of his favourite puppy that ran to and fro across the room from Maria's father to himself before 'sitting up on its hind legs and doing everything but speak'. In reply Maria wrote: 'How can I express my delight and thanks for your affectionate letter. I kissed it as I could not kiss the dear person that wrote it. I am overjoyed at the thought of seeing you soon.'

Maria's elder sister Elizabeth combined good looks with a vivacious personality, and George enjoyed treating her with mock gallantry, to which she responded with such flirtatiousness that some of his guests wondered if it were the daughter rather the mother that the king really loved. Thomas Creevey noted in his diary in December 1822, when Lady Elizabeth was twenty-three, that 'many are perfectly convinced of the truth of the report that dear Prinny is really to marry Lady Elizabeth'. Nor were George's affections reserved for the Conyngham girls alone for George formed a close bond with their brother Lord Francis Conyngham, a particularly attractive young man, who in many ways took the place of Lord Yarmouth in his affections. George became exceptionally fond of Francis, 'dearest Frank', who often performed the duties of a second, unofficial secretary for him. As a reward George nominated him for the Grand Cross of the Guelphic Order, a Hanoverian decoration that told the world how much he loved and respected him.

11

EXTRAVAGANT FRIENDS

In an age of extravagance, few were more lavish spenders than George, Prince of Wales, and his friends, Georgiana, Duchess of Devonshire, and Louis Philippe Joseph, Duke of Chartres. Whereas Chartres' early life represented the old world of male aristocratic privilege, Georgiana displayed an independence of thinking and a social boldness that heralded the new age of female liberation. Fascinated by politics and with a passion for gambling, Georgiana used her pre-eminent position in society to invade these male preserves. Eventually, both she and the prince would look to Chartres to rescue them from overwhelming debt. This was understandable, as Chartres, the senior prince of the French royal blood and a cousin of Louis XVI, stood to inherit approximately one-tenth of all France. Moreover, he was married to the greatest heiress in all Europe and owned the Palais-Royal in Paris, a vast mansion that rivalled the Louvre in splendour.

In contrast, the Duchess of Devonshire could not, as a woman, have access to the family fortune. Her husband, William Cavendish, the fifth Duke of Devonshire, was the owner of Chatsworth and one of the richest men in England with an income of over £73,000 a year. When he inherited the title at sixteen he also became *de facto* leader of the Whig Party. Raised in the architectural splendour of Chatsworth by two cold and emotionless uncles, William Cavendish was described as being lethargic, ill mannered and wooden. His daughter said that her little dog was the only subject they ever conversed about. When in London he frequented Brook's

Club where he ate the same supper of boiled mutton every night but gambled compulsively. In 7 June 1774 he entered into a loveless marriage with the beautiful Georgiana Spencer, who spent as much on her trousseau as Marie Antoinette had done when marrying Louis XVI of France four years earlier. In the complicated sexual behaviour of the time, Devonshire's mistress gave birth to a daughter who was taken in by his new bride. She was joined later by Devonshire's new mistress, Lady Elizabeth Foster, who supplied the duke with the domesticity he needed, leaving Georgiana to her own devices.

On 18 January 1781 Georgiana attended a ball given to mark the Prince of Wales's official presentation to society, at which the *Morning Herald* reported: 'The court beauties looked with an eye of envy on her Grace of Devonshire, as the only woman honoured with the hand of the heir apparent, during Thursday night's ball at St James.' The prince, newly released from Windsor and vulnerable to emotional attachments, became obsessed with Georgiana and solicited her opinion on nearly everything he did. Georgiana was equally taken with the twenty-year-old prince, although her description of him was ruthlessly objective:

> He is inclined to be too fat and looks too much like a woman in men's cloaths but the gracefulness of his manner and his height certainly make him a pleasing figure . . . He appears to have an inclination to meddle in politics, he loves being of consequence and whether it is in intrigue of state or gallantry, he often thinks more intended than really.

On the last point Georgiana was uncannily accurate for the prince took her relaxed and friendly attitude as a sign of encouragement and was soon romantically pursuing her. Certainly there was a deep mutual attachment, but Georgiana did not allow this to become a physical romance and the relationship was never consummated. From then on they considered themselves the closest of friends, addressing each other as 'brother' and 'sister'; it was a relationship more companionable than amorous for George was already being drawn to more passive and matronly women.

Georgiana was very much a tomboy, happy to take risks, particularly at the gaming-table where she began to play recklessly and inevitably lose large sums of money. When questioned by her husband about the size of her debts, Georgiana lied and disclosed only a fifth of the total. From that moment on she was condemned to a life of subterfuge, constantly looking for ways to borrow money without the duke knowing and dreading the moment when someone would reveal the truth. One of the first people she turned to for help was her friend and fellow gambler, the Prince of Wales. Georgiana was, in character, more like the prince himself than any other of his male or even female friends for she often drank to excess and had an exhibitionist streak that once led her to dance on stage in an opera. Her mother, Lady Spencer, was apprehensive for her daughter, believing that gambling in particular would be her downfall. She wrote, warning Georgiana about the dangers of gambling and urging her 'to decline taking any part in it'. She also advised the headstrong Georgiana to behave with a decorum more appropriate to her position as the wife of the greatest magnate in England and to avoid bad company: 'While you [mix] with the vicious and the profligate you will be like them, pert familiar, noisy and indelicate, not to say indecent in their contempt for the censure of the grave' – in short, displaying the very characteristics that would make her attractive to the Prince of Wales. While Georgiana attempted to follow her mother's advice and curb her natural impulsiveness, she remained unable to control her appetite for gambling, and this was to lead to her near disgrace in society and alienation from her husband.

Like her friend the Prince of Wales, Georgiana was captivated by the Whig leader Charles James Fox and organized a series of grand political dinners for him at Devonshire House. Georgiana's involvement with the Whig Party made her a public figure in her own right, and in the 1783 election she was an ardent canvasser for Fox, driving through the London streets in an open carriage with a fox's brush pinned to her hat and knocking on doors in his Westminster constituency. Her most famous exploit was to outrage convention by offering a kiss to anyone who would vote for Fox. When he was duly returned as a member, Georgiana celebrated the victory by standing on the wall of Devonshire House with the Prince of Wales beside her and waving to the victory parade as it passed. Such antics, unheard of in a lady of the aristocracy, captured the public imagination, and the newspapers reported her doings on an almost daily basis. In the satirical cartoons she was often shown with the prince in tow, the implication being that they were lovers. The *Morning Herald* reported on her public activities, such as launching a new ship for the Royal Navy and describing to its readers what she was wearing when riding out in Hyde Park – 'a smart cocked hat, scarlet riding habit and a man's domino' and looking 'divine'. Her popular fame even led to one of the first examples in London of celebrity endorsement when the perfumers Sharp of Fleet Street used her image to promote their brand of French hair powder.

As the undisputed queen of the London political salons, Georgiana often held dinners at which leading Whigs were joined by important foreign visitors, particularly from France where radical discontent was threatening the overthrow of the Bourbon monarchy. One such guest was the Duke of Chartres, who had shocked English society by appearing at Newmarket Races wearing a coat with oversize buttons depicting animals copulating – a stallion mounting a mare, a dog a bitch and so on. Georgiana, who had seen him there, felt his need to shock both stupid and childish, although she admitted to enjoying his conversation. Chartres had developed a long-standing admiration for England and all things English even before he made his first visit to London in May 1783, three months after hostilities between Britain and France had ended. The duke was as much a gambler as either Georgiana or the Prince of Wales. As he set off for England he had wagered a friend that he could travel from Paris to London in less than thirty hours – and easily won the bet. What he also shared with George was a passion for horse racing – his arrival in England on an April day at the start of the flat-racing season led the then French ambassador, the Comte de Moustier, to comment sarcastically that this was no coincidence. Chartres was delighted with the broad avenues and paved streets in London, and with the help of his English agent Nathaniel Parker Forth he found a spacious and elegant house to rent in Portland Place, less than a mile from the prince's residence at Carlton House. Such an important visitor with close ties to the French court was immediately welcomed by London society and by the friends of the Prince of Wales.

When invited to dine with George III, he found the lifestyle at Windsor far less sophisticated than the more formal atmosphere at Versailles. To Chartres' great annoyance, the king and queen, although polite, were cautious of their foreign guest and aware of his dissolute reputation, fearing he might be yet another bad influence on their already wayward son. Nor was Chartres' first meeting with the prince particularly friendly, given the great similarity in their lifestyle. George later told his brother Frederick that he found Chartres 'rather clever but a great beast'. It appeared that Chartres' conversation was as risqué as his coat buttons. Although their initial meeting was a disappointment, the duke was delighted by London itself and rapidly became involved in the social scene. Long an admirer of British constitutional politics, one of his first visits was to Westminster to listen to a debate in Parliament. What he found contrasted most with the formality of the Estates General at Versailles was the club-like atmosphere of the House of Lords. He thought it more comparable to a London coffee house than to a formal political debating chamber and was amused to see the members arriving 'in their greatcoats and boots and spurs'. He added: 'It is not uncommon to see a member lying stretched out on one of the benches while others are speaking. Some crack nuts; others eat oranges or whatever else is in season.' Above all, it was the open-mindedness of the British that most impressed him after experiencing the highly controlled society of Bourbon France.

Chartres was further heartened in the thawing of the Prince of Wales's initial hostility towards him as he began to receive invitations to dinner at Carlton House. Soon they were meeting and playing cards at Brook's Club or travelling to Newmarket together where the distinctive Chartres racing colours of pink and black were often to be seen on the backs of winning jockeys. On 12 May 1783 the *Morning Herald* reported that the previous day the Duke of Chartres had watched the running of the Claret Stakes and that his face 'rather than reflecting his lily ancestry was suffused with a rosy glow' – a reference to the vast amounts of claret drunk to celebrate the race.

When not on the racecourse with Chartres, George was continuing what appeared to be his pursuit of the Duchess of Devonshire. Whenever they met at a ball, the prince refused to partner any other lady until Georgiana arrived and then insisted on dancing with her for the rest of the evening. In reality, Georgiana had become his romantic confidante, and he now shared with her all the details of his new fascination with Maria Fitzherbert. As his closest female friend, he implored her advice on how best to persuade Maria to respond to his declarations of love. As often happened with him in these situations, George became so obsessed that his emotions affected both his judgement and his behaviour. Whenever he met Maria he would be reduced to passionate turmoil, making reckless promises to marry her in scenes of wild behaviour during which he wept, sobbed and fell screaming on the floor, often tugging at his hair like a spoilt child denied a favourite toy. Matters were made worse by Maria's resentment and jealousy of the far more beautiful and witty Georgiana, whom she mistakenly saw as her rival for the prince's affections.

Matters came to a head when, on 8 July 1784, Georgiana was visited by two of the prince's friends, Tommy Onslow and Edward Bouverie, who urged her to come with them and collect Maria Fitzherbert, who had told them that she would not go without Georgiana to see the 'dying' prince. Arriving at Carlton House, they found him draped romantically across a sofa and swathed in blood-stained bandages. He claimed to have run himself through with a sword and declared that his last wish was for Maria to become his wife. He then asked if anyone had a ring, as he wanted one to place on her finger to seal the bargain. As none could be found, Georgiana helpfully took off one of her own and the prince duly placed it on Maria's plump finger. Wisely, and probably at Georgiana's insistence, both women then drew up a simple document stating that 'promises obtained in such a manner were entirely void'. Each then signed the document before leaving Carlton House together. The next morning Maria took flight by making an early departure for France, leaving Georgiana to deal with the frustrated but swiftly recovered prince. With his quarry gone the prince switched his attentions back to Georgiana. When she gave birth to her daughter Harriet a few months later, he visited her several times a day so giving new credence to the continuing rumour that they were indeed lovers and he was the father of the baby. Yet the sole motive for these visits was to bombard Georgiana with pleas for advice on how to get Maria back, accompanied, as usual, by emotional scenes that involved much weeping and kneeling on the floor clasping Georgiana's legs as she lay on a sofa. Relief came a few months later when Maria returned, now reconciled to the idea that she should marry the Prince of Wales, even if the wedding must be kept a secret.

When he returned to England the following year, 1785, the Duke of Chartres resumed his close friendship with the Prince of Wales, and they were again constantly seen together at the races and theatres, with Chartres often in the company of the prettiest actresses. Now resident in Brighton with Mrs Fitzherbert, George invited the duke to join them at the Pavilion where he stayed on until late August. Later he wrote to his host from Paris: 'Nothing has given me greater pleasure than your assurances of friendship. Please count me as one of your closest and most devoted admirers.'

Returning to London on yet another visit, Chartres insisted on attending a parliamentary debate, this time at the House of Commons, an institution more democratic than any that then existed in France. By chance the debate included a powerful speech by Pitt the Younger, attacking the power of the Crown and blaming it for the growing corruption and infringement of civil liberties that were against the interests of the British people. Chartres was ecstatic at the conclusion, telling several MPs as he left the House that he had just witnessed the workings of a true democracy. His words were overheard and reported back to Versailles for throughout his stay in London French government agents monitored his movements and eavesdropped on his conversations. As his visit coincided with a General Election in England, Chartres was then able to observe at first hand the rumbustuous campaigning carried out by the Whigs and Tories. To his astonishment, the candidates openly abused each other, provoking rioting and mayhem and generally behaving in a manner that would have been unthinkable in France. What was particularly surprising was the involvement of the British aristocracy on the political hustings and the sight of the prince's friend, the Duchess of Devonshire, riding in an open carriage with Charles James Fox, openly campaigning for him. A society that could conduct such serious political business in so open and so amusing a manner set a good example to the new France that was emerging across the Channel. Although the French ambassador, the Comte d'Adhémar, wrote approvingly of Chartres' behaviour in London, the French King considered his flirtation with the English Whigs to be shocking and near traitorous, an opinion that was leaked by royalist sympathizers to the *Morning Herald*, which wrote with uncanny accuracy: 'The Court of Versailles, it is said, are really afraid that the Gallic prince should imbibe certain Whig principles during the present political struggle in England which may not be easily shaken off.'

That Chartres should be drawn to the Whigs was understandable, given that the Prince of Wales consorted openly with their leader Fox and spoke approvingly of them to his French guest. George and Louis Philippe Joseph had by now discovered that they had much in common besides gambling and horseracing. Both were in open conflict with their respective monarchs and were seen to consort with the political opposition. They also shared a controversial lifestyle characterized by sexual scandal and heavy drinking. The *Morning Herald* reported seeing them both walking arm in arm in Hyde Park:

> The prince appearing rather *pale* and the *Mons le Duc* very *rubrified*, it
> was observed that the Heir of Great Britain had taken up with the *lilies
> of France* and resigned the *rose of England* to the Prince of Bourbon.

Fifteen years the senior, Chartres now assumed the role of elder brother to George, offering him advice and support in the numerous scrapes and embarrassments that plagued him. As a token of their newfound friendship they agreed that summer to exchange portraits. Nathaniel Parker Forth was instructed by Louis Philippe Joseph to commission the greatest English portraitist of the day, Sir Joshua Reynolds, to paint a full-length portrait of him as Colonel-General of Hussars. Reynolds's bill was 250 guineas, a large sum that was promptly settled by Chartres before taking the painting to Carlton House and presenting it to the prince. Nor during his London sojourn did Chartres neglect his reputation as one of France's greatest libertines, seeking out notorious places of debauchery and attending such scandalous entertainments as *The Calendar of a Man of Pleasure* and *Nocturnal Revels*. Behaving like an early sexual tourist, he also sampled – with the help of George's friend Charles James Fox – the ladies of easy virtue who frequented the numerous taverns in the Strand and as testimony to his growing taste for democracy did not avoid an encounter with even the cheapest whores.

While Chartres was able to spend money freely and to develop his Paris home, the Palais-Royal in Paris, into the most important shopping centre of his day, both the Prince of Wales and the Duchess of Devonshire were becoming evermore desperate in their struggle to satisfy their creditors. Georgiana's plight was the worse, as she had to continue concealing her extravagance and wild gambling debts from her husband. In desperation she began borrowing money from, among others, the banker Thomas Coutts and the French ex-Minister Charles Calonne. By the start of 1789 her creditors were threatening to reveal all, forcing her to make a desperate appeal to the Prince of Wales. He suggested that she obtain a loan from Cornelius Denne, one of his personal bankers. Denne, with deep reservations but not wanting to offend the

prince, advanced her the sum of £5,000, most of which she immediately sent to William Galley at the Lottery Office. He was
instructed to place heavy bets on the Oaks, Derby and Oatland
races in a desperate gamble to recover Georgiana's past losses.
Needless to say, she lost, and the money that might have bought
her more time to clear her debts had evaporated. Now in a state of
near panic, she appealed again to George, this time for a personal
loan of £2,000, addressing him as her 'dear brother' and imploring
him to keep her secret:

> If you can get the £2,000 get it in common notes . . . I am quite made
> and distracted at what I am doing . . . I don't dare read over what I
> have written and if I do not think I could depend on you I should go
> quite mad. God bless you – what trouble I give you. I don't sign my
> name in case of accidents.

Meanwhile, events in France had also begun to threaten the
financial security of the Duke of Chartres, who, following the death
of his father, was now known as the Duke of Orléans. With the
storming of the Bastille in July 1789 in Paris, the political climate
in France changed irrevocably, and as one of the leaders of the
opposition to Louis XVI Orléans was hated by the royalist *émigrés*,
many of whom had gone into exile in England. When he again
returned to London that same year, he received a far cooler welcome
from his English friends. Now he faced cold reserve where once
there had been warmth and open friendship. With his customary
disregard for public opinion, he ignored his detractors and lived
quietly at Chapel Street, his consolations being the presence of his
mistress Agnès de Buffon, the still convivial atmosphere of his old
club and the continuing friendship of the Prince of Wales.
Indeed, his welcome at Carlton House was particularly warm for
George was being vigorously pursued by his own creditors, and he
saw in the return of Orléans an opportunity to escape their
clutches. George and his equally spendthrift brother, the Duke of
York, were constantly mocked in such cartoons as *The Insolvent
Brothers*. As the wealthiest man in Europe, albeit with his financial

future under threat from political extremism, the Duke of Orléans might well provide a substantial loan to the prince that could, at a stroke, restore his own fortunes and those of his brother Frederick and his 'sister' Georgiana. When the suggestion was made to Louis Philippe Joseph he responded positively – he realized that George's indebtedness towards him would be an invaluable asset if ever he were forced to flee France and settle in England. A secret deal was brokered by Forth by which George would borrow the colossal sum of £300,000. The loan would be secured on the revenues of the Duchy of Cornwall and would be redeemed once George came to the throne. By signing such an agreement without his father's knowledge or consent – such security would have needed the permission of the ruling sovereign – the prince had once again committed an act of treason, comparable to his earlier morganatic marriage to the Catholic Maria Fitzherbert.

Negotiations dragged on for many months, only to be abandoned when the new French government made the transfer of such a large sum illegal. Orléans now took the fatal step of changing his name to Philippe Égalité and throwing in his lot with the extreme Jacobins. After signing his cousin King Louis XVI's death warrant, he was arrested, tried and guillotined by Robespierre in 1794. Knowing that her last hope of salvation had evaporated, Georgiana decided to confess the horrendous scale of her gambling debts to her husband, who behaved, she said, 'nobly, kindly, touchingly'. This description seems at odds with his actions for he then announced that they must separate and Georgiana leave Chatsworth and go to live in one of the Devonshire country properties while he sold off land and property to pay her creditors. On no account must she be allowed anywhere near London and the gambling clubs that had been her downfall. As the months passed his attitude softened and a reconciliation eventually took place that lasted until her sudden illness and swift death on 30 March 1806. When told that his 'sister' Georgina had died, the Prince of Wales said mournfully: 'The best natured and best bred woman in England is gone.'

12

THE CONQUEST OF
IRELAND

No English ruler had ever been welcomed in Ireland. Henry II's invading Norman knights had brought devastation, Cromwell and William III had arrived with vengeful Protestant armies and even the Catholic James II had left nothing but defeat and misery. So, having recently experienced the destructive fury of the English mob at the time of his divorce from Queen Caroline, George must have considered the prospect of his state visit to Ireland in 1821 with some trepidation. For it was a mere twenty years since the Great Rising of 1798 had been bloodily suppressed by British and Hanoverian troops and the peasants slaughtered in their thousands on Vinegar Hill. Moreover, the last monarch to land on Irish soil, William of Orange, had arrived to destroy the last vestiges of Catholic power and to drive James II into permanent exile in France. Yet George IV enjoyed one priceless advantage that no other British monarch ever possessed; he already had many Irish friends and was, unusually for an Englishman, aware of the religious and political situation in the country. In 1787, when Ireland was in yet another period of unrest, he had even written to the then prime minister, William Pitt, suggesting that England should take the political initiative and make him the next Lord-Lieutenant of Ireland and that a military solution to the Irish problem was useless:

> A strong military force may secure temporary advantages but no force
> can long coerce a nation of four million people united in sentiments

and interests. I must once more most earnestly recommend concilia-
tory measures and I abjure you to pause on the awful brink of civil
war and to avert its fateful consequences.

His appointment would indeed have been a bold act of faith in
the country and might well have altered the political climate
there. But the prospect of his errant son holding court in Dublin
and hobnobbing with republicans and Catholics was too much for
George III. Predictably, he dismissed the suggestion as Whig-
inspired nonsense and ordered his son to keep his nose out of Irish
politics. But the prince maintained his sympathy for Ireland and
continued to speak in favour of limited tolerance for the Catholic
religion and to remonstrate with his brother the Duke of Cumberland, a notorious Protestant bigot.

Uniquely for a British monarch, George had always enjoyed
the company of Irishmen. The closest friends of his youth included
the playwright Richard Brinsley Sheridan, the soldier and
statesman the Earl of Moira, his secretary Colonel John McMahon
and George Hanger, the most famous drunk in London. They
shared with George an enjoyment of the more obvious pleasures
of life, combined with the capacity for prodigious drinking. In
this, George could be said to be more Irish in his behaviour than
English, and least of all Hanoverian. His romantic obsessions,
roistering enjoyment of sensual pleasures and instant rapport with
people from every social background combined with a cavalier
attitude to expenditure were those shared by many an Irishman.
This was all the more remarkable given his antecedence and
would stand him in good stead in Ireland.

When he set off for Dublin on 31 July 1821 George was in
remarkably good spirits. To avoid the discomforts of the long,
uncomfortable coach journey to Holyhead in North Wales, the
king, accompanied by members of his household, including the
Marquess of Buckingham and the Tory politician W.H. Freemantle, took the more leisurely sea route and boarded the yacht
the *Royal George* at Portsmouth, cruising in a leisurely fashion
around the coast to arrive at Holyhead on 9 August. He was no

sooner ashore than a messenger arrived, carrying a dispatch from London warning that Queen Caroline was dangerously ill. In consultation with those ministers accompanying him, he decided to wait a day before proceeding on to Ireland. The obvious venue for an overnight stay was nearby Plas Newydd, the home of old friend the Marquis of Anglesea, who had famously lost his leg at Waterloo. They had barely sat down to dinner when a second messenger galloped up with news that the queen's condition had worsened. After further discussion, the king decided to remain at Plas Newydd rather than risk alienating public opinion by continuing with what could be seen as pleasure trip to Ireland. The next morning, as the *Royal George* waited at Holyhead for a favourable wind, another messenger arrived, this time with the news that Queen Caroline was dead.

It was barely three weeks since Caroline had been refused entry to the coronation at Westminster Abbey, and the humiliation of that day appears to have destroyed both her spirit and her health. This 'Bedlam Bitch of a Queen', as Sir Walter Scott called her, had suddenly developed a serious stomach condition, making her appear haggard and depressed. Ignoring doctors' advice, she dosed herself heavily with laudanum and went off to the Drury Lane theatre to watch a dramatic reenactment of the coronation with the famous actor Robert Elliston playing the part of the king. Caroline was taken home, suffering stomach pains of such intensity that even doses of opium and castor oil large enough to 'turn the stomach of a horse', as Henry Brougham said, had little effect on her suffering. After nine days of torment she died at Brandenburg House on 8 August, having whispered to her friend, the faithful Lord Hood: 'I do not die without sadness. but I do die without regret.'

For George, the queen's death was a release from the anger and embarrassment that she continued to cause him and to have shown sorrow at the news would have been a gross act of hypocrisy. He did, however, manage to disguise his obvious relief and behaved at first, or so his companions claimed, with commendable dignity and compassion, ordering the flags of the royal squadron to be lowered to half-mast as an act of mourning. 'He reacted', said Lord Castlereagh, 'as we could have wished.' Yet it is not difficult to imagine his true feelings now that the threat of Caroline's unpredictable behaviour was removed from him.

After ordering a period of court mourning of six days, the king decided to press on with all speed to Ireland. Rather than make the crossing under sail in the *Royal George* he embarked on the new steam packet the *Lightning*, which set off at full speed on the morning of 12 August, the king's fifty-ninth birthday. His friends noticed that he was 'uncommonly well during his passage and gayer than it might be proper to tell'. Throughout the six-and-a-half hour crossing, the king never once appeared on deck, remaining below with his companions. Hardly had the ship left port when, led by the king, the entire royal party began downing liberal measures of brandy and water followed by large quantities of wine and whisky punch. The drink and sea air must have sharpened George's appetite for, according to the Duke of Buckingham, the whole party were encouraged to join him in eating goose pie and drinking whisky, 'of which his Majesty partook most abundantly, singing many joyous songs, and being in a state, on his arrival, to double in sight even the numbers of his gracious subjects assembled on the pier to receive him'.

When the *Lightning* docked at Howth Harbour a few miles from Dublin late that afternoon, the king was obviously the worse for drink. As a gesture of mourning he had ordered a black crape band to be sewn on the left sleeve of his plain blue coat, while on his head he had placed, at a jaunty angle, a yachting cap with a gold band. He stood waiting to step ashore, his face bronzed by the sunshine. As the crowd spotted his portly figure waving from the deck, it roared with enthusiasm. The king stepped ashore to be shown a symbolic outline of his first footsteps on Irish soil on the quayside, which had been carved in anticipation of his visit. As the king passed under a rickety triumphal arch, described by Creevey as being only fit for Jack-in-the Green on a May Day, a burly local fisherman, Pat Farrell, came forward to shake his hand vigorously.

The king, mellowed by drink, was delighted by his warm reception and, catching sight of his friend the Earl of Kingston in the crowd, called out: 'Kingston, you black whiskered good natured fellow! I am happy to see you in this friendly country!' Then, spotting another old friend from London, Denis Bowers Daly, George stepped unsteadily forward and pumped his hand, too. Unfortunately, at that very moment, a quick-fingered thief took the opportunity of relieving Bowers of both a sixty-guinea watch and his wallet. Jostling through the crowd, the king noticed a large, rural-looking man waving at him. 'Are you a farmer?' he enquired unnecessarily. 'Troth I am, your Majesty's honour,' the man replied, whipping off his hat and bowing deeply. Eager to demonstrate his knowledge of rural affairs, the king asked him if he had a cow. 'Troth sir, I haven't,' the rustic replied. 'Then,' declared the king, 'you shall have one. I think every poor Irishman should have at least a cow, a pig and some fowl.' These words of wisdom were greeted with rapturous applause by the crowd. An aide must have made a note of this encounter for a few days later the king's secretary Sir Benjamin Bloomfield quietly presented the farmer with a milch cow and two pigs 'with his Majesty's compliments'.

There could hardly have been a more auspicious start to the royal visit than this, and the king set off for Dublin already convinced that the Irish were the finest people in Europe. The Countess of Glengall, however, had lived in Dublin long enough to be suspicious of all this boisterous enthusiasm. She claimed to be appalled and embarrassed by the crowd's wild behaviour as the royal procession entered the city. Thomas Creevey, too, was shocked to see not a single token of mourning for the late queen, although his own sable dress provoked one Irishman later that day to enquire who exactly he was commemorating. Creevey's first sight of Dublin was not auspicious either:

> Rags hung from every window which are called flags . . . no one in mourning. They clawed and pawed him all over, and called him his Ethereal Majesty . . . They absolutely kiss his knees and feet, and he is enchanted with it all. Alas! poor degraded country! I cannot but blush for you.

But it was already clear, not least to the king, that the Irish looked upon him in a far more favourable light than did his English subjects. For their part, they considered his visit a favourable omen for the improvement of their own miserable lot. As Mr Gregory, a typical Irish country gentleman, recalled in his memoirs twenty years later: 'What hopes were raised by his Majesty's visit! The Catholic Bishops, the Catholic nobility and gentry came from the provinces to hear the message of peace and goodwill. The peasants of Galway and Mayo laid by their pikes and blunderbusses and listened for it.'

George's ministers back in London were astonished by the glowing reception he had received in Dublin and were quick to capitalize on it, issuing an official statement that eulogized his arrival in glowing terms: 'what a scene . . . the greatest Monarch in the world sails in a common steam packet, lands among his subjects, unaffected, unattended, unguarded'. Astonishingly, given that the Rising had occurred little more than twenty years earlier, not a single soldier lined the route as the cavalcade passed along the North Circular Road – the Rotten Row of Dublin – the streets of which, Lord Norbury observed, 'were ill paved but well flagged'. As they approached Phoenix Park, the cortege had grown to over five hundred carriages, accompanied by a reputed three thousand gentlemen on horseback. Everyone in the king's party was cheered by the dense crowds lining the streets and even the foreign secretary, Lord Castlereagh, the most hated man in Ireland, was given a desultory cheer. The crowd's ironic cheer for Castlereagh puzzled Thomas Creevey, who wrote:

> Think of their having applauded Castlereagh! It is exactly as if a murderer were brought to view the body of his victim, and that he was to be applauded for his crime; for Dublin is but the mangled corpse of what it was; and he – the man whom they huzza – the cut throat who brought it to its present condition.

The procession stretched back through the city for over a mile. George had by now pinned a huge bunch of shamrock to his hat, which he repeatedly pointed to with one hand while placing the other sentimentally over his heart. The crowd loved the whole performance and, in a way that seemed peculiar to the English visitors, shouted enthusiastically rather than cheering or hooraying. Perhaps the Irish did not know how to cheer, observed John Wilson Croker caustically, 'for they have not had much practice in the expression of public joy'. The English were further amused to see two drunks stopping a third from cavorting on the pavement. 'He is a scandal to our country,' they shouted in explanation. 'What would strangers think if they saw him!'

News of the king's arrival had by now spread to the countryside around Dublin, and two peasants on their way to market, hearing the commotion, abandoned their cart in a ditch, mounted the horses and galloped excitedly to catch up with the cavalcade. They even managed to trot alongside the royal carriage, much to the king's amusement. One brave Dublin urchin leapt on to the royal carriage step and crouched there throughout the journey, braving a constant whipping from the coachman and earning a hearty handshake from the king when they reached Phoenix Park. At the Viceregal Lodge where the king was stay, the king's servants leapt down and attempted to close the gates on the following crowd, but the George waved them angrily aside and beckoned the cheering mob to follow him all the way up to the house. Stepping from his carriage on to the lawn, he made a short, brilliant and impromptu speech expressing sentiments that no other British monarch before or after him would even have contemplated:

> Rank, honour and station are nothing; but to feel that I live in the hearts of my Irish subjects is to me the most exalted happiness . . . I assure you my dear friends, I have an Irish heart and will this night give proof of my affection towards you in bumpers of whiskey punch!

That evening the king, in clear violation of mourning dress for his late wife, appeared at dinner dressed in a bright-blue coat with yellow buttons. Clearly in the best of form, he ate heartily then began excitedly discussing the day's events with his companions. All agreed that they were astonished and overwhelmed by the unexpected friendliness of the Irish people. One of the party, Lord Sidmouth, later claimed that throughout the entire visit he had not heard an unpleasant word spoken nor seen a sullen look from anyone. What amazed them most, as Englishmen, was that it was 'the lowest classes' who seemed the most delighted with the king. After dinner, as Lords Sidmouth and Londonderry strolled together in the park, they were accosted by a Dublin whore who told them excitedly that 'this night is the King to have all the fat women in Ireland'. In view of the king's current predilection for plump mistresses, both lords thought her comments highly appropriate.

The next day even the Irish papers, usually highly critical of the English, were wildly enthusiastic about the royal visit and full of vehement declarations of loyalty to the king. Curiously, George's popularity appeared non-sectarian, being shared by Orangeman and Catholic alike. Many remembered that as Prince of Wales he had shown his sympathy for Ireland and that his Carlton House faction in Parliament had often voted in support of the twelve Irish members. More importantly, he had openly opposed the military coercion of the Irish people in 1797 when the country had stood on the brink of rebellion. Knowledge of this intervention may well have led one rebel survivor of the 1798 Rising to tell the king on the second day of his visit that although he had fought against his father George III he was now prepared to die for his son. It was a sentiment endorsed by Lord Cloncurry, an Irish peer who had been imprisoned in the Tower of London for supporting the United Irishmen. Cloncurry approached the king and suggested 'a waiver of all bygones', warmly inviting him to visit his house. Yet, whatever their appreciation of the king's political sympathies, the Irish also warmed to his easygoing character and were understandably delighted to discover an Englishman who, like themselves, was no stranger to the temptations of strong drink and emotional excess.

When the doors of the Viceregal Lodge eventually closed that first afternoon, George was able to relax and enjoy the less boisterous pleasures of Ireland. The *Dublin Advertiser* reported that the king was seen to delight in 'the fresh beauty of the Irish ladies with their graceful and symmetrical forms and their soft and silvery voices'. At an Installation Ball a few days later he was said to have been in excellent form as he was introduced to a thousand young Irish ladies. They were all, he declared, as well dressed as any he had seen at St James's. When told that a hundred more had arrived too late to meet him, the king good-naturedly put his coat back on again and returned from his dressing-room to give them each a smacking kiss. On 18 August George attended a splendid military review in Phoenix Park and two days later received the leading Irish clergy of both denominations. More dinners and receptions followed, but on the very day that his late wife Queen Caroline was to be buried in her family tomb in Brunswick he brusquely cut short a public breakfast in his honour at the Royal Dublin Society and set off to visit the Marquis of Conyngham and his wife at Slane Castle. His obvious impatience and desire to be gone annoyed the rest of the royal party, who thought that he should have given the assembled guests more than just a few minutes of his time. With barely a waved goodbye to the assembled crowd, he climbed aboard his carriage and, accompanied by a small troop of cavalry, set off at full speed for Slane. Travelling at the brisk rate of ten Irish miles an hour, the cavalcade was soon clear of the city and cantering out into the countryside. Bystanders cheered them all the way to Finglas where the king, realizing that there was no danger, sent half his mounted escort back to Dublin. Maintaining full speed they changed horses at the village of Ashbourne, halfway to Slane. Just an hour after leaving Dublin, the royal carriage rushed through the lodge gates at Slane and arrived at the main door of the castle.

News of the king's impending arrival must have gone ahead of him, and his hosts were waiting on the castle steps 'dressed out as for a drawing-room'. George climbed down eagerly from the carriage and took his hostess, to the astonishment of the servants, in a pro-longed and passionate embrace. After a brief but cheery greeting to the marquess and the rest of the Conyngham family, who had already arrived from England, they hurried off together for a more intimate reunion in her private drawing-room. There they remained alone for the rest of the afternoon until reappearing for dinner. George was relaxed and in the very best of humour as they assembled for dinner beneath chandeliers blazing with candlelight. His host had ordered the outside of the castle to be illuminated, and the whole village of Slane had joined in the celebrations by putting lighted candles in their windows. For miles around, bonfires blazed on hilltops along the Boyne Valley in welcome for the king.

Always an admirer of innovative architecture, George was able to explore the castle and its grounds in detail the next morning. According to Mr Gregory, a frequent guest during the king's visit, George was entranced by the whole romantic aspect of Slane Castle. Standing high on the north bank of the River Boyne, it overlooks a sweep in the river bordered by fine woods. The castle itself had been rebuilt in the Gothic revival style a decade before by the architects James Wyatt and Francis Johnston and clearly pleased the king. 'The house he is justly delighted with,' wrote Mr Gregory, 'especially one round room, and he praised the good taste of a drawing-room in the Country having no window curtains but white muslin.'

It had been decided that the king should meet some real Irish people, in this case the local County Meath gentry, and the following day they all set off in carriages and drove the short distance to Townley Hall, the home of a celebrated local character, Blaney Balfour Esquire. After some merry banter with the jovial Balfour, the king and his party got back in their carriages and 'without a guard of any kind' set off alongside the River Boyne. At Oldbridge they paused to inspect the obelisk that marked the site of the decisive battle in 1690 then carried on, taking in the small grey villages and low rugged hills until they arrived at the mouth of the Boyne and enjoyed a fine view of the Irish Sea.

That night the king enjoyed another good dinner and was seen to be still in the very best of form. As the next day was Sunday, the king decided to attend morning service at the local church. But so many of the local peasantry had gathered in the village to see their sovereign pass that the cheering crowd had to be held back by his small escort of soldiers. Alarmed by what he considered overzealous pushing and shoving by the military, the king angrily intervened and ordered them to stand back. 'Don't mind them,' he called out. 'The people mean no harm.' As the party returned to the castle, a young woman from the village pushed her small daughter forward and urged her to kneel and kiss the king's hand. But with characteristic bonhomie George gently refused the gesture. 'No,' he said, 'but I will kiss her.' Stooping down to the delight of both the crowd and his hostess, he kissed the child's cheek.

At yet another enjoyable dinner in the candle-lit ballroom that evening, the king remained in splendid form. Such was his enthusiasm for Ireland he told the assembled company that he had devised a novel plan to enjoy it more. Turning to the Irish Attorney General he asked him, quite seriously, if it would be possible to send the current Lord-Lieutenant of Ireland, Lord Talbot, back to London and for him, the king, to take over the job himself! Everyone roared with laughter at this except Princess Esterhazy, who had accompanied her husband, the Austrian ambassador, on the trip. She was more concerned in watching the more cautious reaction of the Irish gentry towards the king. She later told Prince Metternich that the Irish ladies seemed far more reserved than their husbands.

The next day the royal guest was taken to meet another member of the local gentry. This time the honour fell, appropriately, to a Mr Smith, who enjoyed local fame by having fathered fourteen living children. When told, a few weeks earlier, that he would be entertaining the King of England to lunch, Mr Smith panicked and decided that his modest residence Annesbrook in the nearby village of Duleek looked far too modest for such a distinguished guest. Smith took immediate steps to improve it in record time, and the result was an architectural folly worthy of the creator of the Royal Pavilion himself. An enormous portico stretching from ground to roof was quickly built on to the front of the existing modest house, together with a large Gothic banqueting hall. Sadly, the latter was never to be seen for when the royal party arrived the king confessed that he was suffering from an annoying bout of diarrhoea. As it was one of the hottest days of the year, George decided to picnic under a shady tree on the lawn outside. Although clearly disappointed, Mr Smith declared himself entirely delighted with the royal visit. Having been completely ruined by his costly home improvements, he was forced to go bankrupt within the year. According to the Countess of Glengall there were many Mr Smiths in Ireland at that time, too ready to spend beyond their means in putting on a grand display for the king. She lamented that: 'Far from doing good to this wretched country, his visit is making people spend money which they don't possess.'

At the final dinner that evening, the Russian and Austrian ambassadors and their wives from London were present along with the ubiquitous Mr Gregory, who wrote a meticulous account of what he considered the most memorable evening of his life. What most delighted Gregory, a man used to the more provincial ways of Dublin than those of London, was the king's charm and relaxed affability to all his fellow guests and above all the impeccable manners that Gregory thought fully justified George's reputation as the First Gentleman of Europe:

> In two minutes after the king came into the room, he thawed the ice and put everyone at ease . . . a wonderful memory, the opportunities he has had of hearing, witnessing and collecting all the good anec-dotes of every kind, and a talent for mimicry quite surprising. He talks a vast deal, but I think not from natural garrulity, but because his rank makes it necessary for him to originate every subject, and perform a kind of solo to which what others say is little more than an accompaniment. He listens with great good breeding, however, assents in an encouraging manner when he agrees with you, and his contradictions, tho' politely given, are frank and peremptory.

Mr Gregory was delighted to see that, as a compliment to his hosts, the king tried every dish on the table and, predictably, sampled every drink 'very heartily, but nothing like excess'. Gregory also noted how he graciously complimented his host on the high standard of the cooking that so contrasted with the poor fare served up by his brother, the Duke of Gloucester, who, he claimed, had a talent for giving bad dinners. With everyone laughing and joking, the king, with his customary concern for the comfort of others, became concerned lest the European diplomats present might feel excluded from the merriment. Gregory again noted approvingly that 'after he had amused us, his subjects, with English and Irish stories he turned to the Foreigners, and for a time giving them French ones, which he does admirably, and with the accent of a Parisian, and perfect power over the language'. Less impressed was Lord Burghesh, who later complained to Mrs Arbuthnot that the king had virtually ignored him the whole evening and seemed more concerned with clinking glasses with the ladies present. As the meal progressed, George moved on from wine to the powerful local brew of hot poteen punch, which he found much to his taste. By the end of the evening it had given him such a thirst that he had returned to downing bottles of claret. Such was the convivial atmosphere that the entire company remained in the drawing-room until half past one o'clock in the morning. When a supper tray was brought in at midnight, everyone was still so replete from the lavish dinner that it was removed again, untouched. Even the quiet-living Mr Gregory had by now succumbed to the heady atmosphere of the evening as well as to the abundant alcohol. The next day he had to apologize to his female friends for not remembering exactly what the European ambassadors' wives had worn the previous evening.

On 27 August the king returned reluctantly to Dublin to perform his official duties for the next few days. One of them was a dinner at Trinity College where the wines were again reported to be good and the music excellent. The king remained in fine spirits, and when one of his party, the elderly Lord Norbury, slipped and fell, George leapt nimbly forward and dragged him to his feet. At this, Norbury, known as an incorrigible jester, thanked him and said, referring to his peerage, and to general amusement:

'This is not the first lift your Majesty has given me.' As he left the college that night, the king was cheered loyally by the students but, for the first time since they arrived in Ireland, some members of the royal party, notably Lord Castlereagh, were booed by the crowd. At a public dinner the next day a local alderman provoked what could have been an even more embarrassing scene by proposing in the king's presence the well-known Orange toast 'to the glorious memory of King William'. Royal embarrassment was averted by the quick-thinking Lord Fingal, who leapt to his feet to intervene with an alternative pledge so saving George from being seen to publicly endorse a naked sectarian ploy. As Croker wrote perceptively: 'If the toast had been put every man, Protestant and Catholic, would have believed that the Alderman acted under the influence of Dublin Castle.' Significantly, the king's own attitude to the Irish problem was revealed when at that same dinner he urged his audience to work for 'peace, no ascendancy . . . kindliness, conciliation'.

The next day, 3 September 1821, as the king prepared to leave Ireland, he was informed that the Irish people had been so moved by his visit that there was a move in Dublin to build him a palace there. When Thomas Creevey was told of the scheme he thought it a melancholy farce and commented cynically: 'Palaces in the air and drunkards under the table are the order of the day. Ireland I am ashamed of you.'

Unaware of the slightest criticism George set off for Dún Laoghaire harbour, which had just been renamed Kingstown in his honour. As he stood on the quayside he graciously accepted farewell gifts from the people of Dublin. One, a marble chimney-piece hewn from the quarries of Connemara, still adorns the Carlton Club in London, but the most significant and unexpected present was a crown of laurel leaves given to him by Daniel O'Connell, the undisputed leader of Catholic nationalist Ireland, which the Liberator, as he was known, presented to the English King on his knees. It was a symbolic gesture of peaceful reconciliation that would, unfortunately, come to nothing. Moved by this obviously sincere tribute, the king replied with tears in his eyes:

I never felt sensations of more delight than since I came to Ireland –
I cannot expect to feel any superior nor many equal till I have the
happiness of seeing you again. Whenever an opportunity offers
wherein I can serve Ireland, I shall seize on it with eagerness. I am a
man of few words. Short adieux are best. God bless you, my friends.
God bless you all.

As the ship sailed slowly out of Kingstown, George could take
satisfaction from the fact that, by sheer force of character, he had
enjoyed in Ireland a general popularity that had always been
denied him in England. To the Irish he had proved that he was a
man of charm, whose graciousness, kind heart and good manners
had appealed to their own instinctive good nature. He had come
to their country with a glass rather than a sword in his hand and
had behaved in a manner that did much to restore the monarchy to
favour. If his ministers had been prepared to reinforce the success
of his visit with political initiatives then the relationship between
the countries might have progressed differently.

Most English politicians agreed that the king's visit to Ireland
had been a great personal success. The Tory John Wilson Croker,
thought it had not only 'assuaged the violence but also removed
the rancour of party in Ireland'. At the other end of the political
spectrum, Irish poet Tom Moore spoke for many of his fellow
countrymen when he declared that from now he was a confirmed
monarchist. Many of the ordinary Irish shared Moore's unexpected
admiration for the king, and one Dublin politician even suggested
that King George IV of England should be rechristened 'King
Paddy the First of Ireland'. The radical press in England, however,
took a far more jaundiced view of the triumphal progress, believing
that the warm and friendly welcome George had received was
totally undeserved. As Lord Dudley commented sourly: 'The King
seems to have behaved not like a sovereign coming in state and
pomp to visit a part of his dominions but like a popular candidate
come down upon an electioneering trip.'

But the euphoria of George's visit was short lived, and by
Christmas it was the violent business of sedition and revolt as

usual in Ireland. The *Dublin Annual Register* spoke for many ordinary Irish people when it said:

> the events of October, November, and December destroyed all the splendid anticipations to which His Majesty's visit had given rise . . . the gaudy and hollow bubble of conciliation soon burst, and a system of outrage, robbery, murder, and assassination commenced.

13

THE SCOTTISH FRIEND

THAT Sir Walter Scott and George, Prince of Wales, could ever become friends seemed most unlikely when Scott published his highly successful epic poem *Marmion* in 1808. For a start, Scott was a confirmed Tory; the prince a close friend of Charles James Fox and an incorrigible supporter of the Whig Party. But an even greater deterrent to friendship or even courtesy was Scott's open support for the cause of Caroline, Princess of Wales, George's estranged and despised wife. Having met her in 1806 Scott was persuaded to introduce a flattering compliment to her father, the Duke of Brunswick, into *Marmion*. An astute manipulator of his own literary career, Scott then realized that this was a mistake and that the patronage of the Prince of Wales would be far more useful. Scott abruptly altered course and set out to ingratiate himself with George through his next poetic work *The Lady of the Lake*. While his earlier works had been set in the Scottish Lowlands, this dealt with the Highlands. Its hero, King James V of Scotland, was depicted as a middle-aged gallant who could not resist the attractions of one particularly lovely woman even if it meant compromising his position as king. The allusion to the Prince of Wales and his relationship with Maria Fitzherbert was obvious to any reader, not least the prince himself. The poem also shows James discovering the virtues of the primitive but noble Highlander and forging an even stronger kingdom with the help of the Highland people.

This theme may well have planted the seed in George's mind

for his own later fascination with Scotland. If the poem was a ploy to gain his favour, then it certainly succeeded for in 1812 Scott's friend Lord Byron told him that the prince preferred his work 'to every bard past or present', and when the Poet Laureate Henry James Pye died the following year, Scott was, at the prince's behest, offered the post, the first Scot ever to be so honoured. That he declined it was more down to his patron, the Duke of Buccleuch, who insisted he refuse it, than to his own instinct to accept. Instead, he suggested that Robert Southey, who needed the money far more than he, would make a better and more deserving Laureate. By now a mutual admiration had developed between prince and poet, with George eagerly telling his friends how much he enjoyed Scott's next work, *Rokeby*. The royal admiration was not shared by Scott's fellow poets who, in the tradition of their trade, looked upon material success as contaminating the purity of the artist. The same strictures did not apply to Lord Byron, however, who awoke one morning in March 1812 to find himself famous as the author of *Childe Harold's Pilgrimage*. This success and his subsequent notoriety made Byron the romantic wanderer of Europe while Sir Walter Scott remained sedately at home, never once setting foot outside his native shores.

In March 1815 Scott accepted George's invitation and sailed down to London to meet him in person. Before leaving he had been warned by a friend that because of his literary success he would be stared at as if he was the 'Czar of Muscovy himself'. His host had been impressed by the gracious manner in which Scott had declined the Laureateship and said that he was 'doubly desirous' of welcoming him to dinner at Carlton House. George went to great trouble to make their first meeting a success, saying to his friend William Adam: 'Let us have just a few friends of his own and the more Scotch the better.' The evening proved a great success, with Scott and his host sharing the honours as entertainers for, as the diarist John Wilson Croker wrote:

> They were the two most brilliant story-tellers in their several ways, that
> I have ever happened to meet; they were both aware of their forte and

both exerted themselves that evening to delightful effect. On going home, I really could not decide which of them had shone the most.

As was customary at Carlton House, the drink flowed freely and at around midnight the prince called for a toast to be drunk 'to the Author of *Waverley*'. When he sat down, Scott filled his own glass to the brim and stood up saying:

> Your Royal Highness looks as if you thought I had some claim to the honours of this toast. I have no such pretensions, but shall take good care that the real Simon Pure [a character in *Waverly*] hears of the high compliment that has now been paid him.

Then raising his glass of claret he drank a return toast to the prince. Once again, before the company could resume their seats, George rose exclaiming: 'Another of the same, if you please, to the Author of *Marmion* and now, Walter, my man, I've checkmated you.' To universal cheers Scott again got up and thanked his host for his splendid hospitality. Croker noted that the prince had addressed Scott all evening simply as Walter, as was his custom with those 'he most delighted to honour'. Yet what the evening produced was more a session of mutual admiration for during the dinner George became fascinated by Sir Walter's anecdotes about Scotland and by his deep knowledge of Scottish history. When Sir Walter eventually departed at midnight, he left his host with an ambition to see the country for himself.

Before he left for Edinburgh a few days later, Scott returned for dinner at Carlton House. The merriment was, if anything, even greater than on the first occasion, with the prince singing an entertaining song that, according to Croker, contained the apposite words: 'I love a Prince who will bid the bottle pass. Exchanging with his subjects glance and glass.' So successful had been the first encounter between prince and author that George presented Scott with a gold snuffbox, set in brilliants and with a medallion of his own head on the lid, as testimony to 'the high opinion his Royal Highness entertains of your genius and merit.'

When Scott was back in Edinburgh he was asked for his first impressions of the heir to the throne. Diplomatically, he declined to be drawn other than to say that the prince was a true gentleman and that there was something about him 'of the prestige and divinity, which hedges a King'. George must have been equally impressed with the famous author for he later recommended him for a baronetcy. The honour was conferred on him, not in consequence of any ministerial suggestion but by the king's personal insistence. When the author returned to London in 1820 to receive it from the new king, Scott bowed to kiss his hand, and George told him: 'I shall always reflect with pleasure on Sir Walter Scott's having been the first creation of my reign.' Had George known that Scott had once clandestinely visited his own estranged wife Caroline, it is possible that he would not have received his honour. Years later Scott's biographer revealed that the writer had accepted an invitation to dine at Blackheath alone so risking the seduction that had been forced on George Canning and Sir Sidney Smith among others. When it became dark, Caroline had taken the quavering author by the hand and led him down to her conservatory, ostensibly to admire the flowers. When Scott appeared to walk slowly behind her, the result of a lame leg, Caroline took his hesitancy to be a sign of moral dilemma and turned to him, saying in mock indignation: 'Ah! False and faint-hearted troubadour! You will not trust yourself with me for fear of your neck!'

Another honour awaited Scott in London. George had decided to celebrate his ascent to the throne by adorning the great gallery walls of the newly renovated Windsor Castle with portraits by leading artists of his most distinguished contemporaries. Already, pictures of reigning European monarchs, their chief ministers and military commanders were in place and now George wanted those of Britain's greatest artists, writers and scientists to hang beside them. The new series would, to Scott's delight, commence with his own portrait, painted by George's favourite artist Sir Thomas Lawrence.

A year later Sir Walter came down to London, this time on the new steam packet the *Comet* to attend his sovereign's coronation at Westminster Abbey. Touched by the honour of his invitation, Scott was nevertheless shocked by the rumoured cost of the preparations and ceremony. Although the most committed of royalists, he was moved to write to his daughter complaining that the vast, ermine-trimmed robes for the peers would cost a whole £400 apiece! Had he known that his friend the prince had ordered no less than nine wigs, each costing fifteen guineas, to try out – then half a year's wages for a working man – and that the final bill for the extravaganza would amount to £243,000, he would have been outraged. Yet Scott, personally in debt for £36,000 at the time, consoled himself with the thought that the event would at least give work to British manufacturers. He ended his letter by reprimanding those 'who sneer coldly at this solemn festival and are disposed to dwell on the expense which attends it, than on the generous feelings which it ought to awaken'. What amused him on coronation day itself was the design of the costumes for the Privy Councillors. So inappropriate were the blue-and-white satin, Elizabethan-style doublets and hose that the unfortunate councillors were forced to wear that they visibly cringed with embarrassment as they emerged from Westminster Abbey. This caused Sir Walter to reflect that 'so gay a garb had an odd effect on the persons of elderly or ill-made men'. At the end of the day Scott thought that, on balance, the fuss and expense of the coronation had been justified by the undoubted success of the occasion. Years later he recalled the scene in the abbey that day as one of almost medieval splendour and worthy of a place in one of his own historical novels. He wrote:

> The aisles crowded with waving plumage, and coronets, and caps of honour, and the sun, which brightened and saddened as if on purpose, and now darting a solitary ray, which catched, as it passed, the glittering folds of a banner, or the edge of a group of battle-axes or partizans, and then rested on some fair form.

What had particularly delighted the new king was the opportunity the coronation provided for dressing up in romantic finery, an appealing prospect for a man with perhaps the greatest collection of military uniforms in Europe. That day George was able to relieve his frustrated yearning to emulate the imperial splendour of Napoleon Bonaparte when he had crowned himself emperor in Paris. Fired up by Sir Walter Scott's tales of the primitive but noble Highlander, he saw his forthcoming visit to Scotland as a second opportunity to indulge this taste for exotic finery. Determined to appear in what he misguidedly believed was traditional Highland dress, George summoned tailors and jewellers to Carlton House and the firm of George Hunter of Edinburgh was specially chosen to provide his formal ensemble of sixty yards of satin plaid tartan, set off by a Highland bonnet decorated with gold and jewelled ornaments, an elegant claymore of polished steel and a large pair of Highland pistols. With his usual disregard for cost, George spent £375 alone on a badge for his Glengarry bonnet and £105 on a sporran made of white goatskin and lined with silk. This theatrical version of Highland dress was a travesty of the truth for the real Highlander wore a simple plaid, a saffron-coloured shirt and a simple knitted hat.

George's enthusiasm for the visit was matched only by that of Sir Walter Scott, who saw his role as that of a traditional Celtic chieftain welcoming a foreign prince to his domain. His offer to mastermind the ceremonies was eagerly accepted by the Lord Provost of Edinburgh, William Arbuthnot, who was only too glad to be rid of the task. Scott's problem was that the only historical precedents were the unfortunate visits of Charles I and Charles II, which had both led to civil disturbance. The new king must avoid politics yet show the people that he was as much the monarch of Scotland as he was of England. Realizing that the task of planning what was virtually a state visit was too much for one man, Scott sensibly coopted a group of his friends, the Committee for the Visit, to share responsibility with him.

Their first decision was that the Scottish royal regalia scattered in various houses and churches should be brought together to await the king's inspection at Holyrood Palace. Next, the royal arrival at the port of Leith had to be planned in meticulous detail, using the skills of two men of the Edinburgh theatre, Daniel Terry and William Murray. Communications were not made any easier by Terry being in London at the time and having to send his written suggestions up to Edinburgh by mail coach. Over the following weeks Sir Walter Scott and his team made plans for a whole series of events, including a Royal Levee, a Drawing-Room at Holyrood, a Peer's Ball, a Caledonian Hunt Ball and a Grand Review of Scottish Regiments and Highland Clans at Portobello Field just outside Edinburgh. Every detail of dress and etiquette was submitted to and personally approved by Scott. When accused by one of the committee, Thomas Mash, of putting too Celtic a slant on the ceremonies, Sir Walter rounded on him angrily, saying: 'If you persist in bringing in English customs, we turn about, one and all and leave you. You take the responsibility on yourself.' What worried the other members of the committee most was that Scott's obsession with reviving what he presumed was his country's lost past might plunge the whole programme into farce. Their fears increased when he suggested the royal bodyguard of the Company of Archers should be dressed in a newly created pantomime costume of Lincoln-green-and-white satin surmounted by large floppy bonnets with feathered plume.

It was a sign of the rapid technological change that had occurred in recent years that when George set off on 10 August 1822 for Scotland, the royal yacht was towed down the Thames by the *Comet*, the same steam packet on which Scott had sailed to London. Four days later the royal yacht arrived safely off Leith in a torrential rainstorm as a barge carrying Scott came up alongside. When told the news that Scott was on board, George shouted to one the crew: 'What! Sir Walter Scott! The man in Scotland I most wish to see. Let him come down.' Within minutes king and author were again toasting each other in cherry brandy, but it was agreed that because of the bad weather the king's landing would have to be postponed. That evening Sir Walter returned home to his house at Abbotsford with the precious glass the king had drunk from still in his coat pocket only to sit on it accidentally at dinner.

The next day the weather abated and George was at last able to land on the quayside at Leith where the first person to greet him when he was rowed ashore was, to Sir Walter's chagrin, not a member of the official welcoming party but a man who just happened to be strolling along the seashore at the time. Waiting on the quayside during this confusion and resplendent in the Campbell tartan stood Sir Walter himself. As the king approached, he stepped forward, bowed deeply and presented his monarch with a splendid silver St Andrews cross 'on behalf of the ladies of Edinburgh'. Others came forward offering him other gifts and words of welcome, among them the Earl of Kellie, who discreetly handed George a small wooden casket that he was told not to open in public. That evening when alone he lifted the lid to find that it contained a merkin, a small wig made of pubic hair collected, as was the custom then, from several of the king's earlier mistresses. When the gifts had been presented, Sir Walter commenced a 'traditional' Scottish welcoming ceremony of his own invention, which included handing his sovereign a libation of his favourite tipple, cherry brandy. To the hurrahs of the excited crowd he downed it in one before climbing clumsily aboard a waiting carriage for the short drive to Edinburgh. On his hat were pinned a St Andrew's cross and a bold sprig of heather, in the manner of the shamrock that he had worn in Ireland.

A few days later at the Royal Levee, George's expensive Highland finery made its first appearance to an awe-struck audience. Dressed from head to foot in the complete costume of a Highlander, including plaid, bonnet and dirk, his large and portly figure was a travesty of what was intended and aroused suppressed giggles among the guests. What made it even more farcical were the flesh-coloured tights that he wore to disguise his pallid and bloated legs protruding from beneath the kilt. 'Since he is to be among us for so short a time, the more we see of him the better,' Lady Hamilton-Dalrymple commented acidly. Others were less amused at the spectacle and blamed Scott for foisting this apparition on the Scottish people. 'Sir Walter had ridiculously made us appear a nation of Highlanders and the bagpipe and the tartan was the order of the day,' complained another guest, James Stuart of Dunearn.

Edinburgh society remained apprehensive of the king's next scheduled appearance at Holyrood Palace a few days later where the king arrived in procession to inspect the Scottish regalia. The participating trumpeters, heralds, yeomen, esquires, macers and grooms were all decked out in garish costumes that approximated to the author's idea of what might have been worn by the attendants at a medieval court. Unfortunately the rain had returned to dampen the costumes if not the spirits of the people. At least the king was dressed sensibly in military uniform this time and escaped the mockery he had received earlier. On his last night in Edinburgh George gave a farewell dinner at Dalkeith House where he had been staying throughout the visit. Proposing one of many toasts, Scott reduced the king to tears by offering his sincere belief that Scotland had not seen the last of its newly discovered king. On the contrary, George replied, his largesse fuelled by the large amounts of Glen Livet whisky he had taken to drinking on this trip, Scotland would now see him frequently. Scott then raised his glass in a final toast to his monarch and friend. 'To the Chief of the Clans ... the King.' The next morning he was on the quayside as George, waving to the last, sailed out of Leith on his return journey to London.

Dismissing any criticism as petty jealousy, Sir Walter Scott remained proud of his key role in the royal visit to Scotland and was convinced that his special knowledge of history had been fundamental in making it a success. In London, however, *The Times* poured scorn on what it saw as clumsy interference in royal matters by the Bard of Abbotsford. 'From first to last Sir Walter Scott permitted himself to be put forward as director of the most trivial matters connected with arrangements for the Edinburgh pageant,' it complained. 'That while meddling in all the details of matters for which his habits and pursuits so ill fitted him, he should ... not have forced these eccentric aberrations into light.'

Although the royal visit had little political significance or repercussions, Scott had unwittingly helped create a whole new role for his country as a tourist destination for the English. Between them, Sir Walter Scott and King George IV had certainly put Scotland on the map. Soon, inspired by her late uncle's visits, Queen Victoria was discovering the delights of the Highlands, and subsequent generations of the British royal family have always spent part of their summer at Balmoral often dressed, if not quite so incongruously as George IV, in kilts and tweeds. The visit of 1822 also spawned the tartan industry and the manufacture of Scottish souvenirs that went on sale throughout the country in a manner and to an extent that would never have been thought possible before. The figure of the noble Highlander, which would adorn a whole host of products, from whisky bottles to short-bread tins, can be seen to have been born out of this royal jaunt to Edinburgh.

Four years later the most prolific author of the age was virtually bankrupt when his partner in a publishing business, James Ballantyne, was sued for the huge sum of £130,000. But Scott did not shirk his responsibility in the matter and set out to pay off the debt by selling the copyrights to his books. Eventually, he managed the task for, as Tom Moore said of him admiringly: 'Scott could spin gold from his entrails.' When first told of his friend's financial disaster, George was deeply saddened and 'melancholy all evening'. When told this Scott replied that he expected little else from a man who has 'as true and kind a heart as any subject in his dominions'. An invitation to visit Windsor was promptly sent to Scott in October 1826, and he arrived to find the king at his entertaining best, 'raising one's spirits and making you forget'. The Lodge itself Scott thought ridiculously large for a cottage and he disliked the way the trees had been planted close to the house. His main criticism, however, was the lack of interesting guests, as most of the king's more colourful friends were now either dead of drink or no longer invited. Scott had not seen the king since his visit to Edinburgh four years earlier and found him a changed man, sad and reclusive. On returning home, Sir Walter wrote a tribute to his friend that eloquently refuted all those who would then and later criticize George IV for not being a latter-day Frederick the Great of Prussia, explaining why he was not more popular than his true human qualities deserved. Scott praised George as a man who was kind towards the distressed and who sincerely desired the best for his people. He wrote:

> I am sure such a man is fitter for us than one who would long to head armies, or be perpetually intermeddling with *la grande politique*. A sort of reserve, which creeps on him daily and prevents his going places of public resort, is a disadvantage, and prevents his being so generally popular as is earnestly to be desired.

In his later years Sir Walter looked back on their friendship as one of the most enjoyable aspects of his life, and the friendly relationship between them continued until both their deaths in 1830. What had delighted Sir Walter most was the cordiality that George showed towards him and with 'what distinction' he always greeted him, insisting on shaking hands with his Scottish visitor ahead of his other guests. When Sir Walter Scott went up to receive his baronetcy, the king 'would scarce permit me to kneel'. 'No subject was ever more graciously received by a Sovereign,' Scott proudly recalled. Few tributes to George after his death were more sincere or effusive than that of Sir Walter, who wrote to Sir William Knighton on 14 July 1830:

> to express my deep sorrow for the loss of a sovereign whose gentle and generous disposition and singular manner and captivating conversation rendered him as much the darling of private society as his heartfelt interest in the general welfare of the country . . . made him justly delighted in by his subjects.

14

BROTHERLY LOVE

EVEN when separated from them in childhood, George IV had always showed great concern for his brothers and sisters. They, in turn, looked to him for the support that an elder brother should provide in a normal well-balanced family. If he had a particular favorite, then naturally it was, of necessity, Frederick, Duke of York, who had shared his brother's early incarceration at Kew. When Frederick returned to England after six years in Hanover, George had driven through the night to meet him at Windsor. Although the prince had been a poor correspondent during his brother's exile, he now more than made up for it by the warmth of his greeting. Seizing his younger brother by the shoulders he warmly hugged him as his eyes filled with tears. The next day he insisted on taking Frederick to Brighton and introducing him to Maria Fitzherbert and his other friends, who all greeted the returned exile with great emotion.

After the cold and conservative atmosphere of Hanover, Frederick was captivated by the delights of Brighton and London, which he now sampled in the company of his elder brother. Others were not so impressed by the brotherly reunion. Frederick's Head of Household, Sir Richard Grenville, complained that the young duke had been 'thoroughly initiated into all the extravagances and debaucheries of the most virtuous metropolis'. Another witness of Frederick's initiation into the dissolution of London society was the MP James Grant, who claimed that George had introduced his brother to heavy drinking, while Frederick, in return, had encouraged the prince to gamble at cards, a hobby he had developed to counter the boredom of the Hanoverian court. Now a compulsive gambler, Frederick soon fell into the clutches of Lady Archer, who ran, with remorseless efficiency, one of the most infamous gaming-houses in London. Described by Robert Huish as 'a living painted sepulchre . . . so bedaubed with cosmetics and the wrinkled deformities of her nature . . . one of nature's vilest abortions', Archer showed no mercy to Frederick, encouraging him to gamble wildly then demanding the prompt payment of his debts.

Taking refuge in drink, Frederick sought consolation in the company of his elder brother. Their mutual drunkenness caused great embarrassment at the time of the Regency crisis, when they entertained guests at a dinner party by imitating their sick father's speech and gestures and speaking of him as 'a compleat lunatick'. The inevitable reaction to such insensitive behaviour was that they were publicly insulted by Colonel Charles Lennox, whose mother was one of the queen's ladies-in-waiting. When Frederick returned the insult he was challenged by Lennox and narrowly escaped a pistol ball in his head during the subsequent duel. At a ball a few weeks after the event George complained to his mother that he noticed that Lennox was present and he should be asked to leave. Queen Charlotte offered instead to leave the room herself so bringing the ball to an end. George agreed that she should go at once for: 'I never will countenance insults given to my family, however they may be treated by others.' The trauma of fighting a duel did little to curtail Frederick's wild behavior nor did it prevent the brothers' disdain for their sick father. At a service of thanksgiving after George III made a sudden recovery, they sat together in St Paul's whispering, laughing and munching biscuits while their father coldly observed them through his opera glass.

The first sign of any dissent between the two brothers occurred over George's controversial association with Maria Fitzherbert. By then Frederick had married Princess Frederica of Prussia, a diminutive and reclusive woman whose tiny feet had started a fashion trend in London society for uncomfortably small shoes. The reclusive Frederica preferred the Yorks' country estate to London, and she lived there, often without her husband but surrounded by over one hundred pet dogs. Driven by a Prussian sense of respectability, she highly disapproved of her brother-in-law's relationship with Maria Fitzherbert and refused to treat her with anything other than a cold civility. Sensitive to any open or implied criticism of herself as the royal mistress, Maria was outraged and ordered George to instruct his brother that his wife treat her in a more friendly manner. The duchess refused to alter her manner, and George, under pressure from Maria, now blamed his brother for not dealing with the problem effectively. For the first time in their lives, George and Frederick were on bad terms. The situation was then exacerbated by the prince being again passed over for a military command in February 1795 while Frederick was made a field marshall. In his frustration George appealed to his brother to support his case for a command, but Frederick, realizing the futility of arguing, politely declined to help. Insult was added to injury during the French invasion scare of 1803, when Frederick personally withdrew the prince's own regiment, the 10th Hussars, from the defensive front line on the Channel coast. George was furious at this perceived humiliation, and his younger brother William, Duke of Clarence, predicted 'an irreparable breach for ever' between his two elder siblings. For a time George refused even to speak to Frederick and instructed the servants not to admit him to Carlton House until further notice. What had made Frederick's actions so hurtful as far as the prince was concerned was that he had given him his full support when Frederick had been criticized for his military failings during the expedition against the French at Den Helder in Holland four years earlier.

An opportunity to even the score came in 1809 when Frederick was accused in Parliament of allowing his mistress, the beautiful Mary Ann Clarke, to make money by selling army commissions that he, as commander-in-chief of the army, had knowingly signed. The issue developed into a scandal. Radical MPs eagerly called for an official inquiry, and satirists had a field day with scurrilous articles and cartoons showing Frederick and Mrs Clarke in bed together. When Frederick appealed for help, George put aside their past differences and sprang unquestioningly to his brother's defence. But, as the incontrovertible evidence was revealed, he was, in spite of his emotions, forced to take a more neutral stand or risk being accused of nepotism himself. Characteristically, he was more outraged by his brother not having paid Mrs Clarke the allowance he had promised her than in his stupidity in allowing her access to military documents. When the vote was taken in Parliament Frederick was found not guilty of conniving in corruption, but there was a price to pay for his naïvety, and he was dismissed from his post. However, George's support for his brother in the face of public opinion had helped restore much of the old relationship between them. By the time of the royal separation and Princess Charlotte's relocation in Warwick House, Frederick was on good terms with his brother again and happy to act as honest broker between the princess and her father, although in reality he achieved little more than infuriating the hot-tempered Charlotte.

For the rest their lives George and Frederick remained the best of friends and were frequent companions at the Brighton Pavilion where Frederick would often entertain the company with amusing anecdotes at his elder brother's expense. When the Duchess of York died in 1820, George set aside his past differences with her and wrote Frederick a moving letter of sympathy in which he stated how much their close friendship throughout their lives meant to him and how he cherished 'the most unvarying, the steadiest affection' for his brother and that 'from the bottom of my soul I do participate and enter into the whole extent of your distress'. Three years later he made a more practical demonstration of his feelings by giving Frederick £50,000 to pay off some of his enormous debts. So generous was George to his brother that the Duke of Wellington's confidante, Harriet Arbuthnot, thought he loved him 'more than any of his family'. When Frederick became seriously ill with dropsy towards the end of 1826, George was 'in great anxiety and uneasiness about him' with, as it turned out, good reason for Frederick died a few months later. Even the cynical diarist Charles Greville was forced to admit that George 'showed great feeling about his brother and exceeding kindness in providing for his servants'. With his customary generosity and humanity George gave £6,000 towards their salaries and the household expenses and took many of the older servants into his own service. As the minute gun sounded at Frederick's funeral on 20 January 1827 George was inconsolable and later said that each shot 'was like a nail driven into my heart'.

Apart from the six years he had spent in Hanover, Frederick had been his eldest brother's closest male friend. Their younger brothers William, Duke of Clarence, and Ernest, Duke of Cumberland, never shared this intimacy but as young children had developed a form of hero worship for their eldest brother, who had had the temerity to stand up to their father. When George reached majority and was given his own establishment at Carlton House, William went to see it and was astonished by the sophisticated lifestyle and fascinating people he found there. Determined that William should not follow George into what he considered an un-Christian and debauched lifestyle, George III did all he could to keep them apart and save William from falling into the clutches of the Carlton House set. At the age of barely fifteen the boy was packed off to sea to serve as a midshipman in the Royal Navy accompanied by the firm instruction from his father that he should be treated 'with no marks of distinction'. For the next ten years William saw little of England but flourished in the career imposed upon him, in spite of developing a growing reputation as a strict disciplinarian. Promotions followed as his career advanced and, at the early age of twenty, he was already captain of his own ship.

Similar precautions were taken with Ernest, Duke of Cumberland, to save him from the contamination of Carlton House. Like Frederick, he was sent off to Hanover to pursue a military career as far away from his eldest brother as possible. Soon on active service within the Hanoverian Hussars, he wrote home to George, telling him how much he missed the family and even after six years abroad could still lament that he had 'not seen a single one out of England except Frederick'. Still deeply homesick, he told George that he would be only too delighted if their father 'would permit of my coming over to you if I was only to stay there but a short time'. Tall, thin, sober and moralistic, Ernest was quite unlike his other brothers in both appearance and attitude: a difference that was further accentuated by the disfiguring facial wound he had suffered in battle. When he eventually left the army and returned to England, Ernest had lost an eye and gained a crippled arm. These wounds were to be a constant reminder to the Prince of Wales that, in spite of his own military posturing and gaudy uniforms, he had been deprived of the opportunity of experiencing war at first hand. Together with Ernest's refusal to join in the bacchanalian activities at Carlton House, this inevitably distanced the brothers, and George now decided that he liked Ernest least of his brothers. In politics, too, Ernest was different, choosing to reject the colourful Whigs in favour of the most reactionary elements in the Tory Party. The situation was made considerably worse by Ernest insisting on pressing these reactionary opinions on his eldest brother, convinced that he had a divine mission to save him from the radical excesses 'that threatened the very foundations of the monarchy and the Constitution . . . that none but a *fool* would credit and none but a *scoundrel* propagate'.

No such political conscience troubled the easygoing William, Duke of Clarence, as he sailed the waves untouched, as his father believed, by the profligacy exhibited by his two elder brothers. But George III's hopes of saving his son from vice were soon dashed – back on shore William displayed a love of drink, gambling and womanizing every bit as contentious as that of George or Frederick. Given an allowance that was minuscule in comparison to theirs, he nevertheless ran up huge debts that put him equally in the hands of his creditors. In desperation he turned to his admired eldest brother, complaining to George of their father's tight fistedness towards them both. 'Does he imagine he will make his sons his friends by this mode of conduct?' he wrote naïvely in 1786. Their shared resentment of George III's attempts to control them became a feature of their growing correspondence with each other. Pursuit of women also featured strongly with William complaining of having to remain with his ship at dock in Plymouth where there was 'not a woman to be touched with tongs, not a house to put your head in after dark'. Driven by a sexual impulse every bit as strong as George's, William embarked on many ill-advised adventures before meeting the love of his life, the actress Dora Jordan. Already the mother of four children by two different men, Mrs Jordan was the ultimate working mother of the age, giving performances on the London stage even when eight month's pregnant. Settling down to sexual and domestic bliss with William, she then pro-duced ten more children and gained the reputation of being the best comedy actress in London. When told of his son's intention to live with a popular actress, George III was surprisingly agree-able, objecting not to the relationship in principle, but to his son's stupidity in giving Mrs Jordan too generous an allowance. 'One thousand a year, sir, too much, too much . . . five hundred quite enough, quite enough!' he announced in his customary peremp-tory manner. Such was Mrs Jordan's natural charm that both the king and queen were won over and soon accepted the relationship, even attending one of her performances at Drury Lane.

In many ways the relationship echoed that of the Prince of Wales and Mrs Fitzherbert, and George made it plain that Dora Jordan should always enjoy the same social status as his own highly respectable mistress. At a birthday party for William one evening, George, with his usual good grace, insisted on taking Mrs Jordan's arm and leading her in to dinner. There he pointedly placed her at the head of the table and then took his seat on her right hand and directed the Duke of York to sit on her left. Such filial support was not always evident on William's part for, although always willing to praise his elder brother in public, William sometimes criticized him in private. On such an occasion he told a lady at a ball that he thought George had behaved badly towards his wife Caroline of Brunswick, even though she was 'a very foolish, disagreeable person'. George, he added, should have 'made the best of a bad bargain as my father had done'. Yet when seeking a new naval command later that month, the first person William turned to was George, who agreed to take up the cause on William's behalf. His efforts were counterproductive, serving only to unite king and government in a firm rejection of William's offer. Disappointed but grateful to his brother for trying, William told him that he considered the prince his truest and best friend.

While relations with William remained amicable, those with Ernest were deteriorating fast, particularly when Cumberland began bullying his ailing father to appoint his favourite Tory, Henry Addington, as prime minister in place of William Pitt. Ernest's increasingly reactionary attitudes made him, according to his younger brother the Duke of Kent, the 'black sheep' of the family. Given a generous allowance of £18,000 a year, Cumberland nevertheless determined to return to military life and demanded a high command in the Peninsula War. When it was refused he became even more critical and embittered with everyone around him for, as William put it: 'If anyone had a corn he was sure to tread on it.' Resentment at being passed over in the Peninsula War appears to have focused Ernest's attention on his eldest brother, whom he now declared was as mad as his father. This led to George refusing to see him alone and Cumberland's furious reaction during a coach trip with George's secretary Benjamin Bloomfield during which Ernest swore 'to destroy with his own hands' whoever had reported his words to the prince. So violent was he that Bloomfield became terrified that he would use the firearms kept in the coach.

Having avoided the company of women for years, Ernest suddenly announced in 1815 that he intended to marry the twice-widowed Princess Frederica of Mecklenburg-Strelitz. Both Parliament and his mother opposed the union, but the infuriated Ernest went ahead anyway, encouraged by the support of the Prince of Wales. In a further affront to the king and queen they married not in a church but at the despised Carlton House, an occasion deliberately ignored by his parents, who disapproved of second marriages. Throughout the ceremony, brother George charmingly held Frederica's left hand while the groom held the right hand and then presented her with a miniature portrait of himself. As a further gesture of disapproval, Queen Charlotte refused point blank to receive her new daughter-in-law and, for once heeding his eldest brother's advice, Cumberland took his new bride off to the Continent until tempers had cooled. Kindly as ever, the prince apologized to his brother for his parent's rudeness, saying that he was unable to shake his mother's determination. Challenging the good relationship that had developed between them, Ernest and his bride refused to believe him, saying that as Regent he should take a firmer stand on their behalf or, as the new Duchess of Cumberland charmingly put it: 'The coal-heaver is master in his own house.' On reflection Ernest realized that his brother had been powerless to intervene, and he wrote to him from Germany acknowledging that George had done his best in the circumstances and expressed his gratitude:

> for all your brotherly kindness to me during my stay in England which will never be effaced from my recollection. In short you ALONE among eleven brothers and sisters have proved to me that you are really a brother and friend. God bless you for it.

William, too, had found himself a German princess to marry after a sad and traumatic separation from Dora Jordan and their ten illegitimate children. With Princess Charlotte dead, it was imperative that at least one of the Prince of Wales's brothers should produce an heir to the throne. His offers of marriage to a succession of heiresses were all rejected, and he finally settled for Princess Adelaide of Saxe-Coburg-Meiningen, described by the diarist Charles Greville as 'frightful, very ugly with a horrid complexion'. The marriage in July 1818 proved an unexpected success, as both preferred rural domesticity at Bushey in Hertfordshire to the social life of London. Two days after the wedding the Prince of Wales called on them and found them 'sitting by the fire exactly like Darby and Joan'. A woman of great natural kindness, Adelaide encouraged her husband's ten children into their household when the unfortunate Mrs Jordan died. When she herself gave birth to a little girl it seemed the culmination of her happy relationship with William, only for the baby to die at four months old. George had grown to admire and respect this prudish but open-spirited woman, and the loss of the child deeply grieved him.

When the government announced that it would support Catholic Emancipation in 1828, the Duke of Cumberland was furious and announced that he would return to England to head the opposition to the bill. George, now a sick man, dreaded his arrival and the bullying he would inevitably receive. When asked why George should be so scared of his brother, the Duke of Wellington explained that although the king was unafraid of anything 'hazardous, perilous or uncertain' he was utterly terrified of ridicule, and Cumberland's ability to mock was, said Wellington, unsurpassed. In a vain attempt to prevent his arrival, George suggested that his infuriated brother be made Governor of Hanover and the present incumbent, the Duke of Cambridge, be recalled and made commander-in-chief of the army. Wellington considered this a ridiculous suggestion, as Cambridge 'was as mad as Bedlam'. Not that he differed from the rest of the family, complained Wellington, who had become convinced that all the Hanoverians were crazy. Why else, he asked Mrs Arbuthnot, did the king persist in claiming that he had taken part in so many battles of the Napoleonic Wars? Had he not claimed to have fought at Waterloo and to have saved the day at Salamanca when leading a daring cavalry charge disguised as General Bock? The king's self-deception was so complete, thought Wellington, that his eyes filled convincingly with tears when he made these absurd claims, leaving his guests so astonished that they could only nod in dumb agreement. To maintain his own integrity during these monologues but without openly contradicting the monarch, the duke had devised a cunning stratagem. Whenever the king appealed to him to confirm that he had indeed been present on the field of Waterloo, the duke replied: 'So I have often heard your Majesty say.'

Even before his dreaded arrival in January 1829, Cumberland had written from Berlin urging his elder brother to 'show publicly, the purity and staunchness of your sentiments on the great question'. In a vain attempt to protect his sovereign, Wellington wrote back imploring Cumberland not to leave Berlin, but Ernest ignored the letter and continued on his grim mission to London. On arrival he made good his threat and began bombarding the king at Windsor with even more violent exhortations to stand firm, honour his coronation oath and protect the supremacy of the Protestant Church. In the face of this new onslaught George continued to dither, but his friends urged him to ignore Cumberland's bluster. Yet the Duke of Cumberland's persistence prevailed, and within a month of his brother's arrival the king appeared to have caved in to all his demands. Wellington was appalled and said he thought that George had become just as fanatical a Protestant as his bigoted brother. Also, having for months refused to discuss Catholic Emancipation at all, he now appeared to speak of little else and was driving everyone in the royal household crazy by endless discussion of the issue.

When told that his brother William had decided speak in support of the bill in the House of Lords, George told Lord Eldon that this was really the last straw. He was sorely tempted to renounce the throne at once, a threat he had made repeatedly when Prince of Wales, and retire to Hanover, leaving the Duke of Clarence to become the new 'Catholic' King of Great Britain. This threat of abdication was serious enough for George repeated it formally to Wellington when the prime minister went down to Windsor a month later. In an emotional audience that lasted well over five hours, the king ranted at the duke, wept repeatedly and appeared completely overwrought. Much of his distress was caused, he claimed, by the members of his household, who kept urging him to ignore Cumberland and support the government's proposals. By now Ernest was threatening to march on Windsor at the head of 20,000 supporters to petition the king against the bill. When told of Cumberland's intention, Wellington informed him by note that if he did so then as prime minister he would order Cumberland to be immediately arrested and taken as a prisoner to the Tower of London. The king must not and would not be bullied by anyone, not even his own brother.

The ordeal, however, was soon to end. When the House of

Lords debated the Emancipation Bill, the Duke of Cumberland, as anticipated, put the Anti-Emancipationist case as follows:

> the moment that there are Roman Catholics admitted into this or the other House of Parliament, this House must cease to be a Protestant House of Peers, and the House of Commons must cease to be a Protestant House of Commons.

The government's position was put simply and sincerely by his younger brother, the Duke of Clarence, who said:

> I maintain that that which is asked for is not concession but Justice. It is merely an act of Justice to raise the Roman Catholics from their present state of degradation. And when an Act is passed for that purpose, I will pledge my life that it will have the effect of uniting and quieting eight millions of His Majesty's subjects.

Clarence ended his speech by warning 'my illustrious relative' that he had lived so long abroad that 'he has almost forgotten what is due to the freedom of debate in this country'. When the vote came on 28 April 1829 the government produced a comfortable majority of 104 for Emancipation. William had demonstrated his public support for his elder brother during the vote by leaning over the rail of the gallery in the House of Lords and yelling 'Content!' at he top of his voice 'like a savage'. A few days later the Duke of Norfolk took his seat in the House of Lords and became the first Catholic to sit there among his peers since the Reformation. Peace again prevailed at Windsor as the Duke of Cumberland was sent packing back to Hanover.

15

A SANCTIMONIOUS COMPANION

THE king's his last years at the Windsor Lodge were far from happy, and his deteriorating health convinced friends he, too, might go blind and mad like his father, although Charles Greville thought he was 'already a little of both'. The death of his favourite brother, the Duke of York, in 1827 and the similarity of their symptoms became an almost daily obsession for him. On 9 January 1828 George apologized to his last secretary, Sir William Knighton, for not replying to a letter sooner, claiming that he did not have the strength to sit up in bed. Of all his household staff, Knighton was now the only one whom George trusted as a friend and adviser, becoming evermore dependent on him. By March 1830 his eyesight had deteriorated badly, and he described himself pathetically as being as 'blind as a beetle'. This debility was now so obvious that the government finally agreed he could sign official papers with an ink stamp of his signature if at least three witnesses were present, one of whom was certain to be the ubiquitous Knighton.

Sir William Knighton was a far different character from any of his predecessors. Where Benjamin Bloomfield, whatever his faults, had been affable and gregarious, Knighton appeared cold and austere. Industrious and conscientious, he was, above all, discreet. At times he could be infuriatingly affected and petulant, having risen, like Bloomfield, from humble origins. Before accepting the post, William Knighton had enjoyed a successful career as a naval doctor and then set up practice in Hanover Square as a fashionable gynaecologist or *accoucheur*. As Benjamin Bloomfield had made himself invaluable by providing mistresses to the aristocracy so Knighton dealt with their unwanted pregnancies. Among his impressive list of clients was the celebrated actress Moll Raffles, one of the many mistresses of Lord Wellesley, the Duke of Wellington's elder brother. Richard Wellesley, once memorably described by George as 'a Spanish grandee grafted on an Irish potato', was once a highly able politician, who had come close to being prime minister twenty years earlier. In 1809 he was sent to head the diplomatic mission in Spain, discreetly accompanied by Moll Raffles, who insisted on bringing along William Knighton as well. Wellesley seems not to have questioned the need for a full-time gynaecologist on the military campaign but agreed to Knighton's colossal demand for £5,000 as compensation for, so he claimed, two years' lost earnings in London.

When Lord Wellesley was unexpectedly recalled after only year in Spain, Knighton complained that his contract had not been honoured. Knighton, like Bloomfield, was not a man to be crossed lightly, knowing as he did the most compromising secrets of his clients. Instead of compensating him financially, Wellesley agreed to recommend him personally to the Prince of Wales, suggesting that he be added to George's growing retinue of doctors. Knighton wrote that he found George intelligent, proud and overbearing but with a most fascinating 'complacency of manner'. When he complained of a persistent lameness in one hand, Knighton, although careful not to offend medical ethics by treating him personally, gave him such good advice that he promptly invited Knighton to become one of his physicians-in-ordinary. Knighton's personal manner was as impressive as his medical skills, and George was soon treating him as a trusted confidant. A baronetcy followed as the doctor became increasingly indispensable. Some of the king's companions, knowing how he relished scandal, attributed his fascination with Knighton to the doctor's unrivalled knowledge of society sex life. His experience as London's leading gynaecologist meant that he knew the complaints of all the ladies who consulted him.

Soon Knighton's duties extended far beyond the medical, and he was soon undertaking delicate personal missions on his sovereign's behalf. The first of these involved dealing with one of his predecessors, the king's blackmailing ex-secretary Colonel John McMahon. Throughout his time as Comptroller of the Prince's Privy Purse McMahon had never lost an opportunity to enrich himself by selling sinecures or contracts in the royal gift. His wife, the lovely woman at the cottage window long ago, joined him in the enterprise so successfully that after her death £14,000 in cash was found hidden in a kitchen drawer. They all came to her for places, Knighton told a friend reprovingly, and it was common knowledge, according to Thomas Creevey, that Lady Beauchamp had paid McMahon £10,000 for getting her husband advanced from baron to earl. Knowledge of McMahon's corrupt activities eventually reached Parliament after McMahon had left his position, and questions were asked as to why he continued to be paid by the Crown when he was no longer in the prince's service. When the radical MP Samuel Whitbread questioned one such demand for £2,000, McMahon explained that it was for the upkeep of sixteen hundred war widows who had remained his personal responsibility. Whitbread, in a witty reference to McMahon's notorious reputation as a libertine, replied that 'if the gallant Colonel would produce a voucher from the ladies that he had performed his duties to their entire satisfaction he should think him well entitled to the salary'.

Throughout his years in royal service McMahon had been careful to retain copies of any documents or letters that might prove embarrassing to his clients in the event of a dispute and provide a form of insurance, a procedure still apparently practised by some royal servants. Among this secret horde were many compromising letters from George to numerous lovers, including some of a highly salacious nature. McMahon looked upon these as his retirement pension, and now, old and enfeebled, he decided to sell the cache and wrote to the king inviting an offer. He hinted that if George did not come up with a generous amount he would then sell off the whole lot to the highest bidder. The king, panic stricken as always in such situations, called in Knighton and asked him to conduct the negotiations on his behalf and to ensure that the documents were either recovered or destroyed at any cost. Knowing that the elderly McMahon was now a hopeless alcoholic, Knighton arrived alone at the McMahon's cottage in Kent clutching a bottle of his favourite brandy. Knighton insisted they down a measure together before getting down to business then, as they bargained, Knighton regularly topped up McMahon's glass until the atmosphere had so mellowed that the old man was happy enough to hand over the entire collection in return for a large but realistic fee. Knighton was delighted with his success and returned to London in triumph, assuring the king unctuously that nothing could have been handled more secretly or satisfactorily than his retrieval of the 'desirable objects'.

When John McMahon died two years later in 1817, leaving a fortune of £90,000, the newspapers were outraged, claiming it was yet another example of the corruption that permeated the Prince Regent's household. *The Times* described the will as 'a large fortune, which never could possibly have been obtained from the income of his several places'. But Knighton proved no better than his predecessor for the king was later to confide to Charles Arbuthnot that he suspected Knighton was up to McMahon's old tricks and had stolen some of his personal letters, pretending disingenuously they were mislaid but that he might know who had them. He wanted, claimed the king, £50,000 to buy them back and a fee of £12,000 for himself as compensation for the disappointment of not getting a sinecure post that the king had recently promised him. These were huge sums, and it is hard to see what unknown secrets the letters contained or why George tolerated such behaviour other than that he was desperate to avoid new scandal.

In his early days of service Knighton made himself useful by taking over most of Benjamin Bloomfield's duties as secretary and financial controller and performing them, as his wife wrote sanctimoniously in her memoir, 'with the unshrinking firmness which its embarrassments required'. Knowing how important he had become, Knighton demanded to be made Keeper of the Privy Purse with a salary doubled to £4,000 a year. His justification for this was, again, that he had given up a lucrative medical practice to serve the king and was losing a small fortune. Knighton also insisted that the king agree to relinquish financial control of his own household, allowing Knighton to inform all royal suppliers that in future only purchase orders signed personally by himself would receive payment. Knighton's boundless ambition continued, and although he had now accrued to himself the offices of Auditor of the Duchy of Cornwall, Secretary and Keeper of his Royal Highness's Privy and Council Seals he still felt them insufficient reward for his many talents and had demanded in 1821 that he be made a Privy Councillor. The king, unwilling to contest the issue, passed on his request to Lord Liverpool, who angrily refused outright to sanction the elevation of such a relative nonentity to one of the most important councils of state. Knighton responded to this rebuff with a display of anger and petulance that suggested he might well turn out to be an even greater irritant than his predecessor. As George's health further declined so Knighton's influence grew, and he became the most trusted of friends, constantly at his master's elbow to reassure and calm him.

Knighton's influence now extended beyond the king's personal affairs to political matters, and the wife of the Austrian Ambassador, Princess Lieven, was convinced that he had engineered the appointment of the Tory George Canning as prime minister. She described him as 'the man-midwife who is really Prime Minister'. Knighton, she believed, was now the real power at court, exercising a malign influence over the king and cultivating Canning to further his own ambition to be appointed a Privy Councillor. But Princess Lieven reported:

> Mr Canning who regards him as his declared enemy, said curtly that he would never consent. The refusal naturally offended the man-midwife, and he is not a man to be offended with impunity . . . everyone is afraid of him from the King downwards. He controls newspapers, caricatures, public business. He works underground.

To many observers, the king's closest friends – his mistress Lady Conyngham and his secretary Sir William Knighton – seemed natural allies at court as both were outsiders who had wormed their way into the his favour and depended entirely on his friendship for advancement. Avarice was also a vice they had in common, according to the diarist Henry Hobhouse, who thought both equally 'fond of lucre'. Lord Lauderdale voiced similar doubts, considering Knighton 'a damned clever fellow' but found it odd that of the four conversations he had with him 'each one of them ended with his asking me what I thought of the price of stocks'. But Knighton's demands for greater rewards were only possible, everyone noticed, because of the king's curious dependence upon him. In March 1820, when Knighton was still just a medical adviser, he was urgently summoned by George on hearing of the death of his brother William's baby daughter. George had even begun discussing matters of state with him before taking any decision. An invitation from the Austrian Emperor to visit Vienna in 1823 required Knighton's immediate presence at Brighton before the king could make up his mind to accept. Knighton was urged to come down to Brighton 'be it only for an hour . . . See you I must.'

William Knighton's years as a practising doctor had given him a canny grasp of the psychology of dependency as well as a polished bedside manner. Knighton was thus able to offer George credible reassurance about his many physical ailments as easily as he gave his opinions on the king's increasingly fraught relationship with his ministers. In return for his comprehensive support, Knighton demanded not only material rewards but insisted the king recognize his literary talents, too, for the doctor considered himself a poet of no mean ability. Yet how could the king, a man renowned for his literary and aesthetic good taste, who had recognized and promoted the genius of Jane Austen, respond as he had done in March 1821 to Knighton's latest banal composition? Hyperbole does not come any greater, as he writes:

It was a very, very, very wonderful poem . . . a most beautiful production of the human mind, perhaps, if not the most grand one certainly of the very grandest and most elegant at the same time that any pen produced, either in our language or any other.

A master at creating an atmosphere of intrigue in the most innocent of daily transactions, Knighton would send the king sealed notes proposing clandestine rendezvous at unlikely hours. One such read: 'I hope to be in your Majesty's bedroom by half past twelve to-night . . . let no one know I am coming with the exception of the one.' Perhaps Knighton was simply coming to say evening prayers for much of the king's sudden and unexpected interest in religion could be attributed to the influence of the pious secretary. Certainly his letters to the king are written with a cloying tone of piety, pomposity and sanctimony worthy of Uriah Heep. One of the most ingratiating reads:

I trust that the Almighty will give you peace, and that your afflicted mind will cease to be tortured by the overwhelming inquietudes . . . your Majesty would scarcely believe the extent of my anxiety and misery respecting you. Burn this if you please . . . I have the honour to be, Sir, your Majesty's most dutiful and most affectionate attached devoted servant.

Knighton was well aware that his fawning had made him well nigh indispensable for, as he boasted to Charles Arbuthnot:

The King perhaps, ought not to have a favourite, but he cannot do without me . . . he is the most helpless creature in the world, he cannot write a letter for himself and he must have a person like me about.

When Knighton foolishly repeated these sentiments to Wellington, the duke, in his usual blunt manner, advised him to confine his activities to the king's private matters and to keep his nose out of politics – advice for which Knighton characteristically profusely thanked him.

Wellington would have been even more outraged had he known that the king was actually asking Knighton's advice as to whether he should sack his Tory ministry and bring in the Whig opposition. Whatever Knighton decided on this matter, the king told him, would be done. But the secretary had become dangerously complacent and, thinking himself invulnerable, had begun to voice his private contempt for his royal master, complaining ill-advisedly to Charles Arbuthnot that the king was 'a great beast who liked nothing so much as indecent conversation'. When this was reported to him George's attitude to his secretary began to change. Knighton's enemies, and there were many, were quick to seize on his sudden and unsuspected vulnerability. One of the king's oldest friends, Sir Thomas Tyrwhitt, declared that he had no doubt that Knighton was 'the greatest villain as well as the lowest blackguard that ever lived'. Princess Lieven, too, confessed her dislike of the man and was convinced that beneath his agreeable and polished exterior Sir William Knighton was in reality a scheming villain. There were, she claimed, even rumours in London that:

> The doctor's chief exploit is having poisoned his wife twenty years ago. The King's household is really the most extraordinary thing in the world. He is head over heels in love [but] the doctor's influence rules him in the first place.

There is no better example of Sir William Knighton's abilities than his key role of protecting his master from damaging publicity in the Harriette Wilson affair. Wilson, the most famous courtesan in England, announced that she was to publish her autobiography, and if her ex-lovers did not want to be mentioned then they must buy themselves out of it. When the first volume of Harriette Wilson's *Memoirs* had appeared in February 1825 it caused a sensation. Cleverly, on the eve of publication, she had placed a notice in the London papers announcing that Lords Londonderry, Byron, Melbourne, Burghesh, Alvanley, Conyngham and dozens more were featured in the work. 'A pretty list indeed,' said

Henry Brougham, 'almost every one of my particular friends is among them.' So great was the demand for the book that it was reprinted thirty times in the first year alone. The next volume, she announced, would contain highly compromising letters written by the king's current mistress, Elizabeth Conyngham, to John Ponsonby. When Ponsonby threatened to sue Wilson, Knighton urged him not to proceed, even though he had prepared his case and hired lawyers, because 'you cannot relieve the feelings of the distinguished lady mentioned in your letter by dragging her name, and for ought you know, even her presence, into the court of Justice'. But when George suggested buying Wilson off, Knighton advised him to stand firm and not to give in to her outrageous demands. But the stress of it all was taking its toll on the king: 'the Wilson business of yesterday has entirely knock'd me up and destroyed me', he told Knighton. Now desperate for money, Harriette Wilson decided to settle for the best terms she could get. Knighton offered her husband a modest but secure minor diplomatic post and an annuity of £100. Harriette herself would receive a cash sum, quietly diverted from the secret-service fund, on the understanding that she cease blackmailing the king and his friends once and for all. It was further agreed with Knighton that any further comments on George IV in her memoirs would be both uncontentious and favourable. Harriette accepted, and the triumphant negotiator returned to London with the letters – which soon mysteriously disappeared – in his pocket to receive, with his usual smugness, the heartfelt gratitude of the king and his mistress.

After his success in the Harriette Wilson affair, Knighton became insufferable. Puffed up with self-importance and considering that he was now irreplaceable for having put the king's personal affairs and his finances in good order, Knighton finally overreached himself. One evening Lady Conyngham, who had been confined to her room with a fever, asked him to come and discuss some important household business. Knighton ignored her request, and when the king reproached him for it the following day he responded petulantly: 'I should like to know whose servant I am in this house.' This insolence could not be ignored, and the king sent him packing to London for a week. That first evening of his absence the king surprised his dinner guests by suddenly shouting out: 'I wish to God somebody would assassinate Knighton.' He was utterly determined, he informed his startled guests, to get rid of Knighton once and for all. Although George's anger appeared genuine, some thought his outburst mere hot air for he could never do without a man he relied on for everything. 'The King's indolence is so great that it is next to impossible to get him to do even the most ordinary business and Knighton is still the only man who can prevail on him to sign papers,' wrote Charles Greville.

A week later George saw the Duke of Wellington for what was to be the last time. During the conversation he appeared unusually optimistic about the future, assuring the Duke that he was feeling much better and would soon be on the move again. That Friday night, 25 June, George retired to his bedroom chair as usual and fell asleep with his head on the table and his hand in that of another physician, Sir Wathen Waller, who had agreed to sit with him. At two o'clock in the morning he awoke and took his medicine together with a sip of tea before falling asleep again. An hour later he awoke in distress and called for a commode and Sir Henry Halford. When Halford arrived he found the king slumped back in his chair with his eyes closed. A moment later a blood vessel burst in his stomach and he lurched up, clutching a page by the shoulder. His last words, according to Sir Henry, were: 'My dear boy! This is death.' As the page supported him, he fell forward on to the young man's shoulder and died.

When George died on 26 June 1830 Sir William Knighton had one last self-imposed duty as a friend. Together with the Duke of Wellington he returned to the king's private rooms and searched through all his possessions for anything that might blemish his master's posthumous reputation. His main concern was to find the huge bundle of letters from various women, which the king was known to have had all his life, together with the copies of his replies. The letters were soon discovered hidden in a cupboard and many were seen to be of 'an ardent nature'. The duke, no prude himself, later claimed to have been shocked by their content. Gathering them up he took them over to the fireplace and carefully burnt them all in an act of historical desecration. This was fast becoming an age of respectability, and only a bowdlerized version of a man's life could be permitted to survive. Even such a past roué as the Duke of Wellington had now to accommodate the pious mores of a man such as Sir William Knighton.

16

A MAN OF THE PEOPLE

WHEN *The Times* correspondent arrived at St George's Chapel in Windsor on 15 July 1830 he was shocked to find that the congregation, apart from the new King William and his party, mainly consisted of servants from the royal household and their friends. The other mourners appeared to be local carpenters, upholsterers and the petty tradesmen of the town who, *The Times* lamented: 'had been admitted to the exclusion of more respectable public servants. Those who arrived first had not only seized the best places but also stopped others from sitting, by reserving places for their friends.' 'Never', *The Times* fulminated, 'have we seen so motley, so rude, so ill-managed a body of persons.' The writer Robert Huish, consistently one of George's greatest critics, was equally shocked by 'the screams of the females and the rude and indecent jokes of the blackguards that gave the whole scene more the appearance of a crowd hastening to some raree-show than to the chamber of death'. What fascinates about these reports is not the absence of most of the aristocracy but the presence of so many working people, a class not generally given to attending royal funerals. Their presence that day was fitting for they were honouring a man who had always displayed a concern and generosity of spirit to ordinary people. Throughout his reign George's popularity among working people was certainly greater than it was with the middle and upper classes, perhaps because he behaved towards them in a natural and unpretentious manner.

When compared with his predecessors, who were isolated by language and a rigid sense of propriety, and his priggish successors, who kept their distance, George IV was a refreshing exception. An ease of manner and lack of pomposity characterized his relationships with friends and servants alike.

While his father preferred the safety of the palace, the young Prince of Wales was quite prepared to venture out into the streets of London with a friend or two without guards of any sort; an action that would have been unthinkable by a foreign prince in any other European capital. Once, when told that an ordinary working-man's pub in Gray's Inn had the best ale in London, he decided to try it for himself, not hesitating to walk in and sample it. Standing at the bar he began chatting to the other customers about the affairs of the day. The landlord was so impressed by his unexpected royal visitor that he later put up a notice announcing himself as 'Purveyor of Burton Ale to His Royal Highness the Prince of Wales'. While happy to participate in horse racing, the traditional sport of kings, George was equally at home in a muddy field watching two sweaty boxers batter away at each other. This interest in boxing in particular, still thought of at the time as a lower-class sport in spite of an aristocratic following, much endeared him to ordinary people. His enthusiasm for the sport ended, however, when he saw a man killed in the ring at Brighton. With typical generosity he settled an annuity on the bereaved widow but said that he would never watch another fight.

Until he withdrew himself away to Windsor he was very much the man of the people, acclaimed by ordinary citizens wherever he went. If the Dublin crowd loved him for his natural, easygoing manner then so, too, did the London mob – although, sadly, the very public quarrel with Queen Caroline brought about a profound change of attitude as he was then portrayed as the guilty party in the marriage. From the time of his divorce he noticed an obvious hostility from the crowd that was never apparent before, making him increasingly fearful of attack.

But in March 1789, at the time of the Regency controversy, he was still in favour. During the incident on the way to the theatre with his brother Frederick, when their carriage became blocked by a crowd shouting support for their father George III, the prince initially joined in the clamour amicably enough, but when a man began bawling 'Pitt for ever' he lost his temper. Leaping out of the carriage, he shouted 'Fox for ever' and appeared fully prepared to take on the man in a brawl. Only the restraining arm of his brother prevented it as Frederick pulled George back into the carriage while beating his assailant over the head with a walking stick held in his free hand as the coachman prepared to drive on.

But the prince's true popularity among working people was revealed later that same night when the royal brothers left the opera. As it was a fine evening, George insisted they walk back on foot along Pall Mall. Astonished to see the heir to the British throne quite prepared to walk unguarded among them, an admiring crowd began to follow, shouting 'God bless your Highness'. When they reached St James's a large gang of butchers suddenly appeared and treated George with great familiarity. Beating the marrowbones and cleavers they carried they formed a rough-and-ready Praetorian Guard and cleared the way ahead as they all proceeded along St James's Street. Knowing he was heading for Brook's Club they halted outside and gave him three rousing cheers as a finale. Cheerfully, the prince gave them a cheer in return before entering the club and sending out ten guineas' worth of ale for the crowd to drink. As witness and fellow club member Sir Gilbert Eliot commented:

> It is to the credit of his spirit and natural manners; and he is out of luck for not being extremely popular, for a tenth part of his popular qualities . . . has made the fortune of many princes and favourites of the people.

There is no doubt that George possessed the common touch, a quality traditionally rare among members of the British royal family. He was able to converse with ordinary people in a natural and friendly manner that encouraged them to respond in kind.

An early experience of this was when he first came to Brighton and liked to enjoy a daily bathe in the sea. One stormy morning, when he emerged from his bathing machine, the attendant, an old sailor called 'Smoker' Miles, barred his way. 'I shall bathe this morning, Smoker,' the prince said firmly. 'No your Royal Highness, it's too dangerous,' Miles replied, pointing towards the raging sea. 'But I will,' said the prince defiantly. 'No,' responded Miles, standing in front of him with raised fists. 'I'll be damned if you shall bathe. What would your royal father think of me if you were drowned . . . he'd say Smoker this is all owing to you, if you'd taken proper care of him poor George would still be alive.' At this the prince roared with laughter and gave way with good grace.

In an age when servants were often treated with disdain or even contempt, the natural ease of manner and good humour with which George dealt with this was remarkable. At Carlton House, Brighton and even in the last years at Windsor, he was a particularly kind master, treating his attendants well and, most unusually, with a great deal of familiarity, whatever their status in the household. When each came to retirement age he or she was given a generous pension to support them in old age. Even the kitchen staff, a class of workers largely ignored in other great houses, were frequently visited by a man who had an unusual interest in the technicalities of cooking. For George was not only a famed gourmet, employing such famous chefs as the Frenchman Jean Baptiste Watier, he was also, unusually for a member of the royal family, fascinated by the mechanics of cooking itself. For this reason he made sure that the kitchens at the Brighton Pavilion were equipped with the very latest catering technology, which included sophisticated ovens, piped steam and hot and cold water everywhere. Whereas in most great houses the design of the kitchens were at best an afterthought, those at the Pavilion were given proper respect and made attractive in appearance with architectural columns in the form of palm trees and decorated bronze lanterns. George was so proud of them that he would occasionally lead his friends along from the drawing-room and sit them down at the servants' table in a reversal of the usual upstairs–downstairs convention. He would then perform the duty of a head butler, meticulously carving joints of meat and passing the plates along the table to his guests. During the Christmas celebrations of 1817 he even gave a supper party exclusively for his own servants. They all assembled in the kitchen, and a large scarlet cloth was thrown over the stone floor as a temporary carpet. George then sat down with them and enjoyed 'a splendid repast'. No servant was missing, even the garden boys being present, and the females in particular were said to be delighted 'with this mark of royal condescension'.

George's ability to deal with the odd or unusual in people was as impressive as his spontaneous generosity. Both were displayed on the eve of the coronation in 1821 when he was visited at Carlton House by the famous Polish dwarf Count Joseph Boruwlaski. After inquiring if the count wanted for anything himself, George then asked him to do him a great service. As the preparations for the coronation made it impossible for him to leave the house, would the count, on George's behalf, visit one of his old valets who was dying? When Boruwlaski arrived at the valet's house he found the man full of praise for his royal master, telling him that the prince had visited him twice a day as he lay ill at Carlton House and making sure that he had everything he needed. What most impressed him, the valet told the count, was that these visits were unhurried, and the prince was happy to pass the time of day with him, telling him all about what was happening in the household. His only wish, the dying man said, was 'to live long enough to greet his dear master after his Coronation' and then he was ready to die in peace.

Where European princes generally conducted their affairs through aristocratic intermediaries, George was unusual in often dealing directly with businessmen and shopkeepers face to face. One of the most remarkable relationships ever conducted between a King of England and a tradesman was that between George and Louis Weltje. Apprenticed to a baker in Westphalia, Weltje had decided to try his luck in London where he opened a high-class confectionery shop in St James's, directly opposite Brook's Club where the prince was a frequent visitor. Given George's predilection for sweets and puddings, they could not have failed to meet. The prince was impressed by Weltje's directness and an obvious business acumen that marked him out from his more inhibited English contemporaries. In a gesture that would have been inconceivable for any other English prince, George persuaded Weltje to leave the running of the shop to his brother and to join him at Carlton House as his steward and *maître d'hôtel*. But the German's role was not confined to household duties alone, and he was soon acting as friend and financial adviser to the prince, using his natural cunning and no-nonsense attitude when dealing with tradesmen. A squat, ugly little man notorious for his bustling manner, Weltje was known to order the prince's cooks about in a 'barbarous Westphalian jargon'. The importance of this strange foreigner in the household intrigued and amused the satirists, and soon Weltje was appearing with George in cartoons alongside other such reprobates as Sheridan, George Hanger and Sir John Lade. The publicity made him a contemporary celebrity in his own right and helped him on his way to acquiring a fortune out of property, mainly in London, where his name still adorns a road in Hammersmith.

In the summer of 1784 George sent the now indispensable Weltje down to Brighton to find him a house. This resulted in the purchase of the lease and later the freehold of a farmhouse on the Steine owned by a local developer Thomas Kemp, of Kemptown fame. Discretely Weltje bought the property in his own name, George not wanting to be castigated by his father for further extravagance and later sold it on to the prince at a considerable profit to himself. So important a role did Weltje play in his master's affairs that, in popular conception at least, he was involved in agreeing the financial arrangements with the government on George's behalf when the Regency was being established. *The Times* even accused him of trying to bribe the prince's political rivals and advised him 'to confine his attentions to his master's stew pans and his influence to his patron's closet or return to keeping a gingerbread stall'. The paper went on to describe, in a xenophobic manner, Weltje as nothing more than 'an itinerant German music grinder raised from earning halfpence by the discordance of a street walking concert'. He was also vitriolically attacked as someone who clearly did not love his new country as he showed a predilection for employing only foreign servants so that true British men 'were out of bread while a German toad-eater had amassed an enormous fortune in the Prince of Wales's service'. Yet this attack came as no surprise to George for he knew that the editor of *The Times*, John Walter, was being paid from secret-service funds by the Tory government to harass the prince and the Whig opposition. At the time of the first Regency, Walter had abused George and Frederick so violently that he was heavily fined by the courts and sent to prison. On release he repeated the slander and was again sent to prison. Only the kind intervention of the Prince of Wales, for which he was given little credit, saved Walter from remaining incarcerated for a very long time.

What was true, however, was that Louis Weltje was now the prince's 'fixer' in matters that extended far beyond the kitchen. He was involved in paying bribes, buying paintings and even securing loans on his master's behalf. Unlike the prince's official secretaries – true gentlemen such as McMahon, Bloomfield and Knighton – Weltje could operate without regard to the conventions of polite behaviour and the mores of the English class system. This gave him considerable freedom as when he acted as initial go-between when George set out to borrow an enormous sum of money from the Duke of Orléans. Weltje was quite happy not even to aspire to being a true English gentleman, and this freedom of attitude made him all the more appealing in the prince's eyes. When Weltje died in 1796 there is no doubt that he left an irreparable gap in George's life both as friend and as his most astute business adviser. He may have also missed him as a drinking companion, too, for they often shared a bottle or two of cherry brandy of an evening or spent hours together at the gambling-table. What motivated this awkward German was the simple desire for prosperity, and this he certainly attained, eventually acquiring a small estate of his own where he entertained many poets, musicians and painters. His great delight in old age, he claimed, was to be able to show his guests around his house and gardens. All this, he told them, he intended to leave to his children, gesturing proudly and saying in his thick German accent, as quoted in the memoirs of Sir Nathaniel Wraxall: 'Dish ish moine, dat ish moine and what ish more, I can leave it all to my posteriors.'

An equally incongruous relationship was that with Sir William Curtis, the sea-biscuit tycoon, who was popularly known as Billy Biscuit. George delighted in the company of this unassuming but highly successful man, who was one of five brothers of humble origins from Wapping in the London docklands. Barely literate – he was widely credited with once proposing a toast, as Lord Mayor of London, to the three Rs: 'reading, riting, and rithmetic' – he was, nevertheless, a brilliant entrepreneur. Curtis's business interests included shipping, the East India Company, banking, and insurance. What made him so interesting to the Prince of Wales was that, like Weltje, he had no great desire to climb the political ladder, preferring to wield influence over a broad spectrum of business activities. Yet he became an alderman and then Lord Mayor of London as well as a Member of Parliament. His politics, he once said, were based on two simple precepts: 'I fear God and honour the King.' In a gesture inconceivable in any other member of a European royal family, George was happy to go and stay with Curtis at his enormous, bad-taste villa at Ramsgate in Kent. Here he rested a night before embarking on the royal yacht for his visit to the Continent in 1821. Guest and host consumed a vast quantity of food and cherry brandy for Sir William's tastes and appetites were similar to that of the prince. A cartoon by William Heath mocks a fat, red-nosed Curtis who declares: 'Just looking out for somthing [sic] to stay my stomach till dinner time,' as he examines a bill of fare while rubbing his protruding belly with delight.

Such close friends did they become that George invited Sir William to join him on the trip to Scotland in 1822. More incongruously dressed even than the king, Curtis appeared beside him at Holyrood Palace. While not having single drop of Scottish blood in his veins, Curtis had decked himself out in another flamboyant approximation of Highland dress, complete with a kilt of the Stuart tartan. One jaundiced Scottish observer, John Lockhart, complained that Curtis 'cast an air of ridicule and caricature over the whole of Sir Walter's Celtified pageantry'. The bizarre appearance of the two pseudo-Highlanders was, of course, a gift to the London satirists, who, for the rest of the year, teased the 'Celtic' king in numerous cartoons and rhymes. George ignored the ridicule and presented his 'fellow Highlander' with a portrait of himself painted by Sir Thomas Lawrence, at which Curtis dutifully repaid him with one of *himself*, again painted by Lawrence.

When researching his pioneering work, *London Labour and the London Poor*, twenty years after the death of George IV, the writer Henry Mayhew met an elderly cab driver who told of an amusing encounter with George when they were both young. Summoned to the British Coffee-house in Cockspur Street one night, he stood waiting on his cab when a waiter ran out and said: 'You jump down and get inside, the prince is a-going to drive hisself.' Then out came the Prince of Wales and four of his drunken friends, including George Hanger. 'The Prince gripped me by the ankle and the waistband of my breeches, and lifted me off the wheel and flung me right into the coach through the open window.' He then took the reins, whipped up the horse, and the coach raced off, cutting corners and ignoring road junctions until they arrived at a gaming-house in King Street, Saint James's. George enjoyed himself immensely and often sent for the same cab driver again. What most impressed the young cabbie was not the adventure itself but the prince's friendly manner towards a young working man for, as he told Mayhew: 'He hadn't no pride to such as me, hadn't the Prince of Wales.'

Throughout his life George IV was as generous with his wealth and patronage as he was with his friendship. There are dozens of instances of his concern for others and the unsolicited help he provided for those in distress. Where others gave words of consolation, George was always ready to provide practical help. A typical story of his generosity concerns a Brighton tradesman who, overwhelmed by business worries, had attempted to commit suicide. Hearing of his distress and realizing that he owed him money, George immediately produced his wallet, took out all the notes and handed it to a page to take to the man. 'Bid him take these,'

he said. 'I may perhaps owe him something and under the circumstances the routine of payment must appear odious.' The
wallet had contained over £700. Again, on hearing that the
painter David Wilkie was seriously ill and worried about some
uncompleted pictures, George did not hesitate to come to his aid.
'Go to Wilkie,' he told Sir William Knighton:

> He is proud and shy he may not want money at all and it would not
> do to offer him. Say to him, however . . . that he has my permission
> to consider me as his banker . . . He may draw whatever he wants and
> repay me at his leisure in the shape of pictures.

Actions such as this marked George out as a man far different
from his parsimonious father or his successors with the exception
perhaps of his good-natured brother William.

Nor was his generosity confined to individuals for many artistic
and cultural institutions were beneficiaries, too. When in 1820 he
was invited to help establish the Society of Literature, he volun-
teered to contribute an initial thousand guineas as well an annual
grant of one hundred guineas. This was mistaken by its president,
the Bishop of St David's, as an annual contribution of one thousand.
Realizing that the bishop had already publicly announced the gift,
to save him from embarrassment George kept silent, and the Royal
Society of Literature was able to purchase premises in London and
to give financial support to such writers as Samuel Taylor Coleridge.
Of equal importance was his donation of his father's 65,000-volume
library to the British Museum, which was to become the centrepiece
of the modern British Library at St Pancras.

George's patronage of literature was only exceeded by the help
he provided in the establishment of Britain's first national art collection, based upon the royal collection that he had inherited from
his father. Under Charles I it had been the best in Europe, but
much had been sold off by Cromwell and his Puritan regime.
Now, with the help of Lord Yarmouth and others, it had been
restored to its former glory, and George was happy to share it with
the nation. His largesse was based on the simple principle that the

contemplation of fine art should not be a selfish enjoyment reserved for princes and nobles in their palaces: 'I have not formed it for my own pleasure alone but to gratify the public taste,' he wrote to the Royal Academy in 1826. In pursuit of this democratization of the arts he helped persuade the government to put up the funds needed to purchase the thirty-eight great paintings that came on to the market with the death of his late friend, the connoisseur John Julius Angerstein in 1823. For once the government listened to his advice and bought them all for the bargain price of £57,000. Initially shown in Angerstein's former residence at Pall Mall, which was opened to the public, the paintings were eventually housed with other publicly owned paintings when the new National Gallery was built in Trafalgar Square in 1838.

From his patronage of the great artists of the day, including Reynolds, Lawrence and Wilkie, George realized that Britain needed to encourage and train young artists to inherit their tradition. When the pope presented him with a number of plaster casts of the marble statues in the Vatican collection, he immediately saw their worth as teaching aids and presented them to the Royal Academy. In the letter announcing their arrival, he even offered to obtain more from Rome if the Academy thought it appropriate. Of even greater significance was his loan to the Academy of the famous Raphael cartoons in his possession and his support for the acquisition of the Elgin Marbles. Such generosity endeared him to the Italian sculptor Antonio Canova, who was visiting London at the time. Canova said that he appreciated his 'fine taste, sound judgement and extensive information' and was certain that 'this King of England combined the suavity of an amiable man and the dignity of the great monarch'. This was praise indeed from a man who had worked for every major European ruler, including the Emperor Napoleon.

Castigated for his public extravagance, George was consistently generous to members of his own family. As well as providing an annual allowance of £50,000 for Frederick, Duke of York, the moment he became king, he gave £10,000 each year to the Duke of Clarence and somewhat less to Princess Elizabeth. To his political friends he was equally munificent, ordering Sir William Knighton to provide an unsolicited £15,000 for Charles Arbuthnot, the Secretary of the Treasury, when he fell seriously ill and asking Arbuthnot never to mention the subject 'or let it be the cause of any shyness or embarrassment between us'. Knighton also recalled that George had only to hear of an actor in severe difficulties caused by illness or poverty and he would provide financial help at once.

His donations to charitable institutions were equally generous. Even the radical politician Henry Brougham had to praise the way he gave to hospitals and orphanages. One small beneficiary was the society formed to abolish 'the present disgraceful trade by Chimney Sweepers'. He was also concerned by cruelty to animals and made a friend of Humanity Dick, the Irish politician Richard Martin, who was largely responsible for founding the Royal Society for the Prevention of Cruelty to Animals and who introduced the first legislation in any parliament in the world to protect them. But it is the payments to individuals that are the most touching, particularly to one Sarah West, who appealed for help, saying:

> I am one of the unfortunate women that have lived with officers – you know there is no provision for them (it would be Encouraging Vice). I resided with Lieutenant Hill of the 64th Regiment in the American War and was the mother of four children.

Then, as now, the dependents of soldiers were treated badly by the government, even worse if unmarried. On George's immediate order, Miss West received six guineas by return of post.

With George IV's generosity went a keen sense of compassion. When he became King of Hanover as well as of Great Britain in 1820, he ordered that the use of torture be abolished in all Hanoverian prisons. He also readily conceded to Lady Conyngham's request that he abolish the flogging of women prisoners in British gaols. Records show that he was constantly interceding with Robert Peel for clemency when Peel was home secretary, particularly when young men were given sentences out of all proportion to their crime, such as the proposed transportation to Australia of a thirteen-year-old boy for theft. The wide use of the death penalty throughout his reign distressed him even more, and George did not hesitate to make his position known to Peel. On the eve of one mass execution he ordered Knighton to write urgently to Peel that:

> The King . . . must say that the executions of to-morrow, from their unusual numbers, weigh most heavily and painfully on his mind . . . The King therefore desires that only four may suffer in the place of eight.

Such compassion was rare, if not unique, among European monarchs at the time. Whenever he succeeded in saving a life, George was delighted. On one occasion Peel was staying at the Brighton Pavilion, having commuted a death sentence at the king's request earlier in the day. In the middle of the night Peel was summoned to the royal bedroom to receive a hearty kiss of gratitude on both cheeks. Then, noticing that the home secretary was wearing a particular flimsy gown, George said: 'Peel where did you get your dressing gown? I'll show you what a dressing gown ought to be,' and he promptly took off his own and handed it to Peel.

Such demonstrations of generosity and understanding were capable of converting those who could be presumed to be his most implacable enemies. None of his friendships was more remarkable than that with Lord Byron. On principle alone, Byron could have been expected to consider George, the king, a prime target for his scathing wit, but remarkably he came to respect and admire him. When his poem *Childe Harold's Pilgrimage* became the literary sensation of 1812, Byron was invited to a ball at which George was present. Etiquette dictated that, as the poet had not been presented at court he could not enter the royal presence. When told of this the prince waved convention aside and summoned Byron at once, heartily congratulating him on his achievement. George's reward was an admiring verse from the great poet:

> Though Royalty was written on his brow,
> He had then the grace, too, rare in every clime,

Of being, without alloy of fop or beau,

A finished Gentleman from top to toe.

What most impressed Byron was George's knowledge of literature and his natural critical ability as well as his genuine respect for writers. As Byron told Sir Walter Scott, the prince had confessed that until he had read *Childe Harold's Pilgrimage* he had thought it impossible for any writer to equal Sir Walter Scott, but now he was not so sure! Praise for Sir Walter, Byron told him, had been delivered by the prince 'with a tone which gave me a very high idea of his abilities and accomplishments, which I hitherto considered as confined to *manners*, certainly superior to any living *gentleman*'. Privately Byron thought that his friendship with the Regent might lead to him being made the next Poet Laureate, an extraordinary prospect for the least conformist of poets. Given Byron's iconoclasm and his radical politics, such an idyllic outcome could never be, and his later waspish poem on the supposed neglect of Princess Charlotte – 'Weep, daughter of a royal line, / A sire's disgrace, a realm's decay; / Ah happy! If a tear of thine, / Could wash a father's fault away' – all but ended the friendship. When George discovered that the lines had been written by Byron rather than the chief suspect Tom Moore, he claimed to be affected 'more in sorrow rather than by anger'. Such a reaction was typical of a man who led his life without rancour – with the notable exception of his disastrous marriage, of course.

Perhaps his most appropriate epitaph was spoken by the Duke of Wellington, who told his friend Thomas Raikes that George had indeed been 'the most extraordinary compound of talent, wit, buffoonery, obstinacy and good feeling – in short, a medley of the most opposite qualities with a great preponderance of good that I ever saw in any character in my life'. The nation, the duke thought, would always have cause to be grateful to the man who had been 'a most magnificent patron of the arts in this country, and in the world'.

APPENDIX: CHRONOLOGY OF THE LIFE OF GEORGE IV

1762 George Augustus, Prince of Wales, born
1763 Frederick, Duke of York, born
1765 William, Duke of Clarence born. George III's first porphyria outbreak
1766 Princess Charlotte, born
1767 Edward Augustus, Duke of Kent, born
1768 Princess Augusta Sophia born
1770 Princess Elizabeth born
1771 Ernest Augustus, Duke of Cumberland, born
1773 Augustus, Duke Frederick, Duke of Sussex, born
1774 Adolphus, Duke of Cambridge, born
1775 Start of American War of Independence
1776 Princess Mary born
1777 Daughter Sophia born
1782 George given Carlton House
1783 General Election. George first visits Brighton
1784 Prince George's first appearance in Parliament
1785 George secretly marries Maria Fitzherbert
1786 George acquires Brighton Pavilion
1788 George III suffers his first major attack of porphyria
1789 Regency Bill debated in Parliament
1793 Outbreak of war between Britain and France
1795 George marries Caroline of Brunswick
1796 Princess Charlotte born
1798 Rebellion in Ireland
1801 George III suffers another attack of porphyria
1802 Treaty of Amiens with France
1804 George III suffers his third attack of his illness
1809 Duke of York involved in Mary Ann Clarke scandal
1811 George becomes Prince Regent;
1813 Ends friendship with Beau Brummell
1815 Defeat of Napoleon at Waterloo
1816 Richard Brinsley Sheridan dies
1817 Princess Charlotte dies in childbirth
1818 Queen Charlotte dies
1820 George III dies. George becomes King
1821 Coronation of George IV
1822 Royal visits to Ireland and Scotland
1827 Duke of York dies
1828 Catholic Emancipation Bill
1830 Death of King George IV

BIBLIOGRAPHY

Anglesey, 7th Marquess of, *One-Leg: The Life and Letters of Henry William Paget, First Marquess of Anglesey 1768–1854*, Jonathan Cape, London, 1961

Armstrong, Walter, *Sir Thomas Lawrence*, Methuen, London, 1913

Aspinall, A. (ed.), *The Correspondence of Charles Arbuthnot*, Royal Historical Society, London, 1941

Aspinall, A. (ed.), *The Correspondence of George, Prince of Wales 1770–1812* (8 vols), Cassell, London, 1963–71

Aspinall, A. (ed.), *The Diary of Henry Hobhouse: 1820–1827*, Home and Van Thal, London, 1947

Aspinall, A. (ed.), *The Later Correspondence of George III* (5 vols), Cambridge University Press, Cambridge, 1962–70

Aspinall, A. (ed.), *Letters of the Princess Charlotte 1811–1817*, Home and Van Thal, London, 1949

Aspinall A. and E. Smith (eds), *English Historical Documents, 1783–1832*, Eyre and Spottiswoode, London, 1959

Ayling, Stanley, *Fox: The Life of Charles James Fox*, John Murray, London, 1991

Bamford, Francis and the Duke of Wellington (eds), *The Journal of Mrs Arbuthnot, 1820–1832* (2 vols), Macmillan, London, 1950

Bessborough, Earl of (ed.), *Georgiana: Extracts from the Correspondence of Georgiana, Duchess of Devonshire*, John Murray, London, 1955

Bickley, Francis (ed.), *The Diaries of Sylvester Douglas, Lord Glenbervie* (2 vols), Constable, London, 1928

Blanch, Lesley (ed.), *The Game of Hearts: Harriette Wilson and Her Memoirs*, Gryphon, London, 1957

Brougham, Henry, *The Life and Times of Henry Lord Brougham Written by Himself* (3 vols), T. Allman, London, 1871

Bruce, John, *The History of Brighton*, Van Voorst, London, 1831

Bryant, Arthur, *The Age of Elegance*, William Collins, London, 1950

Buckingham and Chandos, Dukes of, *Memoirs of the Courts and Cabinets of George III* (4 vols), Hurst and Blackett, London, 1853–5

Bury, Lady Charlotte, *The Court of England Under George IV: Founded on a Diary* (2 vols), John Macqueen, London, 1896

Calvert, Hon. Frances, *An Irish Beauty of the Regency*, John Lane, London, 1911

Campbell, Lord, *Lives of the Lord Chancellors* (10 vols), John Murray, London, 1857

Castle, Egerton (ed.), *The Jerningham Letters, 1780–1843, Being Excerpts from the Correspondence and Diaries of Lady Jerningham and Her Daughter Lady Bedingfield* (2 vols), Chatto and Windus, London, 1919

Clarke, John, *The Life and Times of George III*, Weidenfeld and Nicolson, London, 1972

Clarke, Mary Anne, *The Rival Princes* (2 vols), M. Jones, London, 1810

Colchester, Lord, *The Diary and Correspondence of Charles Abbot, Lord Colchester* (3 vols), John Murray, London, 1861

Cole, Hubert, *Beau Brummell*, Granada, London, 1977

Dale, Antony, *Fashionable Brighton 1820–1860*, Country Life, London, 1947

de Beflaigue, Sir Geoffrey, *Carlton House: The Past Glories of George IV's Palace*, Royal Collection Publications, London, 1991

Delves Broughton, Mrs Vernon (ed.), *Court and Private Life in the Time of Queen Charlotte: Being the Journals of Mrs Papendiek* (2 vols), R. Bentley, London, 1887

Dowden, Wilfrid S. (ed.), *The Letters of Thomas Moore* (2 vols), Oxford University Press, Oxford, 1964

Ehrman, John, *The Younger Pitt* (3 vols), Constable, London, 1969, 1983, 1996

Ford, John, *Prizefighting: The Age of Regency Boximania*, David and Charles, Newton Abbot, 1971

Foreman, Amanda, *Georgiana, Duchess of Devonshire*, HarperCollins, London, 1998

Fraser, Flora, *The Unruly Queen: The Life of Queen Caroline*, Macmillan, London, 1996

George, M. Dorothy, *English Political Caricature to 1792*, Clarendon Press, Oxford, 1959

George, M. Dorothy, *English Political Caricature 1793–1832*, Clarendon Press, Oxford, 1959

Godden, Angelica, *The Sweetness of Life*, André Deutsch, London, 1997

Granville, Castalia, Countess (ed.), *Lord Granville Leveson-Gower (Ist Earl Granville): Private Correspondence, 1781–1821* (2 vols), John Murray, London, 1916

Gray, Robert, *The King's Wife: Five Queen Consorts*, Secker and Warburg, London, 1990

Greig, James (ed.), *The Farington Diary* (8 vols), Hutchinson, London, 1922–8

Gronow, Rees Howell, *The Reminiscences and Recollections of Captain Gronow 1810–60* (2 vols), Bodley Head, London, 1964

Hamilton, Lady Anne, *Secret History of the Court of England, from the Accession of George III to the Death of George IV* (2 vols), L.C. Page, Boston, 1901

Harcourt, Edward William (ed.), *The Harcourt Papers* (14 vols), James Parker, Oxford, 1880–1905

Hare, Augustus (ed.), *The Life and Letters of Maria Edgeworth*, Houghton Mifflin, Boston, 1894

Hibbert, Christopher, *George IV: Prince of Wales 1762–1811*, Longmans, London, 1972

Hibbert, Christopher, *George IV: Regent and King 1811–1830*, Allen Lane, London, 1973

Holland, Henry Edward, Lord (ed.), *Henry Richard, Lord Holland: Memoirs of the Whig Party During My Time* (2 vols), Longmans, London, 1852–4

Holmes, Geoffrey, and Daniel Szechi, *The Age of Oligarchy: Pre-industrial Britain 1722–1783*, Longmans, London, 1993

Huish, Robert, *Memoirs of George IV* (2 vols), Thomas Kelly, London, 1830–31

Jennings, Louis J. (ed.), *The Correspondence and Diaries of the Late Right Honourable John Wilson Croker* (3 vols), Batsford, London, 1967

Jesse, Captain, *The Life of Beau Brummell* , W. Swann Sonnenschein, London, 1893

Knight, Cornelia, *Autobiography of Miss Cornelia Knight: With Extracts from Her Journals and Anecdote Books* (2 vols), W.H. Allen, 1861

Leslie, Anita, *Mrs Fitzherbert*, Hutchinson, London, 1960

Leslie, Shane, *George the Fourth*, Ernest Benn, London, 1926

Leslie, Shane (ed.), *The Letters of Mrs Fitzherbert and Connected Papers*, Burns Oates, London, 1940

Lewis, Lady Theresa (ed.), *Extracts of the Journals and Correspondence of Miss Berry from the Year 1783 to 1852* (3 vols), Longmans, London, 1865

Lewis, W.S. (ed.), *The Yale Edition of Horace Walpole's Correspondence* (34 vols), Oxford University Press, Oxford, 1937–65

Lindstrum, Derek, *Sir Jeffrey Wyatville: Architect to the King*, Clarendon Press, Oxford, 1973

Londonderry, Charles, 3rd Marquess of, *Memoirs and Correspondence of Viscount Castlereagh, 2nd Marquess of Londonderry* (12 vols), Henry Colburn, London, 1853

Longford, Elizabeth, *Wellington: Vol. 1 – Years of the Sword*, Weidenfeld and Nicolson, London, 1970

Longford, Elizabeth, *Wellington: Vol 2 – Pillar of State*, Weidenfeld and Nicolson, London, 1972

Low, Donald, *Thieves' Kitchen*, Weidenfeld and Nicolson, London, 1993

Macalpine, Ida and Richard Hunter, *George III and the Mad Business*, Pimlico, London, 1991

Malmesbury, 3rd Earl of (ed.), *The Diaries and Correspondence of James Harris, First Earl of Malmesbury* (4 vols), Longmans Green, London, 1884

Marchand, Leslie (ed.), *Byron's Letters and Journals* (12 vols), Belknap Press, Cambridge, Massachusetts, 1973

Marples, Morris, *Six Royal Sisters: Daughters of George III*, Michael Joseph, London, 1969

Marshall, Dorothy, *Eighteenth Century England*, Longmans, London, 1968

Melville, Lewis, *Beau Brummell: His Life and Letters*, Hutchinson, London, 1924

Memes, J.S., *Memoirs of Antonio Canova*, Constable, Edinburgh, 1825

Mitchell, Austin, *The Whigs in Opposition, 1815–1830*, Oxford University Press, Oxford, 1967

Moore, Thomas (ed.), *Letters and Journals of Lord Byron*, Gahgnani, London, 1831

Murray, Hon. Ameba, *Recollections of the Early Years of the Present Century*, John Murray, London, 1868

New, Chester W., *The Life of Henry Brougham to 1830*, Oxford University Press, Oxford, 1961

Nightingale, J., *Memoir of the Public and Private Life of Caroline, Queen of Great Britain*, Folio Society, London, 1978

O'Toole, Fintan, *A Traitor's Kiss: The Life of Richard Brinsley Sheridan*, Granta, London, 1997

Pasquin, Anthony, *The Life of the Late Earl of Barrymore*, H.D. Symonds,

London, 1793

Perceval, Hon. Spencer, *The Genuine Book – An Inquiry or Delicate Investigation into the Conduct of Her Royal Highness the Princes of Wales*, John Fairburn, London, 1813

Plowden, Alison, *Caroline and Charlotte*, London, Sidgwick and Jackson, London, 1989

Plumb, J.H., *The First Four Georges*, Fontana Press, London, 1956

Powell, Anthony (ed.), *Barnard Letters 1778–1824*, Duckworth, London, 1928

Price, Cecil (ed.), *The Letters of Richard Brinsley Sheridan*, Oxford University Press, Oxford, 1960

Pyne, W.H., *The History of the Royal Residences*, A. Dry, London, 1819

Quennell, Peter (ed.), *The Private Letters of Princess Lieven to Prince Metternich 1820–26*, John Murray, London, 1948

Royal Pavilion, *The Prince and His Pleasures, The: Satirical Images of George IV and His Circle*, Royal Pavilion, Brighton, 1997

Rudé, George, *Hanoverian London 1714–1808*, Secker and Warburg, London, 1971

Russell, Lord John (ed.), *Memorials and Correspondence of Charles James Fox* (2 vols), Blanchard and Lea, London, 1853

Rutherford, Jessica, *The Royal Pavilion*, Royal Pavilion, Brighton, 1997

Smith, E.A., *A Queen on Trial: The Affair of Queen Caroline*, Alan Sutton, Gloucester, 1993

Somerset, Anne, *The Life and Times of William IV*, Weidenfeld and Nicholson, London, 1980

Stanhope, Earl, and E. Cardwell (eds), *The Memoirs of Sir Robert Peel* (2 vols), John Murray, London, 1857

Strachey, Lytton and Roger Fulford (eds), *The Greville Memoirs 1814–1860* (3 vols), Macmillan, London, 1938

Times Newspapers, *The History of the Times: Vol. 1 –The Thunderer in the Making 1785–1841*, Times Newspapers, London, 1935

Tomalin, Claire, *Mrs Jordan's Profession*, Viking, London, 1994

Watson, J. Steven, *The Reign of George III 1760–1815*, Oxford University Press, Oxford, 1960

Wellington, 7th Duke of (ed.), *Wellington and His Friends: Letters of the First Duke of Wellington*, Macmillan, London, 1965

Wheatley, Henry (ed.), *Memoirs of Sir Nathaniel William Wraxall: 1772–1784* (5 vols), Bickers, London, 1884

Wheatley, Henry B., *London Past and Present* (3 vols), John Murray, London, 1891

Whitley, William, *Art in England 1800–20*, Cambridge University Press, Cambridge, 1928

Wilkins, W.H., *Mrs Fitzherbert and George IV* (2 vols), Longmans, London, 1905

Williams, E.N., *Life in Georgian England*, Batsford, London, 1962

Woodham-Smith, Cecil, *Queen Victoria: Her Life and Times 1819–1861*, Penguin, London, 1994

Wyndham, Hon. Mrs Hugh (ed.), *Correspondence of Sarah Spencer Lady Lyttelton, 1787–1870*, Charles Scribner, New York, 1912

INDEX